Teaching Adolescents
Religious Literacy
in a Post-9/11 World

AUTHORS' COMMENTARY ON THE COVER

We, the authors, hope that our readers are as moved by the cover of our book as we were when we first saw it. For us, the cover is a dramatic reminder that what we are writing about—the necessity of teaching religious literacy to adolescents in our nation's public schools—is more than simply another top-down add-on to already packed middle-school and high school curricula. The image illustrates with tragic poignancy that religious illiteracy among youth both in the United States and throughout the world leads, ultimately, to the devastation, desolation, and utter destruction that the cover so vividly depicts.

Yes, the cover is dark, but the dire warning it conveys is inescapable. How can any of us ever forget 9/11/2001? During those first hours, the television networks replayed over and over the horror of airplanes becoming deadly, exploding bombs and flying into buildings. Also, early on that day, the networks photographed desperate people jumping to their deaths from the top floors of the burning New York skyscrapers. Later in the day, and forever after, mercifully, they never showed those suicidal leaps again. But the grisly memories will linger forever.

For us, our book cover illustrates a central truth for the third millennium: religious literacy is crucial if we are to understand what is important to others, and if we are to avoid going to war with them. This, for us, is where the real payoff of religious literacy lies, and why we wrote our book. We must understand clearly what religious beliefs others throughout the world live, kill, and die for, or we, ourselves, will have nothing to live for; worse, we will end up killing others because what they believe seems evil and dangerous compared to what we believe.

As we write, dozens of religiously motivated wars are raging throughout the world. Some of these wars are small, it is true, but people are suffering and dying nonetheless. Francis Bacon said that "knowledge is power." We would amend this by saying that the greatest power a genuine knowledge of diverse worldviews will confer upon us is that we might be able to stop the world from being torn apart by an irreconcilable clash of religious absolutes—completely misunderstood by those who are not adherents. This, sadly, is history's long, terrible legacy to all of us.

Robert J. Nash
Penny A. Bishop
2009

Teaching Adolescents Religious Literacy in a Post-9/11 World

Robert J. Nash
College of Education and Social Services,
University of Vermont

Penny A. Bishop
College of Education and Social Services,
University of Vermont

INFORMATION AGE PUBLISHING, INC.
Charlotte, NC • www.infoagepub.com

Library of Congress Cataloging-in-Publication Data

Nash, Robert J.
    Teaching adolescents religious literacy in a post-9/11 world / Robert J.
Nash, Penny A. Bishop.
        p. cm.
    Includes bibliographical references.
    ISBN 978-1-60752-311-6 (pbk.) – ISBN 978-1-60752-312-3 (hardcover) –
ISBN 978-1-60752-313-0 (e-book)
    1. Religion in the public schools–United States. 2. Religion–Study and
teaching (Secondary)–United States. I. Bishop, Penny, 1969- II. Title.
    LC111.N27 2009
    379.2'8–dc22

                                                    2009039170

Printed in the United States of America

Dedication

To all the public school teachers and administrators who have been my students throughout a 40+ year career as a college professor. It is because of your inspiration and encouragement that, many years ago, I created a course in religious literacy for public school educators.

—Robert J. Nash

To John "Jack" Daniels, longtime peace activist, civil rights advocate, and religious believer, whose tireless work over the past century has blazed a trail for greater human understanding.

—Penny A. Bishop

Contents

Acknowledgments...xi

Foreword...xiii

Preface...xvii

1 Making the Case 1

Teaching about Religion in Middle and Secondary Schools...........1

Why the Study of Religion in Secular Public Schools is So
Controversial..2

Why Things Must Change 5

Extending the Reach of Multiculturalism....................................6

The Changing Global Religious Landscape................................8

The Impact of 9/11 on the Need for Religious Literacy 9

First Amendment and Civil Rights Considerations 10

Are Adolescents Developmentally Ready for an Education
in Religious Literacy? 12

Who We are as Authors 13

The Scope and Approach of the Book 14

Let our Method Mirror our Message..15

The Language of Narrative..16

The Meaning of Spirituality...17

The Meaning of Pluralistic Classroom Dialogue 18

Conclusions 19

Through Pedagogy..22

Through Partnership 23

Preliminary Words of Advice and Caution 24

Religious Pluralism Resources for Teachers:
A Brief Bibliographic Essay 25

2 The Narrative of Judaism 27

Case Study #1: "Christ Killer!" 27

The Universal Fear of Examining Religious Stereotypes
in the Classroom 28

Is Judeo-Phobia Inevitable in Christian America? 30

Core Beliefs and Practices in the Judaism Narrative 32

The Narrative Dimension 32

The Doctrinal Dimension 34

The Ethical Dimension 37

The Ritual Dimension 38

Judaism Resources for Teachers: A Brief Bibliographic Essay 41

3 The Narrative of Christianity 45

Case Study #2: "What Do You Mean, 'Christ's Birthday'?" 45

The Pedagogical Challenge 46

Is Christianity the Most Pluralistic Religious Narrative of All? 48

Core Beliefs and Practices in the Christian Narrative 49

The Narrative Dimension 49

The Doctrinal Dimension 52

The Ethical Dimension 54

The Ritual Dimension 56

Christianity Resources for Teachers: A Brief Bibliographic Essay ... 58

4 The Narrative of Islam 61

Case Study #3: "Watch Out for People who Look Like the
Taliban!" 61

Dealing with Islamophobia in the Classroom 63

Core Beliefs and Practices in the Islam Narrative 65

The Narrative Dimension 65

The Doctrinal Dimension 70

The Ethical Dimension 73

The Ritual Dimension 74

Islam Resources for Teachers: A Brief Bibliographic Essay 76

5   The Narrative of Hinduism 77

Case Study #4: "Isn't it Illegal to Teach Yoga in Public Schools?" ... 77

Stereotyping Eastern Religions 78

Core Beliefs and Practices in the Hindu Narrative 80

The Narrative Dimension 80

The Doctrinal Dimension 84

The Ethical Dimension 87

The Ritual Dimension 89

Hinduism Resources for Teachers:
A Brief Bibliographic Essay 91

6   The Narrative of Buddhism 93

Case Study #5: "Aren't Buddhists Atheists who Hate Life?" 93

Can the East Ever Meet the West in a Public School Classroom? 95

Core Beliefs and Practices in the Buddhist Narrative 96

The Narrative Dimension 96

The Doctrinal Dimension 99

The Ethical Dimension 102

The Ritual Dimension 105

Buddhism Resources for Teachers: A Brief Bibliographic Essay ... 107

7   Religious Controversies and Misconceptions 109

Controversies and Challenges in Judaism 110

Controversies and Challenges in Christianity 114

Controversies and Challenges in Islam 117

Controversies and Challenges in Hinduism 122

Controversies and Challenges in Buddhism 127

8   The Religious Literacy Toolbox 133

Constructivism in a Nutshell 134

Establish a Safe Classroom Culture 135

Classroom as Community 136

Moral Conversation 137

Emphasize Student-Centered Learning 138

    Student Choice 138

    From Teacher-Talk to Student-Talk 140

    Student Questions 141

Make Interdisciplinary Connections 143

    Mathematics and Sciences... 143

    Literature 144

    The Creative and Visual Arts 146

    Social Studies 148

    Reflective Writing and Personal Narrative.............................. 150

Teach from the Inside-Out... 152

9 **Some Lesser Known Religious Narratives** 155

Case Study #6: "Isn't There Something in This Proposal
to Offend Everyone?" 155

Nothing Ventured, Nothing Gained... 157

A Letter to Eileen 159

    The Chinese Religions.. 159

    Lesser-Known Religious Movements in the United States 167

Lesser-Known Religions Resources for Teachers:
A Brief Bibliographic Essay... 177

Appendix

Constructing a Spirituality of Teaching:
A Personal Perspective... 179

References 201

Acknowledgments

To Penny A. Bishop, my colleague, coauthor, and dear friend, who inspired me, a philosopher of education and a religious studies scholar, to branch out and write a practical book for middle and high school teachers. Our collaboration on this project has been a wonderful learning experience for me. To Ed Ducharme, my former departmental chair, past editor of the *Journal of Teacher Education*, and coauthor on a number of publications, who always insisted that jargon-free, accessible writing is, in the end, the most scholarly writing of all. Finally, to my partner of 50 years, Madelyn, a public school guidance counselor, who keeps me honest in my scholarship by insisting that I write what I believe and I believe what I write.

—Robert J. Nash

Thanks to the many middle and high school teachers who described their successes, questions, and challenges in teaching about religion in public school classrooms. Their insights were an essential part of my understanding what constitutes effective teaching practice about such potentially controversial issues. Without them, there would be no book. To my coauthor, Robert J. Nash, I offer my deepest gratitude for his interest in blending our two areas of expertise into a useful resource for teachers and for his deeply inspiring friendship and collegiality over the past decade. I thank my wonderful faculty in our Middle Level Teacher Education Program at the University of Vermont, who do such extraordinary work with our students that I'm free to focus on projects such as this. And I thank my husband Marc, a high school social studies teacher, and our sons Drake and Alden for constantly supporting everything I do with such good nature.

—Penny A. Bishop

Teaching Adolescents Religious Literacy in a Post-9/11 World, page xi
Copyright © 2010 by Information Age Publishing

Foreword

Fayneese Miller

Dean of the College of Education and Social Services
Professor of Human Development

It is a privilege to have been asked to write a foreword for Robert J. Nash's and Penny A. Bishop's book—*Teaching Adolescents Religious Literacy in a Post 9/11 World*. This is a book for every teacher who has ever had to address a question pertaining to religion arising in the course of a class discussion. Nash and Bishop provide the kind of dynamic understanding of the issues teachers face in those circumstances, making their book a turn-to resource for both intelligent guidance and practical advice for navigating these off-times thorny moments. Teachers in every discipline know what it is like when such a question arises. This impressive book provides both the content and application knowledge necessary to turn them into teachable moments. Rather than the cause of conflict, the cogent advice the authors present can transform these potentially contentious moments into what Piaget refers to as the most natural state-as sources of *curiosity*.

But Nash and Bishop have more in mind than how to navigate teachable moments. Beyond the power of their prose, or the wealth of explanatory information about the world's religions they offer, or the true-to-life class-room specific case studies they present, Nash and Bishop put forward a clearly articulated rationale and reasoned argument for including a for-

Teaching Adolescents Religious Literacy in a Post-9/11 World, pages xiii–xvi
Copyright © 2010 by Information Age Publishing

xiii

mal plan of study of the world's religions in our nations schools. Their project is to address in our classrooms the woeful lack of student's knowledge of religious distinctions, at the same time issuing a direct and forthright challenge to any who might consider it impossible to do so. "The status quo of religious illiteracy in our nation's classrooms must not continue, indeed, *cannot* continue," they say. "There is simply too much at stake."

This is a book about teaching religious literacy. Still, as critically necessary as this project is in our post-9/11 world, the content provided by Nash and Bishop contains such sound and practical advice that any teacher who believes in the importance of feeding the mind, of encouraging curiosity, and providing for a student-generated knowledge-based classroom, will want to read this book. Each chapter begins with a case study and is followed with descriptive information about one of the five major religions—Judaism, Christianity, Islam, Hinduism, and Buddhism. As Nash and Bishop move from case study to a particular religion, they provide the reader with what they see as the teaching challenges inherent in each. The brilliant job they do in comparing and contrasting aspects of each religion within the chapters is one of its central pleasures. And in one must-read chapter, the authors, in laying out the controversies within and the misconceptions about each religion, raise the "red flags" teachers should expect to hear when dealing with each.

As I read each chapter, I thought back on my own high school experience and my sophomore English teacher who assigned us different novels to read, like *Night* by Elie Wiesel, using it to teach us about Judaism and the Holocaust. The time was the 1970s, at the end of the Civil Rights period, and long before 9/11. I was growing up in a town in the south that was one of the last in the United States to fully desegregate all of its schools. The racial disturbances that I witnessed at the high school were to my eyes inevitable because two racially segregated groups of bright and inquisitive minds were now being forced into one academic space—the only high school left in my town.

My sophomore English teacher found an ingenious way to get us to talk about multiculturalism, tolerance, diversity, and pluralism without ever mentioning the word *race*. She taught us about the five major religions through novels and poetry. She did not shy away from the sensitive questions we raised but used them as an opportunity to provide us with basic information about the various religions. Reading Nash and Bishop's book reminded me of the wonders of that English class. Like Nash and Bishop, the purpose of the class was not to indoctrinate but to encourage critical thinking, stage informed debates, and create a desire to learn more. It was also an opportunity to press the lesson that in every area of difference there is, to use Nash's and Bishop's words, "the wonderful potential of binding us together...instead of tearing us apart."

Unlike my sophomore English teacher, who took a back-door approach to adolescent religious literacy, Nash and Bishop are proposing that the teaching be intentional. They are "committed multicultural pluralists" who see teaching students "to understand and respect diverse religious beliefs" as core to teaching young people how to become fully participating and informed members of a civil society.

In Chapter 9 of their book, Nash and Bishop provide tools useful for teaching adolescents religious literacy. They invoke the spirit of developmental and cognitive psychologists (e.g., Piaget, Bruner) who see knowledge as constructed and therefore continually evolving. A constructivist begins with what the student already knows. Then guiding their attempt to understand how they know it, they provide additional information to problematize what they think they know. As constructivists, Nash and Bishop make use of commonly occurring classroom situations, and then provide the information a teacher would need to help his or her students develop religious literacy.

At first glance, a teacher might choose to shy away from a book with the word "religious" in its title. This would be a mistake. This book is about more than teaching adolescents religious literacy. It is about learning how to create a safe space for students to learn about a topic that outside the classroom walls is cause for disagreement and sometimes violent conflict. In their book, Nash and Bishop provide the valuable guidance teachers will need to navigate this thorny path, as the young people in their charge prepare to take their place in a civil and global society.

Nash and Bishop's book, *Teaching Adolescent Religious Literacy in a Post 9/11 World*, is long overdue. The types of diverse contacts young people might have today are no longer between Blacks and Whites, or Christians and Jews, but broader, deeper, richer. The borders surrounding countries are permeable, our young people transnational in their digital ability to cross them even as they remain incognizant of those with whom they communicate.

It is, therefore, imperative that teachers develop the skills and knowledge to teach effectively within a global context. Nash and Bishop provide a remarkable service recognizing and then providing for opportunities to teach what I would call, "religious literacy across the disciplines." Whether how to structure meaningful discussions among students in math, social studies, science, English, health, and so on, the authors provide concrete pathways to answering the complex religious and/or moral questions when they arise. This is a book for every teacher who cares about the cognitive, emotional, moral, and emotional growth of young people in schools. The power of the narrative knowledge and the passion of the authors for its efficacy are evident on every page. Every teacher who picks up and reads this book will see its benefit for more than the teaching of religious literacy.

In the mid-1970s, my teacher understood the importance of intentional teaching in helping her students understand the changing world in which they lived. I believe she got it right. I urge with confidence that many more will learn to help their students achieve an even greater level of religious literacy by reading Nash's and Bishop's book and putting into practice the lessons it provides. They do not offer their book as a panacea to this most difficult undertaking, or shy away from admitting that their book will not smooth every bump in the road. Perhaps the greatest compliment I can pay them is that after reading their book it will motivate you to make the attempt. What a wonderful gift Nash and Bishop have made to the profession!

Preface

Michele S. Moses, Ph.D.,

Chair, Educational Foundations, Policy, and Practice,
University of Colorado at Boulder
(author of *Embracing Race: Why We Need Race-
Conscious Education Policy*)

On May 31, 2009, Dr. George Tiller was murdered. I do not think it is going too far to say that he was murdered because of religion. Dr. Tiller was the head of a women's medical clinic in Kansas—one of the few places where women could go to terminate their pregnancies after the first trimester if they so wished. Described as very religious, the man suspected of killing Dr. Tiller was a long-time anti-abortion activist (CNN.com, 2009). This tragedy profoundly underscores the importance of this book.

With the publication of *Teaching Adolescents Religious Literacy in a Post 9/11 World*, Robert Nash and Penny Bishop fill a large gap in the literature, and they do so in an incredibly thoughtful and nuanced way. Their work is grounded in actual case studies as well as the legal landscape of school-related church-state court cases. They present all sides of the issues—not just the sensational or extreme pros and cons—and recognize the diversity of perspectives represented within these debates. The case studies they detail bring the central issues to light including realistic responses by educators, students, parents, and community members. The cases allow Nash and

Teaching Adolescents Religious Literacy in a Post-9/11 World, pages xvii–xix
Copyright © 2010 by Information Age Publishing
All rights of reproduction in any form reserved.

Bishop to address relevant policy issues as well, such as the debate between teaching evolution and creationism in science classes.

A scan of popular multicultural education books shows that the topic of religion often has been left out of books on multicultural education and diversity (see, e.g., Marshall, 2002; Nieto & Bode, 2007; Perry & Fraser, 1993). Yet in our current sociopolitical climate, religion is more important than ever. Advocating a constructivist approach to teaching for religious literacy, Nash and Bishop stress that teachers ought to take on the role of facilitators of the dialogue about religious conflicts. As they explain, "pluralistic dialogue about religions and spiritualities in the classroom, as in the world-at-large, requires direct, give-and-take participation with all types of religious otherness. It insists that we allow the "other" to get under our skins, to engage with us, to disturb us, and even, if the circumstances warrant, to *change* us" (p. 13). Key to their findings and recommendations is the idea of the moral conversation, or pluralistic dialogue, especially for multicultural education that includes religion. In addition, stories are at the center of this work. Nash and Bishop recognize the difficulties present in teaching for religious literacy, but they do not shy away from their strong call for teachers to incorporate reciprocal dialogue about religion into the curriculum.

They argue that there is a deep need for "comparative religious and spiritual understanding" (Nash & Bishop, 2009, p. 18) in what adolescents learn in school. The book is rich—with nuanced information about today's salient religious worldviews and analyses of how middle and high school teachers can teach religious literacy and engage their students in respectful dialogue on the deep-seated debates connected with diverse religious beliefs and values. It is, at heart, a passionate plea to educators to teach for religious understanding. But it is also much more—a smart and cogent primer for schoolteachers and administrators regarding prominent religions and their concomitant social and educational controversies. It really has exactly what educators need to learn to teach for religious literacy, all in one place, including vast information on where we can go for more detailed information on each topic.

I began this Preface linking an extreme kind of violence to religious zealotry. But, along with the catastrophic events of 9/11 that Nash and Bishop reference, tragedies such as these provide the larger social context for this book. Perhaps it is not fair of me to say that Nash and Bishop's work might contribute to greater understanding in such a way that tragedies like the murder of Dr. Tiller would become fewer and farther between. I realize that is a heavy burden to place on one book. Yet, the information and messages in this book are a significant step toward the education that teachers and students alike so desperately need.

References

CNN.com. (2009, June 4). Slaying suspect 'obsessed' with Kansas doctor, ex-roommate says. Retrieved July 24, 2009 from http://www.cnn.com/2009/CRIME/06/04/kansas.doctor.killed/index.html?iref=newssearch

Marshall, P. L. (2002). *Cultural diversity in our schools.* Belmont, CA: Wadsworth/Thompson.

Nieto, S., & Bode, P. (2007). *Affirming diversity: The sociopolitical context of multicultural education,* 5th ed. Boston: Pearson/Allyn & Bacon.

Perry, T., & Fraser, J. (1993). *Freedom's plow: Teaching in the multicultural classroom.* New York: Routledge.

1

Making the Case

Teaching about Religion in Middle and Secondary Schools

Keri Jenkins sighed and leaned back from her desk at the end of a long teaching week. As a first-year teacher in a small, rural school in the Southeast, she found herself as part of a three-teacher team working with seventh- and eighth-graders. Her strong liberal arts background and double major in biology and botany prepared her well for the science curriculum she was expected to teach, and she enjoyed making learning come alive for the young adolescents on her team. She routinely relied on the wooded school grounds to serve as her classroom, bringing out groups of students to examine their curriculum in its natural context.

Last week, her team had completed a highly successful river study, analyzing water quality, flora, and fauna for the community. The students appeared in the local paper, and the team had been invited to present their work at a community meeting. In the wake of such success and positive emotions, she had been entirely unprepared for last night's angry phone call and subsequent parent meeting that was about to ensue.

Teaching Adolescents Religious Literacy in a Post-9/11 World, pages 1–26

1

She thought back to the conversation in class yesterday that provoked this afternoon's meeting. Most of her students had been enthusiastic about the river study, and were deeply engaged in posing questions. Having been trained in her teacher education program to honor students' questions as the basis for curriculum, Keri had excitedly followed the students' inquiries. What fish are found in this river? How do fish swim? Why do certain plants grow in water? The answers to these questions then raised deeper questions: How did fish come to be that way? What is the advantage to fish of swimming? How did river plants come to differ from others?

Before she knew it, the class had arrived at the questions: What process created this extraordinary variation of life as we know it? How did we/the world get here? Seizing the moment, Keri passionately spoke of Darwin's *On the Origin of the Species*, which had been an influential and thought-provoking text in her own learning of science. She was animated and enthused about the opportunity to open young learners' eyes and minds to the very ideas that had motivated her own study of science in college.

When she arrived home that evening, her answering machine was blinking brightly. Taking off her coat with one arm and juggling folders of student work in the other, she pressed the button and listened. Immediately, she heard the voice of one student's mother, berating her for teaching the theory of evolution to her son. "Just who do you think you are?" the mother asked angrily, "Coming to our community and teaching our children that God doesn't exist? That God didn't create man and the world that surrounds him?" Keri was speechless.

She certainly didn't mean to interfere with families' beliefs, nor did she want to make waves in her newly adopted community. After all, she attended a local church herself every Sunday. At the same time, how could she teach the central ideas in her curriculum regarding the diversity of life on earth without reference to how natural selection and environmental factors work together? After garnering her courage, she called their house and opted not to enter into such a debate on the telephone. Instead, she invited the mother to join her in a face-to-face meeting to discuss the matter. Now, tapping her foot and waiting anxiously for her to arrive, she wished she had asked her principal or a teammate to join her.

Why the Study of Religion in Secular Public Schools is So Controversial

Keri Jenkins is about to face many teachers' worst nightmare: the prospect of meeting with an angry parent whose indignation with her teaching is grounded in strong religious beliefs. For her part, Keri believes that she is doing what every self-respecting science teacher should be doing in their classrooms, and that is teaching the scientifically agreed-upon facts about evolution, particularly when students ask questions that entail this type of knowledge. After all, isn't evolution a proven scientific theory, and a conceptual framework that all students will need to know in order to understand their natural and social worlds as they progress through their education?

How is it possible, Keri ponders, for students to understand the variations in plant, animal, and human life without examining the evolutionary theories of natural selection and adaptation? Also, how will students who are studying environmental science understand the principles of biodiversity and sustainability without exploring such concepts in depth? How will students understand the origins, and meanings, of human behavior without knowing something about sociobiology or evolutionary psychology? Also, why on principle, Keri wonders, will her foray into introducing students to a few of Darwin's pivotal ideas necessarily contradict the teachings of their religious faiths? Can't there be complementarity between the two?

Keri, herself, is a believing Christian, and she does not perceive that her love for science contradicts her faith in God. In fact, if she were ever to be asked in private, she would probably acknowledge that her faith in the plausibility of science actually strengthens her religious faith. For Keri, a proponent of Big Bang Theory, it seems logical that one complements the other, because she believes that evolution is mainly a process created by an all-powerful Deity at a particular moment in time in order to set His Creation in motion.

From the parent's perspective, however, there are two distinct worldviews in conflict in Keri's classroom: the supernatural and the natural. In public schools, and in most colleges for that matter, it always seems that the secular or natural worldview wins out. Why, according to the parent, can't Keri teach the concepts of Intelligent Design and Creationism right alongside evolution? Why can't Keri underscore to her students, more than she appears willing to, that evolution is only a theory with no more intrinsic validity than any other theory? In fact, why does it seem that science has become the official secular "religion" in public education? The parent resents the glaring absence of religion in Keri's science curriculum, as well as in the history, civics, science, and English curricula in her child's school.

In one sense, this parent may even be more open-minded and "liberal" than a separatist, fundamentalist, or orthodox Christian, Jew, or Muslim parent might be. Many of these types of religious believers want religion kept completely out of secular schools in the name of the First Amendment principle of the absolute separation of church and state. They do not want religion to be contaminated in public school classrooms by secular educators with vested philosophical or political interests.

Thus, for most separatist, sectarian parents, religion should be left exclusively to the home and the church to propagate. For them, the home and the church are two of the three legs of the socialization stool in any society, and they are the strongest ones at that. The other leg is the state school, and as every biblically-based Christian knows, believers are commanded to give to Caesar that which is Caesar's and to God that which is God's, and never the twain should meet. The state school, as every orthodox Christian believes, ought *not* to be the venue for religious education of any kind.

If Keri were ever to teach her students that there is potential compatibility between faith and reason, religion and science, many orthodox religious parents in her community would be outraged. They would see her pedagogy as being nothing more than a transparent attempt to transgress the constitutionally protected boundaries between the private and public spheres in the United States. They would suspect her motives. They might accuse her of surreptitiously trying to water down the sanctity of religious truth. Why, Keri might even lose her job over the brouhaha, because she knows that her local school board is made up predominantly of conservative Christians.

We believe, if our own experience with educators in middle schools and high schools is any indication, that there is an increasing number of Keris in the public school classrooms of America. Many of these teachers, all their good intentions notwithstanding, know very little about how to negotiate religious issues whenever they arise in the classroom. In responding to her students' excellent environmental questions, Keri, herself, is probably unaware of the deep-seated religious concerns that teaching about evolution would raise in her community.

What she thought might have been a perfectly appropriate and teachable moment in her science classroom—one that lent itself to a beneficial conversation about Darwin and evolution—turned out to be a lightning rod for some parents in her school system. Unfortunately, Keri had limited knowledge of the creationism–intelligent design–evolution controversy sweeping through school systems in this country, because she never had examined the controversy anywhere in her own teacher preparation.

Likewise, the vast majority of students who pass through the public schools of America during these early years of the 21st century, like millions before them through the decades, have had little, or no, formal academic background in the study of any of the world's religions, including their own. As teachers and teacher educators, we have found the general level of religious literacy in this country to be alarming.

Most Americans are completely out of touch with what is at stake in the global community as groups and nations war with one another over their religious differences. They lack even the most rudimentary understandings of the content and practices of the world's major and minor religions. Even more disturbing is the complete absence of any kind of religious literacy study in teacher education programs.

To Keri's credit, however, few teachers we know, even science teachers, would be willing to touch the subject of religion with a 10-foot pole, especially its possible conflicts with the study of evolution. Sadly, even fewer school administrators would sanction the attempt for fear of alienating many religious believers in the larger community. Remarks we have heard, whenever we talk about teaching for religious literacy, from professors of education, teachers in training, teachers, and administrators range all the way from "What the hell do I know about religion?" to "There's no way I'm going to stir up that hornets' nest. Why not leave well enough alone?" to "Haven't you heard about the 'wall of separation' between the church and the state? Why invite a law suit?" to "Isn't this just another add-on that you people in teacher education expect us public school teachers to incorporate into our curricula? Don't we have enough to do?"

Even though we understand these well-intended concerns, we have decided not to leave well enough alone. The status quo of religious illiteracy in our nation's classrooms must not continue, indeed, *cannot* continue. There is simply too much at stake, in our estimation.

Yes, it is apparent that Keri has her work cut out for her as she anxiously awaits the arrival of the angry parent in her classroom. She feels caught between two implacable forces, one secular and the other religious, and, therefore, she is stuck in a no-win situation. Whatever, she will be damned if she does and damned if she doesn't. She wonders why she has to be put in this situation in the first place. Why is there so much hostility today between those who reside in the religious square and those who reside in the public square, between those who choose faith over reason and vice versa, between those who want to teach about religions in the classrooms and those who don't? Will things ever change?

Why Things Must Change

There are a number of significant and defensible reasons, we contend, why middle-level and high school teachers and administrators need to become more religiously literate and to teach their students to be the same. We describe some of these reasons below, with further elaboration later in this chapter and throughout the book.

Extending the Reach of Multiculturalism

As teachers, we are committed to the basic ideals and practices of multicultural education. Moses (2002) cogently sums up our beliefs.

> Multicultural education is a broad educational approach in which students learn what is necessary in order for them to live and prosper in a multicultural society. They learn that different cultures deserve public recognition, understanding, and respect; that coercive assimilation into the dominant culture should not be endorsed; and that unjust societal structures ought to be questioned. (p. 87)

Also, Moses identifies three "critical goals" regarding multicultural education that we, in turn, endorse.

1. Shaping attitudes that not only honor multiculturalism, but also embody the disposition to evaluate, challenge, and end racism and oppression.

2. Creating social contexts where students—regardless of culture, ethnicity, religion, gender, ability, sexual orientation, and social class—are treated and treat others with equal respect.

3. Fostering empowered, self-determining students. (p. 87)

We have chosen in this book to emphasize, perhaps for the first time in any sustained and systematic way, the ideal that teaching students to understand and respect diverse religious beliefs is yet another, very important way to "honor" multiculturalism. To put it succinctly, as committed multicultural pluralists, we believe that students, regardless of their religious beliefs (or lack of them), ought always to be treated with respect, understanding, and integrity. Moreover, they ought to be enthusiastically invited into the multicultural conversation as worthy participants who have much to teach all of us.

To achieve this worthy end, we seek to expand and deepen the meaning of multiculturalism to include religious difference, in addition to racial, ethnic, gender, and sexual orientation differences. We also seek to explain how the practice of pluralistic dialogue (what we call "moral conversation") in an adolescent classroom setting can further the aims of multicultural education. In order for us to proceed any further, however, we need to make the following important semantic distinctions.

We think of *tolerance* as a minimal, moral duty calling for simple noninterference. It is the obligation to bear, or to put up with, different points of view and beliefs. We think of *diversity* as an empirical term that carries with it no moral obligation. It merely describes a state of difference or variety. It does not enjoin us even to respect this difference, let alone celebrate it, as so many educators think.

Furthermore, as we have suggested earlier, we think of *multiculturalism* as an honest, no-holds-barred look at a multiplicity of cultural identities. Multiculturalism educates us about the histories and cultures that are very much the product of America's checkered past. It also points out the existence of oppression and exclusion that has taken, and is still taking, place in this country. This includes institutionalized racism, sexism, homophobia, classism, and a number of other isms and phobias.

Pluralism, however, is a much thicker term than each of these, containing significant moral meaning and implications for us as educators, and, by implication, for our students as well. Pluralism, according to the comparative religions scholar Diana Eck, aims to "build bridges of exchange and dialogue . . . and this must include constant communication—meeting, exchange, traffic, criticism, reflection, reparation, and renewal" (1993, p. 196).

In our opinion, pluralistic dialogue about religions and spiritualities in the classroom, as in the world-at-large, requires direct, give-and-take participation with all types of religious otherness. It insists that we allow the "other" to get under our skins, to engage with us, to disturb us, and even, if the circumstances warrant, to *change* us.

Simple tolerance, respect, and celebration of difference must always give way to the active seeking of understanding, and a willingness to consider transforming or modifying our previous religious views. We believe that an appreciation of religious pluralism begins with an understanding that the religious world is radically diverse and constantly changing. We contend that for middle and high school teachers and students to be ignorant of the expanding, diverse religious landscape throughout the world is to court international disaster in the decades ahead.

Knowledge of religious difference, like all the other differences, is power, and we hope that teachers and students can use this power to build bridges of dialogue and communication between those among us, as well as those outside, who hold differing religious and spiritual worldviews. By cultivating a religiously literate generation, teachers can help students to avoid further religious misunderstandings and conflicts.

The Changing Global Religious Landscape

In this respect, here are some up-to-date statistical reminders of how, globally, the religious world is in enormous flux: By the year 2050, India's population alone will reach 1.5 billion people, of whom 1.2 billion will be Hindus. By 2050, Muslims worldwide will outnumber Jews by over a hundred to one, and will even outnumber Christians. At the present time, Buddhism is the fourth largest religion in the world, at one time in its 20th century history claiming 20% of the world's people. By 2050, Buddhism will be the main religion of East and Southeast Asia, in such populous nations as China, Vietnam, and Thailand. Also in China, and in parts of Japan, Taoism and Confucianism will total about 1.2 billion adherents in another few decades.

By the year 2050 in the United States, 100 million Americans will claim Hispanic origin, and upward of 60 million citizens will claim Chicano descent. At the present time, 70% of Latinos are Catholic and 30% are evangelical Protestants in the United States. It is also estimated that no less than one billion people worldwide self-identify as atheist, agnostic, secular humanist, freethinker, or uninterested. This segment of unbelievers is a fast-growing international group, more prevalent in countries outside the United States, especially in Canada, Western Europe, and in Communist countries.

Moreover, although very conservative forms of Christianity are on the rise in Latino America, in European nations, the figures are quite different due to increasing secularization. Forty-four percent of the British claim no religious affiliation whatsoever. In France, only 8% of the population identifies as practicing Catholics. And in Italy, despite the influential presence of the Vatican, religious identity has declined steeply in recent years, as less than 10% of Italian Christians claim to be active practitioners of their faiths. Finally, in Africa at the present time, there is a stunning growth of Christianity, especially its most conservative, evangelical, and Pentecostal forms. Eight and one-half million people on that continent convert to Christianity every year, an average of 23,000 a day.

In the United States alone, especially after President Lyndon Johnson signed into law the Immigration Act of 1965, religious pluralism is booming. Thanks to President Johnson, there are no more quotas that limit immigration to a person's national origin. In a post-9/11 era, some Americans are urging the federal government to exercise more stringent oversight by amending, maybe even overturning, the Immigration Act, but, thus far, these efforts have been resisted.

And, so, at this time in our nation's history, cities and suburbs are thriving with the presence of Buddhists, Jews, Hindus, Muslims, and Sikhs, among a host of other religious practitioners. The fact is irrefutable that just as we live in a multifaith world, closer to home we also live in a multifaith, religiously pluralistic United States. Adolescents will need to understand the religious differences that exist among their peers, next-door neighbors, and even among family members, if they are to live knowledgeably, and peacefully, in a multifaith country.

Educating for religious literacy, therefore, is all about bringing adolescents and their teachers into the 21st century of teeming religious diversity. It is about teaching students the whats and whys of differing religious and spiritual beliefs, both in their own country and in the world at large. It is about looking for commonalities, as well as differences, between and among the great wisdom traditions. It is about understanding how teachers and students might live effectively in a religiously diverse world.

It is about transcending religious stereotyping. It is about helping students to understand, in Thomas Merton's wonderful words, that religion speaks to people in three different places: holy scriptures, the deepest self, and, most of all, in the voices of strangers. Teaching for religious literacy, if successful, will enable all of us in these years of the early 21st century to listen to the voices of these "strangers" in order to understand and, perhaps, even to embrace and love them. It is this consequence, we affirm, that will ultimately bring peace to the individual, and to an embattled world as well. (See the website www.adherents.com for up-to-date statistics on church and religious membership; see also Kimball, 2002; Lewy, 1996.)

The Impact of 9/11 on the Need for Religious Literacy

Prior to the calamitous events of that fateful day, most public school teachers in the United States were content to assume an official stance of dispassionate religious neutrality in the classroom. However, in an age marked by acts of terrorism throughout the world, largely based in extremist religious fundamentalisms of all kinds, a globally aware, religiously literate citizen needs to understand the meanings and content of the world's major and minor monotheistic and polytheistic religions. Our nation's adolescents need to learn the complexities of others' beliefs now in order to live peacefully with others in the future.

We ask the following question about the need for religious literacy for our readers to contemplate: Is there any subject matter more essential today for students to understand if they are to grow up and prosper in a peaceful world? We add another question: If teachers themselves actually know little or nothing about this subject matter, how will adolescents ever learn it? Finally, we ask: Isn't it true that unless administrators and parents support the schools in their efforts to teach for religious literacy, an informed religious literacy is unlikely to happen?

Middle school and secondary students must be knowledgeable about, and receptive to, the complexity and richness of religious diversity throughout the world. They need to know that it is impossible to understand the history, culture, and politics of most modern societies today if they are ignorant of the fundamental role that religions of all types have played in every country.

Most important, however, students need to understand that what many in the United States believe to be moral and ethical is largely a legacy of the Judeo-Christian heritage, as well as of the European Enlightenment. Similarly, what much of the rest of the world believes to be the crux of morality for themselves is based on the teachings of their own endemic religions and philosophies.

As a growing reaction to that eleventh day in September 2001 when three airplanes became deadly missiles, and another threatened to, we educators are reminded once again that we are, indeed, interconnected citizens of the world. No longer can any of us continue to think of religions outside the Judeo-Christian axis to be unimportant, or inferior, in the global scheme of things. No longer can we be content to ignore the need for comparative religious and spiritual understandings in our school curricula. No longer can we, as teachers, afford merely to intellectualize religious and spiritual differences in a bemused or detached manner; or to adopt a folkloric approach with our students wherein we do some superficial ceremonial "sharing," or to mention this content only in passing, if we bother to do so at all.

No longer is it enough for those of us who might be more cosmopolitan in our worldviews to do a whirlwind, text-bookish tour through the three major monotheistic religions in a world history, or world literature course, and let it go at that. In the global society we live in, no longer do we have the luxury of thinking about religion as merely a private affair, something best left to the home, church, synagogue, mosque, or temple. And no longer can we marginalize the teaching of religions in our public schools (see Nash, 2002).

First Amendment and Civil Rights Considerations

> *"Congress shall make no law respecting an establishment of religion, or prohibiting the free exercise thereof."*

Many teachers assume that the First Amendment to the Constitution, reproduced above, with its well-established, constitutional wall of separation between church and state, dictates that academic material rightfully belongs to the province of the schools while religious material rightfully belongs to the province of the churches, temples, and other sacred sites. But, in this post-9/11 era, we contend that educators in the public schools need to reexamine the very core of what, and how, they teach students in order to help them become more globally aware, religiously literate citizens.

Contrary to the conventional impression of public school educators that the First Amendment of the United States Constitution requires a strict separation between church and state, thus ruling "out of order" any conversation about religion in secular, state-supported schools, the constitutional wall of separation is actually a low wall rather than a high one. While public schools, like the state, must avoid favoring, as well as discriminating against, religion, they are free to study religion. We contend that educators have a right, indeed a professional responsibility, to further an understanding of religious differences in public schools. This, of course, should be done in such a way that teachers neither pander, promote, proselytize, nor practice a specific religion or religious worldview.

In the *Abington School District v. Shempp* (374 U.S. 203, 1963) Supreme Court decision in 1963 that outlawed school-sponsored prayer, Justice Thomas Clark declared that "Nothing we have said here indicates that such study . . . , when presented objectively as part of a secular program of education, may not be effected consistently with the First Amendment." This ruling suggests that teachers will need constantly to try to achieve a salient balance between representing the pros and the cons of religions throughout the world. They should not favor one over the other. They need to create an educationally safe, conversational classroom space for what we will call "respectful, yet robust, religious dialogue."

This type of respectful and robust conversation begins with an acknowledgment that religion, for at least 3,000 years, has been a fundamental part of human existence. To exclude, minimize, deny, or trivialize in public school curricula what has meant so much to so many human beings is, in our opinion, an unfortunate act of educational neglect.

Too many educators in schools and colleges whom we have taught believe that reason and faith are, of necessity, diametrically opposed. In fact, many believe that religion is more about the heart than the head, and, therefore, it should not be part of a formal academic experience. In contrast, we believe that educators have an intellectual responsibility to correct this misimpression, and that the study of religions deserves a place in any academic curriculum. Religion is as much about the head as the heart, as any historical study of comparative religions will show, and, therefore, the dichotomy does not hold.

As a consequence of the above dichotomy, the secular worldview ends up being dominant in the humanities, social sciences, and sciences. Worse, it drives out other worldviews. Wittingly or not, educators tend to promote a secular humanist account of their disciplines. We believe that this one-sidedness is a violation of the establishment clause of the First Amendment, which states that there is a need for fairness and neutrality in religious matters.

Furthermore, all students, but especially those who come from strong religious backgrounds, have a civil right to explore the tensions that exist in the United States and elsewhere between "tradition and modernity, community and individualism, consensus and pluralism, faith and reason, and religion and secularity" (Nord, 1995, p. 380).

Are Adolescents Developmentally Ready for an Education in Religious Literacy?

We believe that adolescents are, indeed, ready, and our research into faith-development theory more than confirms this belief for us. For example, a growing body of evidence agrees on the fact that a majority of adolescents, starting as early as age 10, no longer believe in a patriarchal God who is often depicted as an old man with a long white beard, whose primary responsibility is to reward and punish and, perhaps along the way, work a few miracles. Adolescents have pretty much left behind this "magic stage" of religious belief.

Instead, most adolescents are trying to discern the tension between dependence and independence in their religious beliefs. Adolescence is a time of life when one begins to ask many of life's quintessential questions: about identity, about the world and how it came to be. Some students, struggling to come to grips with their difficult puberty issues, yearn for a personal relationship with a god or gods. Others, seeking autonomy from parents and controlling adults, yearn to be completely independent of a paternalistic god. Often, the latter, as early as 14 years of age, will refer to themselves as "spiritual but not religious."

Still other adolescents remain regular, mainline churchgoers, holding fast to the traditional faiths of their parents. Some adolescents become "functional deists," whose beliefs are no longer in a personal god but in the existence of natural and human laws that a "disappeared" and "disinterested" deity has left for human beings to figure out on their own. In addition, there is an increasing cadre of adolescents, with little or no formal religious training or traditions, who, nevertheless, retain an intellectual or conceptual interest regarding questions of metaphysical beginnings, endings, purposes, and meanings.

Very few adolescents, according to the research on faith stage development, are cognitively unable to understand religious questions and ideas. And fewer still are emotionally or intellectually uninterested in asking such questions, or in exploring religious meanings in a formal educational environment. All the empirical research on cognitive development and faith stage theory that we know confirms for us the reality that adolescents are ready and eager to discuss religious issues. If they don't have the opportunity to do this in informed and guided conversation with teachers and peers, then we believe they will seek it elsewhere. This alternative, in our opinion, rarely produces beneficial, educational consequences.

Furthermore, moral formation at all levels of schooling is ultimately unattainable unless students, particularly in middle schools and high schools, undertake a serious study of religion's contribution to ethics and morality. Despite claims to the contrary, certain traditional religious virtues (e.g., faith, hope, love, compassion, forgiveness, obedience, integrity, self-respect) still have considerable value in secular pluralist societies such as the United States.

We would go so far as to say that there is such an empirically validated, universal "hunger" for religious understandings among the vast majority of adolescents in the United States and throughout the world that, unless it is satisfied, will lead to all kinds of problems. Among these are a tendency to live and understand life at the most superficial levels; an ignorant stereotyping of all religions by melting them into a false sameness or a false incompatibility; and a sense of exclusivism and triumphalism among those who belong to certain monotheistic religions claiming to be in sole possession of absolute theological truths (for studies on adolescent spiritual development, see Fowler, 1981; Oser & Scarlett, 1991; Shelton, 1989).

Who We are as Authors

We are Robert J. Nash and Penny A. Bishop, the former a religious studies scholar and philosopher of religion and education, and the latter a teacher educator and past middle school teacher. We are both religious pluralists. We steadfastly believe that the time has come for educators at the middle and high school levels to deal openly with the reality of religious difference, both across the curriculum and in separate academic experiences. The book before you examines a number of world religions and spiritualities, and our central purpose will be to inform, explain, and enrich teachers'—and, by implication, students'—understandings of many of the world's most predominant belief systems.

Our intention, therefore, is to make our book informative, practical, experiential, and case-based, but, above all, accessible to classroom teachers and administrators who may not possess an extensive knowledge of the world religions and spiritualities. We write our book from the viewpoint of two lifelong classroom teachers who are also highly respectful, participant observers of a variety of religious beliefs and practices in the United States and throughout the world. Thus, it is our hope that this book will speak primarily to teachers and secondarily to administrators at both the middle and high school levels.

The Scope and Approach of the Book

Obviously, we cannot cover the entire landscape of religions in the United States and throughout the world in one brief book. This will require a lifetime of study, because expertise in any subject matter builds slowly and steadily over a lengthy period of time. The best way for teachers to learn about comparative religions, in our estimation, is to read widely and deeply on their own, sign up for relevant courses in neighboring universities, and attend workshops.

Above all, teachers must make an ongoing commitment to engage in frequent conversations with one another about religious issues, as these might come up in their classroom teaching, as well as in their out-of-classroom interactions with students and parents. What better way than this, we ask, for school colleagues to exchange pertinent information about controversial religious content and innovative pedagogical approaches?

We will be talking here, mainly, about those religious worldviews that are most visible on the world scene at this time in history. The main criteria we have used for including the religions we have in this book are three. First, the largest faith traditions throughout the world require more attention in an introductory book than the smaller ones, simply because many more adherents live and die by them, and, yes, some even cause *others* to die by them. In a classroom, we have found that the best introduction to new material starts small before it is able to spread out and grow tall. We hope that by starting with a half dozen or so of the more popular religious narratives we might spark some interest among teachers in exploring a host of alternative, lesser known religious narratives on their own.

Second, obviously because of space limitations, we will not be able to present an in-depth and extensive presentation of each of these religions. Thus, we will leave it to our readers, if inspired and interested enough, to continue the work themselves of supplementing our introductory remarks about the content of a number of religions, as well as our suggestions for using some creative pedagogy in order to deliver this content. This will entail a consistent self-study course for teachers that ranges more widely and deeply. To this end, we include a brief bibliography of useful religious studies materials at the conclusion of each chapter.

Also, we will be following Ninian Smart's (2000) conceptual framework of how to explore different worldviews. He provides "six dimensions" of all religions, some more important to particular religions than others. These dimensions include: narrative; doctrinal/philosophical; ethical; ritual/practical; experiential/emotional; and social/institutional. We concentrate on the first four of Smart's dimensions—narrative, doctrinal, ethical, and ritual—and conflate the last two into a chapter we call "Religious Controversies and Misconceptions: Red Flags for Teachers."

Our religious overviews of each of these dimensions in the chapters ahead will necessarily be brief, but we want them to be informative. To this end, we concentrate on the central "dimensions" of each of the religions, rather than delving deeply into the academic sidebars—the complexities, details, and esoterica of comparative religious study. Our primary intention, frankly, is to whet teachers' appetites for this subject matter rather than to subject them to a total immersion experience that demands too much for an introductory study.

Finally, we contend that the several religions we discuss in this book contain ideas common to all faith systems. In other words, we believe that there is something in each of these narratives for everyone to appreciate, and, maybe, even to integrate into their own religious worldviews in a way that preserves the integrity of the believer. This, we feel, is a fitting outcome whenever one studies some of the world's greatest, and oldest, wisdom traditions.

Let our Method Mirror our Message

In order to model respectful dialogue, we began this project by consulting our audience directly. We emailed and spoke face-to-face with over one hundred middle and secondary school educators from a variety of disciplines, in both formal and informal discussions. Those teachers who have embraced the need to enhance adolescents' religious literacy were extraordinarily generous with their time and thoughts, sharing with us their challenges and successes in this important endeavor. As a result, we have embedded within our text many of their perspectives, struggles, and helpful approaches. We are deeply grateful to them, both for the crucial work they continue to do, and for their willingness to share so openly.

We hope that how we actually think and write about religion in this book will also serve as a kind of template for our readers as they go about the task of implementing a pedagogy of religious pluralism in their classrooms. May our authorial method, therefore, be consistent with our pedagogical message. This is our intent, even though we know that we will frequently fall short of fully realizing our ideal.

The Language of Narrative

First, a few comments about our use of the language of *narrative*. We believe that stories are indispensable in communicating meaning, inspiring praiseworthy behavior, and in bringing people together in a spirit of compassion and social justice. All the great religious traditions teach best by telling stories. Neil Postman (1996) goes so far as to assert that "... the word 'narrative' is actually a synonym for god—with a small 'g'. God is the name of a great narrative, one that has sufficient credibility, complexity, and symbolic power to enable one to organize our lives around it" (p. 5).

We hold that the brilliance of all the religions and spiritualities the world has ever known lies in their peculiar narrative power. Religion is basically a story lived out by people to give meaning to their lives at various times throughout human history. If this is true, then we must continually ask how a particular narrative created at a particular point in history still speaks to our needs today. How does it help us to understand who we are, to whom we belong, how we should behave, and how we might come to grips with the mystery of our existence?

Thus, we will be using the word *narrative* to describe each of the various religious traditions. We mean no disrespect. We do not mean to imply at all that religions are mere "fictions" or "myths" manufactured mainly to comfort and placate people. Rather, we use the word *narrative* in its original Greek, Latin, and Sanskrit senses: a way of knowing and telling that confers important survival benefits on both the tellers and hearers.

For example, we agree with sociobiologists and evolutionary psychologists that narrativizing could very well be a deep-structure behavior hardwired into the human brain. Thus, the ability to construct religious narratives in our lives allows us to create order and meaning out of apparent chaos. It also enables us to reach out to others across our differences and to unite with them. This skill is as fundamental to human survival as our ability to satisfy our needs for love, food, sex, and shelter. All of these needs define, and complete, our basic humanity.

The Meaning of Spirituality

Second, we hold no particular brief either for, or against, the word *spiritual*. At times, we will use the word as practically synonymous with the word *religious*, as some scholars do today. On principle, they refuse to separate accounts of religion from spirituality, and vice versa, because they know that one without the other is incomplete and artificial. For them, one is head, the other heart. One is public, the other private. One is creedal, the other poetic. One is institutional, the other personal. And, historically, each has often existed in tandem with the other. Thus, we have coined a term to represent this unity: "religio-spirituality." We apologize beforehand for its awkward-sounding tone.

At other times, however, we use the word *spiritual* to differentiate an institutionally-based belief system from a personally-based one, as do so many young and older people today. This distinction is crucial to some adolescents, and to some teachers as well, and we want to be respectful of the strong sentiments behind it.

However, there is an older, more mystical sense of the word that frequently gets lost in modern understandings. Here is Bede Griffiths (1996) on the mystical meaning of spirituality:

> Something breaks suddenly into our lives and upsets their normal pattern, and we have to begin to adjust ourselves to a new kind of existence. The experience may come through nature or poetry, or through art and music; or it may come through the adventure of flying or mountaineering, or of war; or it may come simply through falling in love, or through some apparent accident, an illness, the death of a friend, a sudden loss of fortune. Anything which breaks through the routine of daily life may be the bearer of this message to the soul. (quoted in Harvey, 1996, p. xi)

What Griffiths is saying is that, at times, spirituality, as separate from the formal teachings and practices of organized religion, can lift a veil, and help us to see our lives as if for the first time. We become aware that there is a deeper level of meaning to existence. We see, if only dimly, what one philosopher calls "fleeting signals of transcendence."

During these moments, we no longer exist only as solitary, existential individuals. Now, we experience the universal oneness of the human condition that binds us all together. We are hit in both our hearts and heads with the sudden realization that no matter what church we might belong to, what sacred book we revere, or even whether we are theists, agnostics, or atheists, in the end, life is pretty much an unfathomable mystery. And each of us is a finite creature struggling in our own ways to experience all that our existence has to offer.

The Meaning of Pluralistic Classroom Dialogue

Finally, we hope that our tone in writing this book will model the kind of respectful and generous dialogue about religions that we hope to encourage in the middle and high school classroom. Thus, we begin our thinking and classroom practice with the proposition from the oldest and most sacred Hindu book in the world, the *Rig Veda*: "Ekam sat vipraha bahudha vadanti"—"Truth is one, but the wise call it by many names."

Therefore, we will proceed throughout the book to urge teachers to operate in their classroom conversations from the following assumption: No single person or group has exclusive knowledge, and ownership, of the Ultimate Religious Truth (this does not preclude, of course, the *private belief* that a particular religious narrative does, indeed, possess an exclusive truth for the religious adherent). Rather, in a pluralistic *classroom* dialogue, each of us, along with our students, must learn to appreciate one another as fellow travelers on a continuing quest to call religious truth by our own, special names.

To do this in a classroom, however, each of us will need information, affirmation, support, and clarification throughout the teaching–learning dialogue. In this spirit, then, we recommend the practice of four particular virtues in all classroom dialogues about religion. Taken together, the four virtues can lead to a type of dialogue about religious pluralism based on what Ninian Smart (2000) calls "structured empathy." This method respects the beliefs and nonbeliefs of students because it means "getting at the feel of what is inside another person or group." It means understanding the "structures of beliefs inside the heads" of a believer or nonbeliever.

Humility means that we work hard to attribute the best motive to others, whenever they take the risk to express their thoughts in public (even, especially, when they honestly acknowledge their ignorance, based on stereotypes, about particular religious beliefs and practices). In the name of humility, then, we need to listen carefully to these publicly expressed beliefs and inquiries. We do this because tolerance and compassion begin with an assumption that we are not the only ones who possess wisdom and insight into religious truth. We, too, tend to stereotype and dismiss. We, too, hold fast to half-truths. We, too, are liable to understate and overstate.

Faith means trusting that what we hear from another is worthwhile in some way, if only, and especially, to the religious speaker. In fact, we need to go one step further. We must have confidence that what others have to offer about their understanding of religious beliefs might even be valuable to us in some way. In the words of Mark R. Schwehn (1993), we need to "believe what we are questioning, and at the same time question what we are believing" (p. 49). In any classroom dialogue about religion, we maintain that success is measured by how well each of us is able to make the other person look good. To the extent that we try to make ourselves look good, and the other person look bad, then *we* look bad.

Self-denial suggests that, at some advanced point in any dialogue about religion (and this will differ according to grade level, personal developmental stage, individual maturity, and intellectual readiness level, personal temperament, etc.), each of us will need to reexamine at least a few of the assumptions (and misassumptions) about religion that we cherish. This includes, of course, our pet unchecked biases and uninformed stereotypes.

We will need to learn how to surrender ourselves to the possibility that what might be true to others could, at least in theory, be true to us as well. Self-denial is the inclination to acknowledge that we are willing and able to search for the truth in what we oppose, and the error in what we espouse, at least initially. It means avoiding the opposites of self-denial: arrogance, unwavering certainty, and self-righteousness.

Finally, *charity* is all about attributing the best motive, and looking for the good in others, including, especially, in what others are willing to fight and maybe even die for. Charity is about exercising generosity and graciousness, even, in some instances, affection. This of course does not mean ignoring, or excusing, errors in judgment, faulty reasoning, or one-sided zealotry. In our estimation, a good education in religious literacy is about achieving the virtues that oppose these vices, including the four we elaborate here. We will be talking a lot in the pages ahead about how to initiate, and foster, pluralistic religious dialogue in the classroom and place a special emphasis on this in Chapter 9.

Conclusions

As veteran teachers ourselves, having worked with hundreds of middle and high school teachers and administrators through the years, we are well aware of the risks on every side of what we are proposing in this book. Isn't it inevitable, for example, that some political and religious constituencies in the communities will be offended by our religious literacy project? Yes. Will some teachers and administrators balk at having to take on this additional educational responsibility, and the formal training it will probably entail? Yes. Will it be difficult to teach such a value-loaded subject matter as religious and spiritual diversity without taking sides, either consciously or unconsciously? Yes.

Will it be an ongoing challenge to decide how best to teach for religious literacy, either within the confines of the separate disciplines or across the curriculum? Yes. Will there be pedagogical struggles for teachers in knowing how to separate the cognitive content of religions from the emotional experiences of students (and teachers) who might also be believers or seekers, or even nonbelievers? Yes. Will it be a challenge for teachers about how to handle those situations when questions come up in the classroom about the "truth" of one religion over another? Yes.

Will teachers and administrators have to get clearer, and actually reach some kind of consensus, about the limits of their academic freedom when it comes to teaching for religion literacy? Yes. Will this be hard? Yes. Will teachers need to seek further training in both the content and pedagogy of comparative religious studies in order to feel intellectually comfortable with this very controversial subject matter? Yes.

More practically, will it be demanding for teachers to know exactly how to test for mastery in religious literacy? Yes. Will this require bold and innovative ways to measure results? Yes. Will teachers always need to be ready for those special, teachable moments in the classroom when opportunities open up for what might be a breakthrough conversation about religious difference? Yes.

In short, we know that our proposals are radical. They will shake up conventional teaching and curriculum protocols at the middle and high school levels. But we also know that teachers will be up for the challenge, as they have been for decades in the United States. Just look at how teachers have responded to the various initiatives through the decades to integrate sex education, drug education, career education, multicultural education, citizenship education, and so on, into their curricula. They have frequently tackled all of these wisely and well, recognizing the importance of the work, and there is no reason to believe that they are any less competent to be on the lookout for opportunities to teach for religious literacy.

Finally, it is important to remember that for every pedagogical risk a teacher runs in the classroom, there is always an incredible learning opportunity. As we have tried to show throughout this book, teaching adolescents to be religiously literate presents an unparalleled opportunity for all of us to enlarge and enrich our own learnings about the depth and complexity of religious worldviews as well as our students'. Like us, our students ask the age-old perennial questions in their own adolescent cognitive styles and unique individual voices: How did we get here? What is our purpose while on Earth? What happens when we die? Such questions are basic to humanity, addressed across religious traditions for thousands of years, and are deeply relevant to the daily lives of middle level and secondary students in our public schools. We believe it is time to broaden and deepen our conceptions of multiculturalism to include religious faith as a central component of diversity. Given the clear and reasonable parameters set forth by the First Amendment of the Unites States Constitution, we put forth that public schools are a critical venue through which to educate adolescents about the diverse and ever-changing religious world of which they are a part.

We believe that many teachers want to tackle such difficult and important curriculum in their classrooms. From Vermont to Thailand, dozens of middle and secondary school teachers were willing to participate in our interviews, both via email and face-to-face, responding to questions such as, "What do you hope to achieve by teaching about religion to middle school or secondary students?", "What have you found to be the most effective instructional methods for teaching about religion?", and "What is the most challenging part of teaching about religion?", among others. Their responses confirmed for us that many teachers recognize the vital importance of teaching for religious pluralism. The educators shared myriad successes and failures, all of which helped us to understand what it means to create a pedagogy for religious literacy.

We are fully aware of how deeply sensitive and political the topic of religion is. Religion is the source of debate and consternation between and among communities across our country on a daily basis. Within the past year alone, we have been witness to hundreds of media accounts, detailing profoundly divisive issues in many states, cities, and towns. A quick trip to the search engine Google will turn up most of these accounts for those who might be interested.

Kansans, for example, experienced the emotional trial in which the board of education attempted to reconcile the role of evolution within its science standards. Texans encountered a heated debate about bible electives in public schools. Minnesotans saw arguments over their recent life science standards, which were revised to include that students must understand how new evidence can challenge accepted theories, including but not limited to cell theory and the theory of evolution. Pennsylvanians felt the challenging divide when one local school board required that evolution be taught alongside the theory that humankind owes its origins to an "intelligent designer" and another faction of the community rapidly brought a lawsuit against the board in response.

Yes, we recognize daily the controversial roots of the topic. Yet it is precisely because religion is so sensitive, heated, and political that the work toward religious literacy is urgent. Prothero (2005) commented on this urgency by reminding us of a tragic event,

> A few days after 9/11, a turbaned Indian American man was shot and killed in Arizona by a bigot who believed the man's dress marked him as a Muslim. But what killed Balbir Singh Sodhi (who was not a Muslim but a Sikh) was not so much bigotry as ignorance. The moral of his story is not just that we need more tolerance. It is that Americans—of both the religious and the secular variety—need to understand religion. (www.csmonitor .com/2005/0120/p09s02-coop.html)

We agree that Americans need to understand religion. And we believe middle and secondary schools are excellent venues for the exploration of such subject matter. How can an educator tackle such potentially volatile topics in his or her own community? The answers lie within both pedagogy and partnership.

Through Pedagogy

First, it is imperative that teachers understand the limitations and possibilities outlined in the First Amendment, which delineates clearly that educators may teach about religion in a way that does not promote or denigrate any particular belief system. In the 1963 case of *Abington vs. Schempp*, Supreme Court Justice Tom Clark wrote in the majority opinion, "It might well be said that one's education is not complete without a study of comparative religion . . . and its relationship to the advance of civilization." If so, then the education of most public school students in this country is indeed, at present, incomplete. Because of misunderstandings and misrepresentations of the First Amendment, too many teachers fail to understand, as Prothero (2005) put it, "the subtle distinction between teaching religion (unconstitutional) and teaching about religion (essential)."

Furthermore, as we will outline in Chapter 8 of this book, to teach about religion, teachers must be diligent about attending to the climate of the classroom. This means creating a safe culture in which to explore sensitive topics and developing community norms. It means introducing the precepts of a moral conversation, in which all members of the dialogue feel both respected and heard.

It means asking and encouraging meaningful questions, questions that are at the heart of adolescent ponderings. It also means adopting a constructivist approach, in which teachers become helpful guides and facilitators, removing themselves from having the one "right" answer. And it means promoting rich inner dialogue, through which adolescents can grapple with life's biggest existential questions.

Finally, the study of religion should be embedded wherever meaningful connections can be made within the curriculum. Religion is not the sole purview of the social studies teacher, nor is it the sole purview of the teacher down the hall who does an annual unit on world cultures. Religion is inherently interdisciplinary, and it has a place throughout the curriculum, in the sciences, humanities, and arts. State or national standards that emphasize critical thinking, comparing and contrasting, analyzing, summarizing, evaluating, interpreting, and debating are a good place for educators to find a fit between teaching for religious literacy and teaching in order to meet mandates for common standards. We have found such a fit in our own state's educational standards, and we did not have to look that hard. The fit is there if only educators will take the time, and make the effort, to read through these documents.

Through Partnership

In order to carry out this challenging and potentially volatile work, we also suggest that teachers find others in their schools, "traveling companions" so to speak, who believe in the importance of teaching for religious literacy. The road to teaching for religious literacy ideally is not traveled alone. One of the public school educators with whom we consulted reflected on her students' learning about religion: "They have shown such profoundly little knowledge of religion before we start this unit that we've become utterly convinced of its importance." Together, she and her colleagues work toward a common goal. Working in partnership with others can provide support, extra resources, and a critical lens for reflecting on one's practice.

Furthermore, enlisting the support of the school's administration is a significant component. To enlist this support, teachers, like Rachel and Jake in Chapter 9, need to clearly present their rationale, the facts that illustrate the vital importance of religious literacy, and their understanding of the First Amendment. Doing so helps anticipate any concerns prior to their emergence.

While building-based partners can be helpful, community partners serve another important role. Local colleges or universities can be helpful, as can community religious groups, as long as one engages multiple diverse groups that are committed to promoting a pluralistic view and are coming together for the sake of global understanding. Without this common agreement, teachers run the risk of being perceived as affiliated with a particular religious organization and, perhaps, as planning to use the public schools to promulgate special religious beliefs of one kind or another. It is also worth talking explicitly with community partners about the ramifications of the First Amendment and the role it plays in the study of religion in public schools.

Preliminary Words of Advice and Caution

Engaging adolescents in exploring religious pluralism in the public school classroom is without question a challenging task. Certainly, it is easier to stick with the tried-and-true approaches to curriculum, and to teach from a place of comfort. Teaching from the inside-out, honoring meaningful questions, adopting a constructivist approach, and creating community within the classroom require time, energy, and practice. They are sure to be met with both failure and success.

Additionally, the concepts and narratives in the world's major and minor religions are complex and challenging for even the most advanced of students. Furthermore, teaching for religious literacy invites controversy. Those who choose to embrace such a pedagogy will undoubtedly meet up with those who oppose it, and because religion is an integral part of many people's lives, such opposition can feel both hurtful and personal.

We recognize all of this and still we believe the benefits of helping students understand the world's vast religious diversity from a pluralistic perspective far outweigh these challenges. The only way to avoid a cycle of religio-political aggression, one that begins with ignorance, leads to fear and violence, and finally to war, is to equip students with a working knowledge of the global population that surrounds them.

Why was our country attacked on 9/11? Who are these attackers, and why do they hate us? What do they believe? What makes us right? What makes them right? Teachers who were with students in middle and secondary school classrooms on that terrible Tuesday, the eleventh of September, in 2001 will hear in these questions echoes of the very ones posed to them in the days that immediately followed. These are important questions indeed, and we do not serve our students or our global community well when we ignore them.

On the contrary, we need to engage such important questions head-on, and continually invite still others to be posed, no matter how provocative or controversial. We need to grapple with such crucial concepts; build a community within our classroom that enables the safe and respectful exploration of difficult and existential questions; and honor multiple perspectives in a deeply pluralistic and moral way. Only then will students understand the motivations and behaviors of those around them. Only then will we achieve a more multicultural, pluralistic world.

For thousands of years, religion has been a central part of humanity. Whenever we, as educators, exclude or minimize religion's vast role in society, we leave out a large part of our world's shared history. This is a serious act of educational omission, even neglect, on the part of our nation's public middle and secondary schools, particularly when adolescents are so very ready to engage in meaningful dialogue about the world that surrounds them.

As Greene (1995) advised educators,

> Our classrooms ought to be nurturing and thoughtful and just all at once; they ought to pulsate with multiple conceptions of what it is to be human and alive. They ought to resound with the voices of articulate young people in dialogues always incomplete because there is always more to be discovered and more to be said. We must want our students to achieve friendship as each one stirs to wide-awakeness, to imaginative action, and to renewed consciousness of possibility. (p. 43)

Such dialogues are the hallmark of teaching for religious literacy in today's middle and secondary schools. These multiple conceptions of humanity are at the very heart of the religious pluralism that we so dearly need and that our adolescents so clearly deserve.

Religious Pluralism Resources for Teachers: A Brief Bibliographic Essay

The best and clearest treatment of the relationship between religion and science is Ian G. Barbour's *Religion and Science: Historical and Contemporary Issues* (San Francisco: Harper, 1997). The fairest, and most accessible, examination of the current brouhaha concerning intelligent design, creationism, and evolution is Michael Ruse's *Can A Darwinian Be A Christian?: The Relationship Between Science and Religion* (New York: Cambridge University Press, 2001).

As preparation for putting together some type of religious literacy curriculum, teachers ought to read Nel Noddings's *Educating for Intelligent Belief or Unbelief* (New York: Teachers College Press, 1993). Noddings's book is thematically constructed for high school teachers. Written from a philosopher's perspective, the book covers such religion-oriented concepts as theism, polytheism, belonging, feminism and religion, immortality, salvation, humanism, unbelief, and ethics.

Another must-read for teachers is Warren A. Nord's and Charles C. Haynes's *Taking Religion Seriously Across the Curriculum* (Alexandria, VA: ASCD, 1998.). Nord and Haynes review the major legal battles fought over the right to teach about religion in public schools. They also focus their attention on how to integrate religious issues into public school curricula from a disciplinary perspective. Finally, no study of the upsides and downsides of teaching for religious literacy in secular educational venues is complete without Warren Nord's majestic *Religion and American Education: Rethinking a National Dilemma.* (Chapel Hill: University of North Carolina Press, 1995).

A valuable primer on religious issues written primarily for lay audiences is Stephen Prothero's *Religious Literacy: What Every American Needs to Know—And Doesn't* (New York: HarperOne, 2008).

For a more focused examination of the evolution of school-prayer conflicts dating from the early 1800s to the present day, see Joan DelFattore, *The Fourth R: Conflicts Over Religion in America's Public Schools* (New Haven, CT: Yale University Press, 2004). DelFattore has the ability to write about complex legal issues without jargon and in a way that is engrossing for lay readers.

For a down-to-earth, highly readable guide to first amendment issues in the public schools, see Charles C. Haynes and Oliver Thomas, *Finding Common Ground: A Guide to Religious Liberty in Public Schools* (Nashville, TN: First Amendment Center, 2001). This guide is a treasure trove of resources, and it includes curricular materials, student religious practices, character education content, and various school district policies regarding religious liberty in schools and communities throughout the United States.

For a wonderful, very readable content overview of the world's major religious wisdom traditions, see Huston Smith's classic work, *The World's Religions: Our Great Wisdom Traditions* (San Francisco: HarperSanFrancisco, 1991). This is a book that has sold in the millions since its initial publication in 1958. It was written for a nonprofessional, as well as a professional, audience, which explains, in part, its great popularity. One other extremely accessible introduction to the enormous growth of religious diversity in the United States is Diana L. Eck's *A New Religious America: How A "Christian Country" Has Become the World's Most Religiously Diverse Nation* (San Francisco: HarperSanFrancisco, 2001). We have drawn generously from both works throughout our book.

2

The Narrative of Judaism

Case Study #1: "Christ Killer!"

As Gina Theodorakos strode down the hall from lunch duty in the cafeteria in the direction of her classroom, she mentally prepped for her next math class. This particular group had been falling more and more behind each day and she worried about their performance on the upcoming state tests. As she turned the corner, she noticed immediately the cluster of girls in front of the row of lockers outside her door. The students' faces were visibly concerned and the group of students appeared to be consoling whomever was in the middle of the group. After fifteen years of teaching at this urban school, Gina was no stranger to the adolescent angst and drama that regularly unfolded in the hallways. While pulling out her keys to unlock the classroom door, she turned to ask the group what was wrong.

"Ms. T," one girl blurted out, "Check out what someone wrote on Susan's locker." Sighing, Gina turned the key in the lock, opened her door, and shooed the group of students into her classroom. Only Susan now remained, standing in disbelief in front of her locker. On it was scrawled

Teaching Adolescents Religious Literacy in a Post-9/11 World, pages 27–43
Copyright © 2010 by Information Age Publishing
All rights of reproduction in any form reserved.

"Christ Killer" in barely legible spray paint. Gina drew in a sharp breath, put an arm around Susan's shoulder, and asked her when the words had appeared.

"I don't know," Susan admitted, "This is the first time I've been to my locker today. And, remember? I was out yesterday for Rosh Hashanah. But I know who wrote it. One of those stupid kids from our math class."

Gina thought back to last week's conversation in their class, when Susan had informed her that she would be missing school in observance of the Jewish New Year. A voice from the back of the room had shouted out, "Hey, that's no fair, man!" And another had joined in, laughing, "Yeah, why should *she* get to miss the exam? Just to go and hang out with a bunch of people wearing funny hats and long beards?"

"You don't understand. This is one of the holiest days of the year," another Jewish student explained. "And besides," he added, "We never even think of having school on Christmas or New Year's Eve, do we?"

The conversation quickly turned into a heated debate, with many students shouting across the room and few students listening. At the time, Gina had been extremely uncomfortable with many of the comments; she had been eager to shut down the conversation as quickly as possible. After all, she couldn't be expected to discuss religion in her math class, could she? Not only was this class a full chapter behind in the mandated curriculum sequence, but Gina also felt completely unprepared to discuss matters of faith with any authority. As a result, she had intervened quickly and steered the class back to their math work. Yet now Gina wondered if she had done the right thing. If she had taken the time to distill some of these misconceptions, she pondered, would she and Susan be standing here now? Had she missed a magnificent, although admittedly difficult, teachable moment due to her own discomfort?

The Universal Fear of Examining Religious Stereotypes in the Classroom

Gina is at that familiar point for all teachers when she wonders if her choice to avoid (rather than tackle head-on) a controversial subject in the classroom is the best pedagogical decision. On the one hand, stereotypical comments made by adolescents in a classroom about a major, monotheistic faith cry out for a teacher's direct intervention. On the other hand, Gina is teaching a math class and feels tremendous pressure from the great emphasis placed on numeracy by the state assessments. And, as everyone knows, math is more about numbers than words, more about calculations than philosophical or religious ideas. At least, this is the way that Gina was trained at the state university to think about her subject matter.

What Gina actually knows about religion is nil. For example, she feels badly that she cannot even put two or three coherent sentences together explaining the meaning of a popular Jewish holiday like Rosh Hashanah. Even her own childhood religious upbringing in the Greek Orthodox Church was conspicuously devoid of theological understandings. She remembers that a student once asked her after school what the difference was between Greek Orthodoxy and Roman Catholicism, and why Greeks were not Roman Catholics. In addition, the student inquired as to why Greek Orthodox priests were allowed to marry and Catholic priests needed to remain celibate. Truth to tell, Gina did not even know where to begin to answer these types of questions. So she faked a few words of response, abruptly changed the subject, and walked away from the conversation feeling very unsatisfied.

Fear! All teachers know the feeling. It manifests in the classroom in many ways: anxiety and agitation in being aware of the nearness of danger; fright, timidity, dread, even sheer terror, over saying the wrong thing at the wrong time. Fear can paralyze. Fear can be unreasonable. Fear can lead to an irrational decision. Fear can tie teachers into knots, and cause them to go against their better professional judgments. Fear can send teachers into frantic flight or fight responses.

Imagine, then, Gina's fear the instant she sees those dreaded words scrawled in spray paint on Susan's locker door; cruel words so often used against the Jewish people throughout the past 2,000 years to justify the worst kinds of religious and political discrimination, persecution, and genocide—"Christ Killer!" Gina second-guesses herself. Could she have possibly headed off such terrible, hurtful graffiti if she had dealt immediately with the ignorant stereotyping of Jews that was circulating that day in her math classroom?

But how might she have done that without causing more problems, indeed, worse problems? What if she ended up inflaming all the old prejudices against Jews? What if she said something stupid based on her own unexamined stereotypes? What if she did not know how to lead an intelligent, more "light-than-heat" conversation on such a controversial topic like religious prejudice? How would she ever explain her failures to her principal or to a Jewish parent? Fear often leads to avoidance in the classroom. And avoidance inevitably leads to problems left unresolved, problems that frequently come back to haunt teachers and students alike. This is what is happening to Gina, and she hates the feeling.

Is Judeo-Phobia Inevitable in Christian America?

We intentionally use the term "Judeo-phobia" in this chapter rather than anti-Semitism. Judeo-phobia is an irrational, excessive, and persistent fear of Jews and, especially, Judaism. It is fanned by the media and politicians, particularly today when Jews are cast as the unjust persecutors of Islamic Palestinians. Moreover, many non-Jews resent the Jewish self-designation of "God's chosen people." Finally, many secular politicians on the left are wary of the Christian United States' apparent unquestioning support of Jewish interests in the Middle East. All of this, of course, feeds the fear of Jews and Judaism in this country, particularly when this phobia is taken only at face value and not subjected to closer scrutiny. In our opinion, Judeo-phobia begins with a grave misunderstanding, and ignorance, of the religion of Judaism.

Not so, anti-Semitism, however. The term "anti-Semitism," coined first by German writer Wilhelm Marr in 1879, describes a far stronger resentment, even hatred, of Jews. (Technically, it is important to understand that the term itself is incorrect, in the sense that Semitic people also include Arabs as well as other Middle Eastern populations. A more accurate term would be "anti-Jew.")

While much, if not most, of this antipathy against the Jews is also based on ignorance and fear, it is, nevertheless, grounded in a willful prejudice and hostility. Some extremist, white supremacists, for example, see Jews as the powerful leaders of a worldwide conspiracy, wielding a disproportionate influence in banking, Hollywood, behind-the-scenes politics, law, education, medicine, and other professional institutions. Some members of radical Christian Identity movements (the Christian militias, the Aryan Nation) do, indeed, think of the Jews as "Christ killers," and, in past years, a few deranged people in these groups have even attempted to injure and kill the "Christ-killing" Jews.

We are concerned in this chapter about dispelling the ubiquity of Judeo-phobia both in the United States and abroad. Perhaps, along the way, this will lead to the dissolution of anti-Semitism, perhaps not. We hope, though, that at the very least it calls into question those stereotypes about Judaism that are rampant throughout this country. One of the best places for this type of critical deconstruction to occur, we believe, is in public school classrooms filled with very impressionable, stereotype-prone adolescents.

While, admittedly, much of this Judeo-phobia is political, racial, and anti-Zionist (a term for those who advocated, and later supported, the establishment of the Jewish national state of Israel), we contend that much of it is also based on blatant religious ignorance. For example, there is as much logic in calling all Jews "Christ killers" as there is in calling all Christians "Jew killers" (because some Nazi officers, who also happened to be devout Protestants and Catholics, played an active role in killing Jews in the death camps of the Holocaust).

Few people we know in our own public school experience really understand the religio-spiritual relationship of Judaism to Christianity beyond a few well-known clichés. One of these is that Jesus came to earth to fulfill, and complete, the teachings of the Jewish prophets. Therefore, the so-called "Old Testament" teachings were eventually replaced by "New Testament" teachings—hence, no longer necessary. The New Testament God now took the place of the Old Testament God. The conclusion to be drawn is a logical one for many Christians: Why then the need for a Jewish God when there is a better one available?

Moreover, some theologians have drawn extra sharp contrasts between Judaism and Christianity (Schoeps, 1968). Early church fathers, like Melito of Sardis and John Chrysostom, went so far as to condemn the Jews themselves, and, in the process, argued that Christianity was self-evidently superior to Judaism. Even St. Paul himself in Galatians 2:21 warned that "If righteousness comes through Torah, then Christ died for nothing." No wonder, then, that Jews through the ages were regarded, even by such famous Enlightenment thinkers as Diderot and Voltaire, as the ultimate aliens in a Christian society. And no wonder as well that historically Jews have been marginalized and unjustly accused of a variety of heinous crimes against Christians.

Surely, at some level, Gina, the math teacher, senses that there is much more for students to know about Jews, and maybe one of the best places to start is with an informed introduction to, and a dialogue about, the religion of Judaism. She is convinced that the place to start is with the phenomenon of Judeo-phobia, because it is her strong position that phobias can be reversed by valid information and honest, give-and-take conversation. She is convinced that they can be unlearned.

She only wishes, however, that she, herself, knew more about Judaism, and its relationship to Christianity, than she actually does. She still does not understand, for example, how God-fearing Christians in Nazi Germany could stand by and go along with the Holocaust. She knows that Christianity and genocide are obvious contradictions in terms. During the time following her upsetting experience with that ugly class stereotyping and that even uglier Judeo-phobic graffiti, Gina resolves to undertake some intensive study of Judaism on her own.

Core Beliefs and Practices in the Judaism Narrative

The Narrative Dimension

Judaism as a whole can best be characterized as a continuing narrative of "exile and return." The history of Judaism is a long, painful story of destruction and restoration, Holocaust and survival. Here is a people who have lived through centuries of the worst kinds of persecution, and yet, despite their relatively tiny numbers, they have suffered and endured, and in many cases, actually prospered. For one, their religious influence has been huge throughout the world, forming, at least in part, the philosophical and theological basis of both Christianity and Islam.

Judaism is the oldest monotheistic religion in the world, dating back anywhere from 2000 B.C.E. (Before the Common Era) to 1260 B.C.E., when thousands of Jews left Egypt, following their prophet, Moses. It was at this time that the Jews settled in Canaan and formed the twelve tribes of Israel. Much of Jewish history has been a time of moving from land to land trying to find a place to rest and to settle. Following the *shofet* (judge) Saul's death, in 1050 B.C.E., David became the king of Judah, and Jerusalem became a religious center where the Ark of the Covenant with God was kept. His son, Solomon, a man of legendary wisdom, reigned after David's death, and built the famous Jerusalem temple that housed the Ark on Mt. Zion.

After Solomon's death, two kingdoms emerged, Israel and Judah, and, in 722 B.C.E., the Assyrian Empire conquered the Jews. In 587 B.C.E., the Babylonian emperor destroyed the first Jerusalem temple. At that time, most of Judah's population went into Babylonian captivity. After being freed by the Persian emperor Cyrus, most Jews went back to Jerusalem and rebuilt the temple. However, in 167 B.C.E., the Seleucid Emperor abolished Jewish law and profaned the temple. This instigated the Jewish Maccabean revolt in 164 B.C.E. Hanukkah, the Jewish holy day, celebrates this revolt and the rededication of the Temple.

In 40 B.C.E., Herod, an unpopular ruler, became King of the Jews, as proclaimed by the Romans. Jewish Zealots (*sicarii*), in reaction, resorted to acts of terrorism and insurgency against the Roman Empire. In retaliation for this rebellion, the Romans destroyed the temple by fire, and the imperial army razed Jerusalem to the ground. The last Jewish resisters were killed in 74 B.C.E. in Masada. And, later, in a final act of retaliation by the Romans, the population of Judah, a remaining stronghold of Jews, was depopulated. Jewish religious practices were banned throughout the Empire, and, at the end of the 4th century C.E. (Common Era), Christianity became the official religion of the Roman Empire.

We believe that this brief history of the Jews is necessary in order for educators to understand the extraordinary plight of the Jewish people right up to the present day. Historically, the Jews are a people of "exile and return." They are an incredibly persistent and courageous people. Despite centuries of persecution, most Jews today refuse to see themselves as history's victims.

At the present time, Judaism is a relatively small global religion, numbering around 20 million followers distributed throughout the world. About 5–7 million Jews live in Israel, and the largest concentration, about 7–10 million, resides in the United States. The remaining Jews live in the former Soviet Union, Western Europe, Canada, Argentina, South Africa, and Brazil. These countries account for almost 95 percent of the world Jewish population.

Despite their tiny size in the global community, religious Jews believe they have endured through centuries of persecution, genocide, and population upheavals (the Diaspora) because of their special status as defined in the Pentateuch (the Five Books of Moses given to him by God, and referred to as the Torah). In these first five books in the Jewish Bible (Genesis, Exodus, Leviticus, Numbers, and Deuteronomy), God identifies the children of Abraham, Isaac, and Jacob as His "chosen people." "Your descendants will be aliens living in a land that is not theirs . . . but I will punish that nation whose slaves they are, and after that they shall come out with great possessions" (Genesis 15:13–14).

The Torah explains the basis for the persistence and power of the Jewish narrative throughout history. Despite current scholarly concern about whether Moses actually authored the Pentateuch, the Torah is still seen by a majority of religious Jews as the divine revelation of God's indomitable will for His special people. This is sometimes referred to by scholars as the "doctrine of election." "It was not because you were more in number than other people . . . but because the Lord loves you [that he] has chosen you to be a people for his own" (Deuteronomy 7:6–8).

Huston Smith (1991), the comparative religions scholar, points out that, today, Jewish opinion about the doctrine of election is sharply divided between those who consider it arrogant and those who consider it necessary in order to give meaning to Jewish pain, suffering, and violent death throughout history. But whatever the final verdict on the doctrine of election, educators need to understand that most religious Jews believe they have been called upon by God to survive history's atrocities against them for a Divine reason.

If not this, how, then, to explain the following crimes of inhumanity committed against a small minority of people: the terrible persecution and dispersal of Jews by dominant Christians and Muslims throughout the centuries; the renewal of Czarist Russian pogroms in 1881 that slaughtered hundreds of thousands of Jews; the Nazi-sponsored Holocaust that obliterated 6 million people (one-third of the entire world's population of Jews); the creation of Israel in 1948, a small Jewish state, that has since faced numerous political, military, and terrorist threats to its existence in the Middle East. The concept of being "God's chosen people" is what has kept Jews alive and prospering for over two-and-one-half millennia.

But what does it mean to be "God's chosen people"? What exactly are the Jews called upon to do in the world, in God's hallowed name? What is it that Jews believe by way of their religion? And how do these beliefs help to define their mission in the world today? Is Judaism a single, internally consistent, religio-spiritual narrative, or is it, like Christianity, an intramural, pluralistic religio-spiritual narrative? If Judaism is, indeed, a religious mansion with many rooms, are there any common religio-spiritual beliefs that transcend particular doctrinal and group differences within Judaism? Is there any validity to a familiar quatrain, sometimes uttered in admiration, sometimes in disdain, that has echoed through the ages: "How odd/ Of God/To choose/The Jews."

The Doctrinal Dimension

At the outset, it is important for educators to know that Jews are as internally diverse a people as any other ethnic, national, religious, or racial group. So, too, are those who believe in, and practice, the religion of Judaism. Although Judaism is not a doctrinally (creedal) driven belief narrative, it does contain certain tenets (principles and beliefs). But how Jews approach these tenets differs markedly according to whether they self-identify as Orthodox, Ultraorthodox, Conservative, and Reform. (Remember, too, that there is considerable heteropraxy [different practices] and heterodoxy [different beliefs] *within* each of these categories.)

Orthodox Jews believe in being strictly loyal to the "faith of the rabbis and prophets," as this has been received from antiquity. This means preserving the rituals, traditions, and doctrines, as set out in the Torah and developed in the Talmud, in as exact a form as possible. Some Orthodox Jews, however, refer to themselves as "observant," or "traditional," preferring these less value-loaded terms.

Ultra-Orthodox Jews are not a homogeneous group. One tradition, the Lithuanian, stresses continuing Talmudic study and analysis in the yeshivah (academy). These ultra-orthodox Jews are the scholars of Judaism. The other tradition, the Hasidism (Hebrew word for "pious"), is a revivalist movement marked by mystical practices. Its main purpose is to deepen spiritual devotion by encouraging joyous activities such as singing and dancing.

Conservative Jews do not stress absolute adherence to the traditional beliefs and practices of Judaism. Conservatives cherish these beliefs and practices, of course, and they strive to achieve a decent continuity with the ancient ideals; but they also see the need to make certain adjustments of the faith based on the social realities of the present. These adaptations must always be compatible with the essence of ancient teachings; however, for Conservatives, it is also important that they find a way to negotiate, and resolve, the tension that exists between tradition and modernity in Judaism that confronts Jews in every culture.

Reform Jews are pragmatists. They are not "strict biblical constructionists." They are more than willing to engage in ongoing conversations about what religious beliefs and practices might best fit the modern world. Certainly, the Law (*Halakhah*) in Hebrew scriptures is central to Reform Jews' understanding of their religion, but so too is a flexible and up-to-date interpretation of the Law. Reform Jews are "autonomous biblical constructionists" in the sense that individuals are granted greater authority in deciding how to understand, and apply, the lessons of the Hebrew scriptures to their own lives.

What follows are a series of precepts that we think most religious Jews—differing interpretations and emphases notwithstanding—would endorse as central to their faith narrative:

- As the world's first major monotheistic religion, Judaism is guided by several central theological precepts. All of them, however, are grounded in one or two pivotal beliefs. The first is expressed in Psalm 19 that "The heavens declare the glory of God; and the firmament showeth his handiwork." Also, as recorded in Deuteronomy 6:4: "Hear, Oh Israel, the Lord our God, the Lord is One." Thus, the Jews' religious legacy to the world—unlike the Greeks, Romans, Syrians, and other Mediterranean peoples who believed in a very different type of deity(ies)—was to experience God as one and indivisible. Moreover, this God was said to be loving, kind, righteous, and just.
- The first chapter of Genesis starts with "In the beginning God created the heavens and the earth . . . [and He decided that] everything that He had made . . . was very good." In key passages throughout the Torah, Judaism teaches that God is *unspeakably*

great (some Orthodox and Conservative Jews take this adverb literally, and respectfully refer to the name of God as G–d). Furthermore, human beings are made in the image and likeness of their God, and, hence, are God's beloved creatures.

■ For religious Jews, human history has a meaning, a Divine destiny, if you will. We do not live in an amoral, purposeless world, with human beings amounting to nothing more than worthless specs in a multigalaxied, infinitely expanding universe. Neither are we, in Victorian poet and novelist Thomas Hardy's words, "mere flies that the gods kill for their sport." No, in contrast, religious Jews believe that human beings are majestic and significant creatures. They are God's chosen people, and they are called upon to love their God with their whole hearts, minds, and souls; and, as important, to love their neighbors as much as they love themselves.

■ In return for their obedience to God and kindness to their neighbors, Jews will enter into a special covenant, and God will establish and sustain them as His precious people.

■ What God asks in particular of His chosen people, in return for the great gifts he has given them, has been revealed to them in the Torah, Judaism's major source of divine revelation. It is in the Torah, as well as in the Mishna (oral, legal interpretations of the Torah) and in the Talmud (a collection of original studies, commentaries, anecdotes, allegories, and interpretations throughout the centuries meant to supplement and elaborate the Torah), where Jews can locate the central doctrinal beliefs.

To summarize: Rabbi Moses ben Maimonides (1135–1204) states his version of common doctrinal truths in his commentary on the Mishna (cited in Schoeps, 1968, p. 223). Among the most crucial are the following:

1. "God is the Creator and Guide of everything that has been created."
2. "God is one, and He alone is our God, who was, is, and will be."
3. "God is not corporeal."
4. "It is proper to pray only to the Creator and to Him alone."
5. "All the words of the prophets are perfectly true."
6. "The prophecy of Moses was true, and he was the chief of the prophets."
7. "The whole Law is the same that was given to Moses."
8. "This Law will not be changed, and there will never be another from the Creator."

9. "The Creator knows every action and every thought of the children of His Creation."
10. "The Creator rewards those who observe his commandments, and punishes those that transgress them."

The Ethical Dimension

A practicing Jew is someone who not only attempts to understand the meanings of the Law in Jewish scripture, but, more important, strives to put the moral laws of God into actual day-to-day actions. In other words, it is not enough simply to *know* God's will. What counts is *doing* God's will. And this means following the Law by doing good to others. One way to do this, according to medieval Jewish philosopher Moses Maimonides, is to act toward others in such a way that every action bespeaks the presence of God in the world.

For religious Jews, God is perfect, the "Creator of heaven and earth." God made human beings in His holy image, and God is both merciful and just. Therefore, as God's chosen people, Jews have a unique responsibility to fulfill His faith in them by actually putting into practice the moral teachings of the Torah. In a nutshell, the most succinct way to capture the essence of Jewish ethics is to hear the words of the Jewish scholar Hillel more than 2,000 years ago when asked by a non-Jew how to become a good Jew: "What is hateful unto you, do not do unto your neighbor. The rest is commentary—now go and study" (cited in Schoeps, 1968, p. 229). Christians know this as the Golden Rule, asserted by Jesus, but it was first put into words by a Jewish Rabbi who preceded him by several years.

"Let justice roll down like waters, and righteousness like an ever-flowing stream," Yahweh (God) says in Amos (5:21–24). Also, here is a contemporary scholar, Jacob Neusner (in Sharma, 1993), commenting on what makes Judaism ethically unique in the history of religion: "...it is the amazing power of what Judaism calls 'the Torah' to exalt the humble, to strengthen the weak, to give joy to the disappointed, and hope to the disheartened, to make ordinary life holy and sacred and significant for people who, in the end, are not much different from everybody else, except that believing has made them so" (p. 353). This is Neusner's contemporary "commentary" on Hillel's, and later Jesus's, Golden Rule of ethics.

What might be considered an additional "commentary" on the Golden Rule of ethics is the Decalogue (the Ten Commandments), first appearing in Exodus 20:2–17, and said to be given to Moses directly by God. Most educators have heard of the Ten Commandments, but it is rare in our experience to find educators who are able to name all of them from memory. In our opinion, students need to learn about these 10 principles of ethical behavior if they are to understand the basic moral precepts of the three major monotheistic religions, each of which embraces them in some fashion.

For example, throughout the *Qur'an*, the holy book of Islam, Moses is considered a major prophet, someone who is on a par with Muhammad. It was Moses, remember, who conveyed Divine Revelation to humanity, including the Decalogue (although the Ten Commandments are never mentioned explicitly in the Qur'an).

The first four commandments of the Decalogue stipulate each person's responsibility to God. The first three forbid polytheism, idolatry, and taking God's name in vain, and the fourth orders people to keep holy the seventh day of the week, the Lord's day. The last six commandments spell out each person's responsibility to others. The fifth commandment is the only commandment that is not stated as a negative injunction. It simply tells people to obey and honor their parents. The final five commandments, all stated as "Thou Shalt Nots," include prohibitions against killing, adultery, stealing, lying, and coveting the possessions of others.

Orthodox and Conservative Jews tend to take the Ten Commandments literally. Reform Jews tend to be much more flexible in their interpretations, seeing them as helpful guides to moral action, to be sure, but rules, nevertheless, that must be adapted to the realities of contemporary cultural contexts.

The Ritual Dimension

As we have seen, religious Jews are a diverse and scattered group. Particular theological emphases differ. Specific interpretations of scriptural passages vary, often dramatically. Ethical obligations tend to shift according to time, context, and culture. And worship activities cover a wide range of practices. Given these differences, however, what remains irrevocably important to all religious Jews is the *ritual* aspect of their faith story.

In fact, it can be argued that rituals and ceremonies define the religious Jew today far more accurately than do stories, doctrines, and ethics. There is a universal aspect regarding the importance of the liturgical dimension of Judaism for most religious, and even for some secular, Jews that is lacking in other areas. Why is this so?

One theory that we find congenial is that, historically, Jews have been forced, as a matter of sheer survival in a hostile world, to be a communal people. Jewish ritual and worship, particularly in the synagogue (a place that brings Jews together for worship and religious study of the Torah), have given Jews the opportunity to gather together in a supportive and tightly-knit community. In fact, it has been in the synagogue/temple where, throughout their history, most Jews experienced the feeling of being one large ethnic family, bonded together by an all-pervasive sacred liturgy and spirituality that defines their common history as a people.

Regardless of theological and cultural differences throughout the world, it is in the synagogue where Jews offer prayers (*beracha*) of praise and thanksgiving. It is in the synagogue where the Jewish community comes together in order to perpetuate its traditions. One way to do this is through prayer. Prayer, for the religious Jew, is the earthly bridge to God. The basic prayer texts have not changed for 1,500 years. And they are supplemented by other texts on certain feast days. In the Jewish service, the rabbi reads the Torah on each Sabbath in 54 weekly sections throughout the liturgical year. Some Jews keep the Sabbath laws more strictly than others, but most Jews use the Sabbath as a necessary day of rest.

The Sabbath service consists of salutations and prayers to God (*Amidah*), pledges of faith (*Sh'ma*), and public readings of passages from the Torah (the *aliyah* [going up] summons Jews from the congregation to actively participate in these readings). Rabbis lead the actual service, and cantors lead the congregation in song.

Briefly, here are the major observant holy days during the liturgical year (from fall to fall) for religious Jews. Rosh Hashanah and Yom Kippur are the "High Holy Days" (sometimes referred to as *Yamim Noraim*, the "Days of Awe") of Jewish worship:

- *Rosh Hashanah.* Literally, this translates to "the New Year," or "Head of the Year," and it is celebrated on the first and second days of *Tishrei*, a month that goes from the middle of September to the middle of October. Rosh Hashanah is the beginning of the penitential season. It is a birthday celebration of the human race. It is during Rosh Hashanah that religious Jews celebrate God the Creator and God's human Creation as well. Here is a phrase that is heard over and over again in the liturgy during this holy day: "Remember us unto life, for You, Oh King, delight in life; inscribe us in the Book of Life, for Your sake, Oh God of life." To which Jews exchange this greeting: "May you be so inscribed and sealed for a good year."
- *Yom Kippur.* This is the holiest day of the Jewish year, following 10 days of penitence and fasting. It takes place on the 10th day of Tishrei, and it is translated as the "Day of Atonement." In one sense, Judaism is all about repentence and atonement. Yom Kippur is a time for Jews to confess their sins in order to

get right with God. They do this through prayer and supplication. Like Moses standing on Mount Sinai—alone, broken, and desolate—after the destruction of the Golden Calf, and looking for the presence of God in the darkness, so too for Jews in the temples of today. They seek God in the darkness, and it is only when they promise to transform their attitudes and behavior that God answers them and grants grace and mercy. Sometimes the Atonement liturgy consumes an entire day (some Jews fast for 24 hours), ended by a blast of the shofar (ram's horn).

■ *Chanukah* (Hanukkah). The term means "Festival of Lights," and Jews are insistent that this holy day is not the equivalent of Christmas for Christians. The holy day occurs around the middle of December, and it celebrates not Jesus's birthday, but the victory of the Maccabees over the Syrians in the 2nd century B.C.E. Hanukkah, like Purim (carnival) in the spring, is a festival of great joy. It also serves to remind Jews that no matter how severe their oppression, God will always be there to rescue them, as long as they remain faithful and do His Will.

■ *Passover* (The "Festival of Unleavened Bread"). This holy week (in late March or early April) celebrates the Jewish people's exodus from Egypt, and emancipation from Egyptian slavery. It also celebrates God's decision to "pass over" Jews who marked their doors with the blood of lambs in order that their first-borns would not be killed. God had warned the Egyptians that their first-borns would be killed if they did not release the Israelites (Exodus 12). The Passover is observed for 7 or 8 days by almost all Jewish believers, regardless of particular philosophical or religious differences. Throughout this time, Jews abstain from eating bread and yeast-based foods. Many Jews also abstain from work at various intervals during this holy week.

■ *Life Cycle Rituals.* We will mention only a few of the more important ones here, particularly those events that non-Jewish adolescents are most likely to hear about but seriously misunderstand, due to ignorance and media stereotyping.

   – Birth (*birt* or covenant) ceremony. For boys, circumcision is the removal of the foreskin of the penis as a sign of the covenant between God and the Jews, as described in Genesis 17:10. Circumcision, a simple surgical procedure, is performed either at home, in a synagogue, or in a hospital, on the 8th day after birth. For girls, also on the 8th day, *birt hayyim* ("covenant of life") is celebrated as a naming ceremony only.

- *Bar mitzvah, bat mitzvah* ("son and daughter of the command-ment"). Bar mitzvah symbolizes that boys, not their fathers, are responsible for their own transgressions at age 13. Bat mitzvah symbolizes religious adulthood for girls at the age of 12 years and one day. During the ceremony, a boy reads from the Torah and a girl reads from the *haftarah* (from the Prophets). These ceremonies usually take place on a Saturday morning as a part of a larger, basic service.
- *Kiddushin* ("sanctification"). This is the Jewish marriage ceremony that takes place under a wedding canopy (*huppah*). The ritual breaking of the glass underfoot sadly commemo-rates the destruction of the Temple in Jerusalem in 70 C.E. For Jewish believers, marriage is a divine command, a sacred bond. Here is what the oral Torah says about the significance of marriage: "A man who has no wife is doomed to an exis-tence without joy, without blessing, without experiencing life's true goodness, without Torah, without protection and without peace" (Yevamot 62b).

Judaism Resources for Teachers: A Brief Bibliographic Essay

Throughout this book, we have drawn generously from the following re-sources, among many others to be mentioned in subsequent bibliographic essays, in delineating the *content* of each of the religions that we examine. Our chief purpose was to choose, and use, references that would speak best to nonscholars of religion. We believe that the resources we cite in this section, and in each of the resource sections that follow in succeed-ing chapters, are more than understandable for teachers and students who know little about religious pluralism. We hope it goes without saying that we have translated and interpreted all this content in our own way, and any deficiencies or excesses of understanding and presentation are entirely our own.

The publication of the Bible that we refer to in this chapter, and the next on Christianity, is the New Revised Standard Version (Iowa Falls, IO: 1989).

The HarperCollins Dictionary of Religion, edited by Jonathan Z. Smith and William Scott Green, in collaboration with the American Academy of Religion (San Francisco: HarperCollins, 1995) is easily the most compre-hensive, one-volume guide to understanding the world's religions in print today. We have used this resource as a basic reference in writing our book—

in order to check the facts of what we think we know about religion and to seek further, expert clarification—more times than we can count.

The "Teach Yourself Books on World Faiths" (London: Hodder & Stoughton) are an invaluable resource for religious studies beginners. Particularly useful for our purposes in this chapter is C.M. Pilkington's book in the "Teach Yourself" series, *Judaism* (1995).

So too, Brandon Toropov's and Luke Buckles's greviously misnamed *The Complete Idiot's Guide to World Religions*, 3rd edition (New York: Alpha Books, 2004) is a valuable resource for teachers. In our opinion, this book, in spite of its insulting title, is a wonderfully concise, informative, and enjoyable introduction to a number of the world's religions. This is also a book that can easily be read by adolescents.

It is a book that will more than whet the appetites of those readers who want to study religions further. In particular, Part 2 on Judaism is an excellent tool for understanding the historical roots of Judaism as well as the modern Jewish experience. The chapters "Jewish Ritual and Celebration" and "Breaking Down Barriers to Judaism" are among the best in the book.

David Levinson's *Religion: A Cross-Cultural Dictionary* (New York: Oxford University Press, 1996) is a fine examination of both the commonalities and differences in how people experience and express their religious beliefs. Levinson, a cultural anthropologist, in a series of brief and clearly written essays, discusses the religious customs, beliefs, and histories of 16 of the world's major faith systems. His treatment of Judaism is masterful.

Another very useful general resource for teachers is Arvind Sharma's *Our Religions* (New York: HarperCollins, 1993), a book he edited with contributions from the preeminent scholars from each of the seven traditions. It is worth knowing that each of the scholars is both a believer and practitioner in the religions they describe. In our opinion, the best single examination of Judaism that we have read anywhere is by one of Sharma's contributors, Jacob Neusner, a world-renowned scholar who has published 500 books (this is not a typo) on Judaism.

In the popular, nonacademic realm, we would be remiss if we failed to mention Harold S. Kushner's extraordinarily popular book *To Life! A Celebration of Jewish Being and Thinking* (New York: Warner Books, 1993). Few popular writers are able to capture the power of Judaism to provide consolation, inspiration, and enlightenment to millions of Jews as well as Kushner. He writes with warmth and wisdom. Another popular book on Judaism that helped us to understand Jewish mysticism is Daniel Gordis's *God Was Not in the Fire: The Search for a Spiritual Judaism* (New York: Touchstone, 1995). A third panoramic, almost poetic narrative of the history of the Jews is by Chaim Potok, *Wanderings: History of the Jews* (New York: Ballantine Books, 1978). Potok is a storyteller without peer.

Finally, a book that we consulted on a regular basis for understanding in a down-to-earth way just how the various religions celebrate their respective services, holidays, rituals, and ceremonies is edited by Stuart M. Matlins and Arthur J. Magida. *How To Be a Perfect Stranger: The Essential Religious Etiquette Handbook*, 3rd edition (Woodstock, VT: Skylight Paths, 2003) is a clear and direct guide as to how outsiders ought to participate in the religious services of a number of faith communities, particularly during weddings, funerals, initiations, holy days and holidays, and prayer services.

3

The Narrative of Christianity

Case Study #2: "What Do You Mean, 'Christ's Birthday'?"

Ricardo hoisted his backpack onto his shoulder and stepped off the school bus into the school's parking lot full of indignation. It hardly seemed fair, he thought to himself, that the school bus driver could decorate her bus for Christmas, when he and his sixth-grade classmates were not allowed to put up a Christmas tree in their classroom and exchange gifts with each other. He recalled with pleasure last year's Christmas parties, in which his teacher had brought in colorfully decorated Santa cookies, and they had walked to the neighborhood's Senior Center in their busy, southwestern suburb to sing carols for the community.

This year his school had been designated as a "holiday-free zone." As a result, they didn't have their annual Halloween parade, and now they were not recognizing Christmas in his classroom this month. So Ricardo could hardly believe it when he saw a cross mounted on the dashboard of his school bus this morning, with a banner beneath it reminding all who boarded to "Keep Christ in Christmas."

Teaching Adolescents Religious Literacy in a Post-9/11 World, pages 45–59
Copyright © 2010 by Information Age Publishing
All rights of reproduction in any form reserved.

He bustled into the building and put away his school gear, stowing his sweatshirt in his cubby. He turned to his friend at the adjoining cubby, also getting ready to begin the school day. "Did you notice the cross on our bus this morning?" Ricardo queried. "She shouldn't get to celebrate Christmas at school if we can't! It's just not fair." His friend began to reply, but was interrupted by their teacher, Mr. Gutierrez, who called the class to gather for their daily Morning Meeting.

The students assembled in a seated circle in the front of the room, and Mr. Gutierrez began with a greeting and reviewed the day's agenda. As was customary, he then invited students to share briefly an item that related to their current learning theme or an event that had occurred in the past day. Ricardo's hand shot up, along with others. He kept his hand straight up while one classmate told the group that her grandfather was visiting. Another shared that he had sold 30 more raffle tickets for the class fundraiser. Finally, Mr. Gutierrez called on Ricardo to speak.

With an exasperated sigh, he described his morning's bus ride, and once again voiced his impassioned plea for fairness. "Why," he wondered aloud, "is my bus driver allowed to put up a cross, and we can't do *anything* here in our classroom? I go to church too. I celebrate Christ's birthday at Christmastime." Two of his classmates joined in with equal indignation, nodding their heads and vocalizing their support. Rosa, however, was perplexed. "What do you mean, Christ's birthday?"

Mr. Gutierrez listened thoughtfully to Ricardo's concerns. At the same time, Rosa's lack of knowledge about Christianity struck him. He recognized an opportunity to make learning relevant for these middle-schoolers, to build on their questions. The class spent the next hour researching Christian symbols, including the cross, on the Internet and in the school library. They then reconvened to share what they had learned and to plan a course of action to remedy what they viewed as a double standard in their school community.

The Pedagogical Challenge

Mr. Gutierrez faces a teachable moment. When he asks Ricardo to speak, little does he suspect that his student will be concerned about the school bus driver's putting up a cross in full sight of everyone on the bus. Also, Ricardo's request for fairness in displaying holy/holiday symbols in the classroom is certainly understandable, even though it could lead to something very controversial both inside the school and outside in the larger community.

Ricardo publicly acknowledges his own Christianity, and in doing so, he rouses the support of others of like mind in his classroom. This is all well and good, Mr. Gutierrez thinks, but what should he do with Rosa's perfectly plausible question: "What do you mean Christ's birthday?"

Mr. Gutierrez knows from past conversations with Rosa's parents, two sociology professors and self-declared secular humanists at the local state university, that they have been intentionally raising their three children as nonbelievers. Additionally, how does Mr. Gutierrez respond to the Jewish students in his class, and to Rosa and others like her, as well as to the two Muslim children from Pakistan, and to the Hindu student from India, who joined the class late after immigrating to this country with his parents who found employment at IBM?

And so, Mr. Gutierrez, being a responsive and pedagogically sensitive veteran teacher, opts to send all his students off to the library for an hour or so to do some independent research on the meaning of Christianity, its significant sacred symbols, and even some representative practices and rituals. Mr. Gutierrez understands that, in his classroom, any question is permissible, because inquiries generated by students are the ones that frequently lead to the best types of learning. They emanate, firsthand, out of students' natural curiosity, and, therefore, students acquire answers to real questions of their own, and not just to teacher-generated questions.

The pedagogical dilemma for Mr. Gutierrez, however, is this: What exactly should the students be learning about Christianity? How far should he go in educating them about the world's largest religious denomination? And, then, how can he help them translate these new learnings into a student-led effort to correct what they feel is a double standard regarding the recognition, and celebration, of religious holidays in public schools?

Moreover, Mr. Gutierrez realizes that, although he himself was baptized a Christian, he actually knows very little about this religion. Being a member of a family that was only nominally Christian while he was growing up, he made the decision in high school to find his own spiritual path outside any institutional church. And this is where he finds himself today.

Finally, Mr. Gutierrez knows that he needs to encourage a spirit of respectful religious dialogue among his students, one that is characterized by empathy, generosity, fairness, and informed understanding. He is under no illusion that any of this will be easy, but he is convinced, nonetheless, that it is necessary. After all, Mr. Gutierrez prides himself on being a teacher's teacher, someone who willingly follows the path of potential learning wherever it might lead.

Is Christianity the Most Pluralistic Religious Narrative of All?

The question that heads this section depends on one's point of view, of course. To us, however, an assumption of wide-ranging religious diversity within a major religious unity (*e pluribus unum*—"out of many one") is the best place for teachers to start dealing with Christianity in public school classrooms. Religious studies scholars, for example, estimate that the number of variations across the Christian denominations in the United States alone is in the hundreds. Throughout the world, the number rises to the thousands. Within individual Christian denominations in this country, the differences in interpretations, teachings, and practices are seemingly incalculable. Imagine what they might be globally.

And so, a logical question for any teacher could easily be: "Is there a single form of Christianity that everyone agrees on, despite the endless permutations and reframings?" We believe there is, and we will refer to this as the "core Christian narrative." Please remember, however, that to arrive at any reasonable consensus on the irreducible core of a religious worldview that commands the allegiance of close to 2 billion self-declared believers and practitioners worldwide will be very difficult, if not impossible.

The core beliefs and practices will necessarily be small in number. A good general rule in religious studies is that the larger the denomination the less it appears that individual practitioners seem to have in common. Size makes for endless intramural variety, multiple interpretations, and sometimes endless turmoil, debate, and conflict.

For example, *cultural* and *historical* differences alone, around the world, and in this country as well, tend to affect Christian beliefs and practices in an unimaginable number of ways. Ask a Catholic Christian from Central America to explain her beliefs regarding the Virgin Mary, or the doctrine of Papal Infallibility, and then compare these to the beliefs on the same topics of a Catholic Christian in the United Kingdom, or in the Netherlands, or in Poland, and be prepared for discord.

Ask an evangelical, Protestant Christian, perhaps on the theologically moderate, evangelical faculty at Calvin or Wheaton Colleges in the Midwestern United States, to explain the "official" Christian position on evolution, creationism, and intelligent design. And then ask an instructor or two at fundamentalist-minded Bob Jones University in the South to do the same. Be prepared here, as well, to stand back when the sparks created by the theological friction start to fly.

Or ask any of the millions of members belonging to several Christian sects in this country to explain the "true" doctrinal meanings of the Trinity, salvation and redemption, the "End Time," the Incarnation, faith versus good works, grace, and a variety of other Christian doctrines. Likewise, get ready to sort through the thicket of variances of a number of strongly opposing views on these doctrinal issues.

To say that "I am a Christian" is, actually, to say as much about one's particular family upbringing, local church community, schooling, theological training, cultural/racial/ethnic frame of reference, national and political habitus, and personal temperament/taste than anything else. There may, indeed, be basic commonalities of belief in the Christian narrative that transcend its vast differences. At times, however, it appears to the non-Christian world, and even to Christians themselves, that Christianity represents an *e plures plures* ("out of many, many") far more than it does an *e pluribus unum.*

In the sections that follow, we attempt to identify a few of these pivotal commonalities across the whole Christian community that teachers can use as a starting point for helping their students learn about the world's largest religion. In addition, keep in mind that, in spite of the ubiquity of intrareligious and interreligious differences, Christianity also has much in common with *different* religions, as do these religions with Christianity, as well as with one another. You will see this clearly as you read our subsequent chapters.

For starters, we think that the Christian Revelation reflects the Eastern and Native American beliefs that all of life is interconnected and sacred. Also, the Christian belief that life exists in a harmonious, organic, natural balance is very Taoist. Christianity has in common with Hinduism the belief that the human soul is immortal and filled with grandeur. With Buddhism, Christianity stresses suffering, compassion, and strong ethical convictions. With Judaism, Christianity shares the mystical assumption that ultimately God is unknowable and unnamable, and those who understand this paradox possess a "higher ignorance" that is profound, indeed sacred. And, with Islam, Christianity shares an understanding that God is great, good, wise, and all-compassionate.

Core Beliefs and Practices in the Christian Narrative

The Narrative Dimension

Sometimes referred to as "myths" by religious studies scholars (in the neutral Greek sense of *mythoi*, which means stories of divine or sacred significance), religious stories or narratives are dramatic accounts of the meaning of religions such as Christianity. Among their multiple functions, these stories serve the purpose of creating, and preserving, an enduring religious history for people. They also help us to make sense of the perennial questions that come up in every generation about the proximate and ultimate meaning of life, as well as the origins and ultimate destiny of the cosmos.

Stories give us a way to continue to celebrate a religion's high points by stressing the miraculous, the numinous (mystical), the life-changing events, and the supernatural qualities of a God, as well as the charismatic strengths of religious leaders and prophets. Stories, encoded in sacred books such as the Qur'an, the Bible, the Tripitaka, and the Rig Veda, and so on, can also function as useful moral tools to continue to persuade, and to inspire, adherents and potential converts to live the ethically praiseworthy life.

Moreover, as any history of each of the various religions has confirmed, for religion to work well on a personal level, it must first be born in narrative. This is the precondition for religion to eventually grow into creed, rite, ritual, and institution. Thus, the way that people in all times and places have been able to make spiritual sense of their personal damage and grief, and of the inevitability of their own suffering and death, has been primarily through the healing power that a good religious story provides.

In summary, at the institutional level, the most captivating religious narratives are those that feature unforgettable characters, momentous events, magnetic ideals, and sonorous and seductive languages. The real power of the Christian narrative, according to many religious studies scholars, lies mainly in the larger story that Christianity itself tells, as well as in the parables that Jesus told and in the life that he led.

The actual story of Jesus's life has been called by some the "greatest story ever told." This 2,000-year old narrative about an obscure Jewish teacher and prophet who claimed to be the Son of God, who lived for a relatively brief 33 years in a remote outpost of the Roman Empire, has set the stage for generations of Christians to hear, and to heed, their Savior's message.

The Christian story comes mainly from the four Gospels ("good tidings")—authored by Matthew, Mark, Luke, and John—who wrote as believers, rather than as dispassionate historians. Biblical scholars claim that Mark was the source of two Gospels (Matthew and Luke), and that Mark's source was actually a collection of *logia* (sayings) of Jesus, often referred to simply as "Q." Although there has been some controversy reaching even into modern times among certain scholars as to whether there was actually a "historical Jesus," there is a general consensus that someone named Jesus did in fact exist. Separating the historical figure from the legendary/divine figure is a task of biblical scholarship that will probably continue for as long as the religion of Christianity endures.

Not much at all is known about Jesus's humble beginnings and early years in Bethlehem, Palestine, and Jerusalem, except that he was born of a virgin, Mary, and a carpenter father, Joseph. As Jesus's young life began to unfold, John the Baptist, a prophet whom Jesus himself thought was the second coming of Elijah, announced the imminent appearance of a Messiah, one who would be even "mightier" than John. This Messiah would free the Jews from Roman rule. After John's eventual arrest and execution by Herod Antipas, who considered John a political revolutionary and a threat to the throne, Jesus began his peripetetic ministry in Galilee.

What we mostly know about the ministry of Jesus occurred during the years 28–33 c.e., when he spent much of his time announcing the coming of the Kingdom of God, while walking throughout the countryside in Palestine and Jerusalem. He performed miracles, healings, exorcisms, and other wonders in the company of his 12 chosen disciples, representative of the Twelve Tribes of Israel.

He also surrounded himself with a close group of women who followed him, and he spent a great deal of time with the everyday people (the sick, poor, outcasts, handicapped, fishermen, farmers, artisans, tax collectors, etc.) whom he met and helped along the way. This was considered to be scandalous behavior in Jesus's day: Here was a self-proclaimed Messiah who preferred to be in the company of common people rather than spend his time with the temple priests and political leaders of the times.

What did Jesus teach? He taught the apocalyptic message that the Kingdom of God was fast approaching. Earthly time was coming to an end. And people had better be prepared. Furthermore, he himself was more than just a messenger of God, as John the Baptist was. He, in fact, was the Son of God. In fact, he was God.

Once again, not much is known in any detail about Jesus' actual, day-to-day affairs as an itinerant preacher, prophet, and Messiah (which he never proclaimed publicly). What we do know in some detail, and the story has been repeated for over 2,000 years, is the cruel persecution and tragic death on the cross that Jesus experienced at the hands of Roman authorities. The Romans treated him as a common criminal, a threat to the state, and they turned him over to Pontius Pilate for punishment.

The Romans feared his popular appeal, as did the Jewish religious hierarchy, and both groups accused him of being seditious and blasphemous. So, Jesus was crucified, died, and was buried. And what followed 3 days later was probably the central event in Jesus' life, because for believing Christians (then and now) it demonstrated that Jesus was truly Lord and Savior. Listen to Paul (considered one of the shapers of Christianity, even though he lived after Jesus died) in Acts 13:29–31: "They took him down from the cross, and laid him in a tomb. But God raised him from the dead; and for many days he appeared to those who came up with him from Galilee to Jerusalem."

After his death, God resurrected Jesus from the dead, and He ascended into Heaven, thus presaging the Final Day of Judgment for all of us. And, so, the life of Jesus ended not as a dismal failure, but as a resounding success. From a nondescript beginning, an anonymous young life, four or five short years as an itinerent preacher, and an ignominious death as a criminal at the age of 33, Jesus became the central symbol of a worldwide religious movement called Christianity.

To this day, over 2,000 years later, Christianity remains the largest religion in the world, with a membership in excess of 2 billion people; and a legacy that has left an undeniably indelible mark on Western music, art, philosophy, theology, history, and politics. It is safe to say that unless one knows the story of Christianity, then the full cultural riches of the Western world will remain inaccessible.

The sum of Jesus's teachings is best captured in such parables as the Good Samaritan (Luke 10:30–37), a man who was a member of a minority race that was scorned by the people of his time. The lesson in this parable is that every person can be saved, regardless of status, wealth, education, or politics. It is the individual alone who must decide whether or not to participate in the "Kingdom of God." Like the Good Samaritan, a member of a despised religious group—who stopped to help a man beaten and robbed by bandits, a man ignored by a priest and a lawyer who passed him by—so, too, for all of us. No matter who we are, we are called upon to act with love and compassion toward our neighbors, and to love God with our whole hearts and minds. This, in a nutshell, is the core teaching of Christianity.

The Doctrinal Dimension

A doctrine is a teaching (theological, historical, and philosophical) embodied, for example, in the basic principles and tenets of faith in the Christian Credo ("I believe"). It is important to note, however, that a doctrine is not *ipso facto* a dogma. A religious dogma is something handed down by an authoritative person and/or scripture, or learned body of a teaching church, that is designated to be true and indisputable. The Catholic magisterium (the official Church teaching office), for example, is vested in the papacy and in the Catholic Bishops, and it alone decides what doctrinal beliefs are to be dogmatic and which are not. Some Christian doctrines in Catholicism, Protestantism, and in Eastern Orthodoxy become dogmas over time; some do not. Some Christian narratives are dogma-thick, some dogma-thin.

Doctrines function in religion in many ways, just as they do in the political, philosophical, educational, or economic realms. The doctrinal dimension in a religious narrative, for example, ensures historical continuity; lends order to the various strands of religious belief within the larger narrative; safeguards and highlights what is truly important in the religious tradition; provides stable reference points; and defines and shapes the meanings in a particular religious community. The emphasis on doctrine is stronger in some Christian communions (e.g., Catholic, Episcopalian, Eastern Orthodox) than in others (e.g., Quaker, Evangelical, Pentecostal).

What follows, therefore, is a very brief summary of doctrinal beliefs that make up the core of Christianity. In its streamlined form, this is the core that apparently underlies all the variations of Christian belief, worship, and practice. Even this minimal claim, however, will be controversial.

During the 2nd century C.E., Christians in Rome met to establish what was called a "baptismal profession." This later became the model for the Apostle's Creed, which articulated the basic elements of the Christian faith:

> I believe in God, the Father, the Almighty; and in Christ Jesus, his only begotten Son, our Lord, born of the Holy Spirit and Mary, the Virgin, who under Pontius Pilate was crucified and buried, was resurrected from the dead on the third day, and rose to heaven, sitting at the right hand of the Father, whence he will come to judge the quick and the dead; and in the Holy Spirit, one holy Church, forgiveness of sins, resurrection of the flesh. Amen.

There have since been a number of official Church Councils since then that have refined the Apostle's Creed, and worked to establish an official Christian canon. What follows are thumbnail descriptions of those Christian dogmas that are binding on all believers right up to the present time:

- There is one God, and this God created heaven and earth. (Christianity is a monotheistic religion.)
- Jesus Christ is the son of God.
- Jesus Christ was born of a virgin. This is called the "Virgin Birth."
- Jesus Christ is both divine and human. This "double nature" is called the "Incarnation."
- While alive, Jesus Christ preached a message of love, forgiveness, personal transformation, and individual salvation. (The primary ac-

count of his life appears in the first four Gospels [the "good news"] of the Christian bible, often referred to as the "New Testament.")

▪ Jesus Christ was crucified and died for the sins of humanity. This is called the "Atonement."

▪ Three days after his death, Jesus Christ was raised from the dead. This is called the Resurrection.

▪ He ascended into Heaven 40 days later. This is called the Ascension.

▪ Just as there was life after death for Jesus, so, too, is there life after death for those Christians who experience a personal conversion (*metanoia*), a drastic change of heart and mind.

▪ The spirit, and saving message, of Jesus Christ lives on today in various Christian communities.

The Ethical Dimension

Historically, *ethics*, from the early Greek and Roman understandings of the term, had more to do with customs and conduct, and certain virtues, than with the specific designation of standards of right or wrong behavior. It is only later, with the advent of Christianity, that ethics took on the more normative *moral* meanings of good and bad—as prescribed and proscribed by God in both the Jewish and Christian bibles.

Christianity, of all the monotheistic religions, is perhaps the most ethically thick belief system. No view of the world is valid, Christians believe, unless it is first predicated on specific ethical ideals. Ask a Christian to name the three most important moral virtues, and chances are that a majority will immediately cite faith, hope, and charity. Ask a Christian what it *really* means to be a Christian, and the response will most likely be an ethical one—along the lines of the Golden Rule, or turning the other cheek, or loving one's neighbors as much as oneself.

The Christian view of God emphasizes particular ethical expectations on the part of the Creator toward his Creation. These ethical precepts are inscribed in the teachings of church leaders, traditions, and scripture, and they have evolved over the course of 2,000 years in a variety of Christian communities. Some of these communities have been religiously conservative, some moderate, and some radical.

Thus, it is very difficult for scholars today to pinpoint a so-called monolithic "Christian ethics" that, in the early 21st century, would be able to win the unanimous backing of all Christian believers. There are just too many variations in Christian interpretations and perspectives for this to happen. So, whatever can be claimed as a Christian ethics, is, at best, a compromised summary of a limited number of moral principles that religious ethics scholars are able to agree upon. What follows are some of the more common ethical principles in Christianity:

- Unlike a system of humanistic, secular ethics, any account of Christian ethics is "transcendent" and "objective." Christians believe that morality is neither subjective nor relative. Rather, it is based on something that exists above and beyond specific human contexts. Christian ethics posits certain absolute, unchanging moral truths as a basis to determine how one ought to act morally.
- For some Christian communions, these truths are rooted in human reason, the natural law, Scripture, other forms of Divine Revelation, church traditions, official magisteria, or in some combination of all, or some, of these. What they all have in common, however, is that each is a means, given to human beings by God, in order to better discern the moral will of the Divine Creator.
- Unlike Judaism and Islam, whose moral teachings are grounded in specific *laws* (Torah and Shari'ah), Christianity puts its moral emphasis instead on following the *example* of the one Lord and Savior, Jesus Christ. For Christians, grace and faith are more important than the law in living an ethical life. The active imitation (not the legal codification) of Jesus's unique way of being in the world—his compassionate spirit, his loving interactions with others, his willingness to forgive even his worst enemies—is the quintessential Christian ethic.
- Jesus's major moral message is one of love. John (2:5–6) says, "Let us love one another. To love is to live according to his commandments. This is the commandment which you have heard since the beginning, to live a life of love." This is the ethical sum and substance of Jesus' Sermon on the Mount (Matthew 5–7).
- The Christian Bible account of Jesus's moral teachings highlights an "ethic of trustful, joyful acceptance of the divine grace and love and a humble, grateful, and wholehearted commitment to the will of the 'Lord of heaven and earth' who has taught people to call upon him as their Father." Throughout the Christian Bible, although Jesus did, at times, refer to rewards and punishments in an afterlife, this was not the most important rationale for his ethic. Instead, the most important justification was a combination of the acceptance of Divine forgiveness, the overcoming of human estrangement from God, and a humble acceptance of doing God's will.

Here are some selected excerpts from the Christian Bible that capture the nub of Christianity's ethic of love, compassion, mystical depth, and social justice.

"Blessed are the meek: for they shall inherit the earth. . . . Blessed are the merciful: for they shall obtain mercy. . . . Blessed are the peacemakers: for they shall be called the children of god. . . . Let your light so shine before men, that they may see your good works, and glorify your Father which is in heaven." (Matthew 5:1–16)

"Ye have heard that it hath been said, An eye for an eye, and a tooth for a tooth: But I say unto you, That ye resist not evil: but whosoever shall smite thee on thy right cheek, turn to him the other also. . . . For if ye love them which love you, what reward have ye?" (Matthew 5:38–48)

"Therefore, all things whatsoever ye would that men should do to you, do ye even so to them: for this is the law and the prophets." (Matthew 7:7–12)

"Lord, when we saw them hungered, or athirst, or a stranger, or naked, or sick, or in prison, and did not minister unto thee? Then shall he answer them, saying, 'Verily I say unto you, Inasmuch as ye did it not to one of the least of these, ye did it not to me.'" (Matthew 25:31–45)

"For what shall it profit a man, if he shall gain the whole world, and lose his own soul?" (Mark 8:34–36)

"He that hath my commandments, and keepeth them, he it is that loveth me; and he that loveth me shall be loved of my Father, and I will love him, and will manifest myself to him." (John 14:15–21)

The Ritual Dimension

Human beings live by ritual. We are ritualistic creatures across a broad range of social, recreational, educational, political, economic, and, especially, religious activities. No aspect of our lives is without ritual. It is instructive to keep track of how many repetitive, formalized, and stylized acts serve as markers each and every day, throughout our lives, for what is important to us. Think of holiday celebrations, birthdays, job interviews, school graduations, eating out, getting ready for bed, taking a shower, or even reading a book or writing a paper.

The chances are that we do all of these things within a set pattern of behaviors. Not only do these rituals provide a sense of order and security for us in our day-to-day lives, but they also function to create and preserve relationships. They mark us as predictable and reliable creatures. They are outward acts of communication that convey warm and friendly, or, in the case of religion, solemn and serious, feelings to others.

The Latin root of the word is *ritualis*, meaning *rite*, or a way to *join* or *fit* into something. Hence, in religion, a rite of passage is a ceremony that marks a major transition in a believer's life. In Christianity such transitional markers, or rites of passage, are baptism, confirmation, matrimony, ordination, and the last rites of death. These rites join or bind the religious community together in mutual relationships. Also, think of such sacred rituals as reading the Torah, receiving the Eucharist, praying in an Islamic mosque while bowing toward Mecca, meditating in a Buddhist ashram, burning incense in front of an altar, attending sacred festivals, offering benedictions, making religious pilgrimages, and so on.

Below are some key examples of Christian rituals:

- The sacraments (L., *sacramentum*, a consecrated oath of allegiance) in the Christian churches provide symbolic spiritual nourishment for worshippers. In a real sense, they are "oaths" or "ordinances" or "outward signs" of allegiance to God. One of the key sacraments is Baptism, a submerging of the religious initiate in water in order to cleanse the sinner. This symbolizes a rebirth, a raising of the sinner to a new life in Jesus Christ. Another significant sacrament, especially for the Catholic and Eastern Orthodox churches, is marriage. The mutual exchange of wedding vows before a priest or minister, and the larger community, represents a couple's binding commitment to one another "in sickness or in health, till death do us part."

- Worship ceremonies are common rituals for Christians. For example, Catholic Christians attend *Mass* (from the Latin, *missa*). Mass is a ritual celebrating the Catholic Eucharistic rite. So, too, in very similar ways, Orthodox and Anglican Christians celebrate the Eucharist. The communion rite is the most important part of the Mass, consisting of the Lord's Prayer, a sign of peace, and the reception of the Eucharist (in the form of consecrated bread and wine).

- Whether Christians belong to such diverse denominations as the Disciples of Christ, Christian Science, Baptist, Lutheran, Methodist, Mennonite/Amish, Eastern Orthodox, Presbyterian, Seventh-day Adventist, Unitarian Universalist, the United Church of Christ, Episcopal and Anglican Churches, or the Roman Catholic Church, each has in common that they celebrate certain life-transition rituals in their own unique ways. These rituals include, among others, holy days and festivals, lifecycle events, initiation ceremonies, ordinations, the wearing of appropriate attire, prayer and meditation, the giving of gifts, and funerals and mourning.

- Of the important, ritual holy days in the liturgical Christian year, none is more sacred than Christmas. It is often referred to as the "Feast of the Nativity of Our Lord and Savior Jesus Christ." Christmas brings the season of "Advent" (the *coming* of the Savior) to a close in the liturgical Christian year. Easter is equally important, because it celebrates the resurrection of Jesus Christ from the dead. Preceding Easter is the season of Lent (L. *Spring*)—40 days of self-examination, penance, and fasting. Also preceding Easter is Good Friday, the most solemn, and saddest, day of the Christian year. During Good Friday, there are often ritual enactments of the crucifixion, the scourging of Jesus's flesh by the Roman soldiers, and the washing of the apostles' feet symbolizing humility. Finally, the season of Pentecost (the 50th day after Passover) represents a Christian festival on the seventh Sunday after Easter, celebrating the descent of the Holy Spirit upon the Apostles.

Christianity Resources for Teachers: A Brief Bibliographic Essay

One very comprehensive, but easy to read, volume on the intellectual, spiritual, and moral horizons of Christianity is *The Oxford Companion to Christian Thought*, edited by Adrian Hastings (New York: Oxford University Press, 2000). Although a scholarly treatment, Hastings's study is written in clear and cogent prose.

An equally scholarly work, but one framed in a crisply told and engaging historical narrative, is Brian Moynahan's *The Faith: A History of Christianity* (New York: Doubleday, 2002). Everything you wanted to know about Christianity, both its strengths and weaknesses, watershed events and people, is told in this unprecedented chronicle of a faith that, in 2,000 years, has literally changed the world. The volume's scope and depth and accessibility are unrivaled as a history of Christianity.

The book that best helped us to identify and understand the Christian biblical texts on a number of issues, including most of those hot-button topics we raised in our Christian Controversies section, is by Harvard professor Peter J. Gomes. Its title is *The Good Book: Reading the Bible with Mind and Heart* (New York: Morrow, 1996). In our estimation, this study is the best contemporary examination of the Bible for nonreligious studies scholars.

Also, for our purposes, Philip Jenkins's *The Next Christendom: The Coming of Global Christianity* (New York: Oxford University Press, 2002) is the best writer on contemporary trends in Christianity around the globe. For example, he asserts that by the year 2050, four out of five Christians worldwide will be Latinos or Africans. He also predicts that by 2050, Christianity and Islam will be the two most dominating religions in the world. Moreover, they will square off in intense, high-tech military conflicts in a far more devastating replay of the religious wars of the Middle Ages.

No study of Christianity would be complete without Marcus Borg's *Jesus: A New Vision* (San Francisco: Harper & Row, 1988). Borg captures both the humanity and the divinity of this man, Jesus. He makes the case, against the one made by Albert Schweitzer, that there was a historical Jesus after all.

4

The Narrative of Islam

Case Study #3: "Watch Out for People who Look Like the Taliban!"

Jim Marcel smiled broadly as he welcomed his class of juniors and seniors into their first period class. Jim was eager to get into the content of the day. As a World War II buff, he favored his American History class over the others he taught. In the past 25 years of teaching he had come to view his country's military history with a passion, and he enjoyed introducing others to it as well. Lately he had been using literature as a means to do so, to the dismay of some of his department members.

Just last week at a department meeting they had argued over the use of fiction to teach history, some feeling there was just too much content to cover. Nevertheless, Jim found historical novels to be a powerful way of conveying the human side of history. This week, he had assigned a short novel in order to introduce the concept of Japanese relocation camps through the story of one family.

Teaching Adolescents Religious Literacy in a Post-9/11 World, pages 61–76
Copyright © 2010 by Information Age Publishing
All rights of reproduction in any form reserved.

He cleared his throat to gather students' attention and jumped in. "OK, so who finished *When the Emperor was Divine* last night?" About three-fourths of the class raised their hands. "And what was the premise of the book?" All but two hands dropped down. "Maureen? What did you think?"

"I thought it was incredibly sad," she offered, shaking her head. "I mean, to watch that nice family being viewed as potential enemies of the state and then sticking them in camps. I can't believe our country would do such a thing, just because they were Japanese. It seems hypocritical to blame the Nazis for putting Jews in concentration camps when we were rounding up people right here in our own country. It makes me ashamed, actually, to be an American."

Jacob jumped in quickly, "Well, that was in the 1940s, right? It's not like America would do something like that *now*. We don't stereotype in that way anymore. We don't see the Japanese as 'potential enemies of the state.'"

Their teacher interjected, recognizing an opportunity to make the concept more relevant. "But who do we see as potential enemies of the state, then? Especially after 9/11?" The class fell silent. Jim probed a bit more. "In 1942, the U.S. placed people of Japanese descent in relocation camps because we feared an attack on our West Coast. Who would you say we fear now, after the attack on the World Trade Center and the Pentagon?"

Karin slowly raised her hand and spoke, "Well, I have to admit that I worry now about suicide bombing happening here in our country. I mean, every time I watch the news with my parents there's another instance of suicide bombing and terrorists. So I guess I fear people who believe in their religion to such an extreme that they want to kill others. Aren't Muslims extremists who talk all the time about Holy Jihad? Don't they want us all to become Muslims like in Iran?"

"Yeah," Clem added, "My dad said it's just a matter of time before those Muslim people are doing those things here in America, and trying to convert us. And that we need to pay attention to people around us, to always be alert and watchful, especially to people who look like the Taliban—you know, turban heads with dark beards, sandals, and all."

Maureen replied quickly, "Yes, but isn't that just the same? When we start making assumptions about people because of the way they look, or the way they worship, isn't that the same as Roosevelt's relocation camps? If we think that way, maybe then it *could* happen all over again . . ." Her voice trailed off in dismay.

Jim looked around the room as the conversation became more and more heated. Some students were nodding, others jumping in to agree or to argue their point. While he was glad they were making meaningful connections between history and present day, the conversation was spiraling a bit out of his comfort zone. Jim wondered how to disarm Clem's perspective without calling Clem's father prejudiced, and how to empathize with Karin's fear without inspiring more. Mostly, however, he wondered how to capitalize on Maureen's concern, to instill in his whole class a commitment to not reliving the mistakes of the past.

Dealing with Islamophobia in the Classroom

Islamophobia: the irrational, excessive, and persistent fear and loathing of Islam and Muslims, based on ignorance, malevolence, half truths, and/or willful fantasy. At the present time, this phobia is rampant throughout the Western world, particularly in Europe and the United States.

Islamophobia is fueled by media oversimplifications and distortions, a priori political and religious agendas, and, most of all, by sheer stubbornness, and stupidity. Regarding the latter, philosophers could have a field day exposing those logical fallacies that fuel Islamophobia: unrepresentative generalizations; faulty analogies; all-or-nothing thinking; word magic; emotive language; self-serving appeals to so-called "authorities"; popular passions; ad hominem attacks; self-righteousness; special pleading; ridicule; non sequiturs; and circular definitions and question begging, among others.

The Cure: a vigorous education in knowledge about Islam at all grade levels, but especially with adolescents in middle schools and high schools. This education would include generous doses of accurate information and hands-on experience, as well as an informed, intellectual exposé of sundry, and popular, fallacies, stereotypes, lies, and religio-political, anti-Islam agendas.

Before we begin to dispense some specific information about Islam as a coherent, religio-spiritual narrative, here are some initial observations about Islam and Muslims that students (and adults) rarely, if ever, see or hear in the Western media or in public schools in the United States. For starters, Islam has much more in common with Judaism and Christianity than it does with any of the other world religions. Islam is a monotheistic religion. Islam respects, indeed reveres, Jesus, Abraham, Moses, and Muhammad, putting them all on the same level as being great prophets.

Islam admiringly refers to Jews and Christians as "people of the book," along with themselves. In fact, one of the most popular verses in the Islamic holy scripture, the Qur'an, is this, spoken by Allah (God): "Do you not know, O people, that I have made you into tribes and nations that you may know each other." And, further, "If God had so willed, He would have made you a single people. But His plan is to test each of you in what He hath given you . . ."

Moreover, Islam, like Judaism and Christianity, is a peaceful religion. The phrase that one hears most often in the everyday speech of Muslims is this: *salam alaikum*, "peace be with you." The response is *alaikum salam*. The word *Islam* actually means "peace, submission to God's will, and commitment." Thus, for Muslims, peace within themselves, and with others, is the ultimate goal of their faith, and it comes through an alignment of the human will with God's will.

If anything, Muslims are a model of restraint and peacefulness throughout the world. Think of what it must be like to live as a scorned, minority religion in every major, non-Arab country in the Western world, surrounded on all sides by such majority religions as Christianity, Hinduism, Buddhism, and Judaism. And in these countries, Muslims experience the most horrible injustices and cruelty, particularly since 9/11. They are truly an oppressed "other." Most have learned to "turn the other cheek," live peacefully, and to preserve their integrity and dignity as best they can.

Adolescents in the United States need to understand that Islam is not a religious monolith. It is as heterogeneous a religious narrative as are Judaism and Christianity. For example, there are moderate Islamic believers and fundamentalist Islamic believers. By the same token, there are moderate Islamic states (e.g., Turkey) and fundamentalist Islamic states (e.g., Saudi Arabia). Some of these are theocratic, others democratic; some secular, some sacred. While it is true that, at bottom, all Muslims believe in the indisputable, monotheistic truth of such surahs (a Qur'an chapter) as 112:1–4, "Say He is God, the One! God the eternally Besought of all! He begetteth not nor was He begotten. And there is none like unto Him." Still, surahs such as this are not the final word on Islamic homogeneity.

As in Christianity, millions of individual Muslims, and dozens of Islamic states, choose to practice their faith, live their lives, and interpret their scriptures in a multiplicity of forms. Pluralism within the same religion is as inescapable a fact of life as is pluralism between and among different religions. To dramatize this point, just ask adolescents to think about the differences in attitudes, beliefs, practices, and lifestyles between parents and parents, parents and children, and siblings and siblings *within their own families*. Suddenly, the phenomenon of an endless array of intramural differences in a single family unit becomes a fitting metaphor for understanding the endless array of differences that exist within a single religio-spiritual narrative. Islam is no exception.

We close this brief, introductory section on Islamophobia in the West with a quotation from a fundamentalist Muslim student from Iran currently studying in the United States. We think the quotation bears examining, and discussing, in middle and high school classrooms because it offers a non-Western perspective on the morality of the Western world that is bound to shake up conventional American attitudes that the "West is best." We hold that ethnocentrism, in all its insidious forms, needs to be dismantled wherever and whenever, if people are to learn how to live nonjudgmentally and nonimperialistically in a religiously pluralistic world.

Listen to Mojtaba (Policano, 1998) on what he thinks is the "depraved" state of American life. From his perspective, there is little that is good in the United States and much that is bad. Keep in mind, though, that while many of his own opinions reflect a phobic kind of thinking, they are as certain to him as Western Islamophobic opinions are to us:

> We are rigid in Iran, to be sure, but we don't kill a million babies a year through abortion; we don't have tens of thousands of unmarried teen-age mothers; we don't have shelters for battered women, because there are no battered women in my country. We don't have homeless people sleeping on street gratings or people being mugged in the nation's capital. We don't have a drug problem; we don't have homosexual marriages or a runaway divorce rate; we don't have abused children or unsafe schools; we don't have an AIDS epidemic; we don't have any of the social problems that are destroying your society.

> Think about that please, and tell me if your right to dance and drink alcohol or look at women half-naked on the streets, or being demeaned in the lyrics of rap songs and being raped in pornographic images on the internet and movie screen, or read political commentary in a press that is as self-censored and self-limiting as any in the world compensates for the sicknesses that are killing your country. (p. 10)

Core Beliefs and Practices in the Islam Narrative

The Narrative Dimension

The recurring thematic motif in the Islamic narrative throughout history is one of withdrawal and return, of rise and fall and rise again, of outsider and insider, as "other" and similar. In some ways, the story of Muhammad is the story of Islam. Muhammad ibn Abdallah ibn Abd al-Muttalib is the full Arabic name of the Islamic Prophet, Muhammad. He was born in 570 c.e. in Mecca in southwestern Arabia, a land of deserts and an array of monotheistic religions; but also a land undergoing considerable religious ferment at the time of his birth.

Throughout the region there existed communities of Christians, Jews, Zoroastrians, Gnostics, and Neoplatonists, as well a number of pagan cults and idol worshippers. Paganism and idolatry were widespread at the time, particularly in the local clans and tribes, and this resulted in the dilution of worship practices in Judaism and Christianity. For example, Muhammad's own tribe, the Quraysh, although theoretically Muslim, practiced idol worship and lived largely without law and order. Theft, murder, and torture were common.

Muhammad was raised by a foster mother, and during his childhood there were many signs and wonders that presaged the time when he would become Allah's Prophet. He spent the early part of his life traveling with his uncle on caravan routes, journeying to Syria, Egypt, and Yemen. As a young adult, he himself became a caravan leader. At age 25, he began to work for a wealthy woman who lived in Mecca. Her name was Khadijah, and she later fell in love with Muhammad, despite being 15 years older than he. Together they parented six children, two of whom died very young.

Eventually, Muhammad became a widely respected tribal leader, and, later, a regional leader. He advocated peace, understanding, civility, and reconciliation in all aspects of his life, at a time when tribal warfare was the order of the day. It was when he was 40 years old, in the year 610, that he began to experience the divine revelations from Allah, conveyed by the angel Gabriel (Jibril), that would later become the sacred content of the Qur'an (recitation).

Because Muhammad was illiterate, like most other Arabs of his time, all the instructions from Allah came to him in oral form as recitations. He memorized everything he heard, and conveyed these teachings to his fellow Arabs through charismatic preaching and service. His message was simple yet powerful, much like the Qur'an that he loved: There is only one God. His name is Allah. This God is great and beneficent, all wise and all compassionate, just and merciful. He asks for obedience and the settlement of human conflicts by peaceful means.

Muhammad was forced to leave Mecca because of political unrest, and also because of the increasing threats of religious persecution from pagan tribal leaders who saw him as an enemy to their way of life. In 622 c.e., Muhammad and his followers journeyed across the desert (called the *hijra*, or "departure") and settled in the city of Medina 400 kilometers away, which he established as an Islamic state.

War and bloodshed occurred between Meccans and the Muslims of Medina, fomented by a growing rivalry between the two cities. Sadly, Muhammad's rule was marked by much bloody conflict and hostility, caused by intragroup and intergroup rivalries over religious and political differences. But throughout it all, Muhammad remained balanced, dedicated to peace, and highly respected by people throughout the Arabic world.

Among his many political gifts, fueled by his love of Allah and the Qur'an, Muhammad worked hard to resolve conflicts primarily through negotiation, based on a sense of mutual obligations, arbitration, and mediation. He believed that this was the will of Allah—the responsibility to settle differences peacefully. Muhammad was not a violent or angry man; rather, he preferred peace agreements and constitutions over declarations of war against his enemies. And, to some extent, he was successful. The Medina constitution that he wrote was the first of its kind anywhere. He died in 632 at the age of 63, leaving a legacy he called the *ummah*, a community of committed Muslim believers. His legacy lives on today with a worldwide Muslim *ummah* that is growing unabated.

In the aftermath of 9/11, what too often gets overlooked in the Western world today are the extraordinary achievements throughout history of this worldwide religious *ummah*. We hear mostly about Islam's failures, its deficiencies and excesses, personified by the actions of extremist terrorist groups (most of whom have nothing to do with Islam) and dogmatic, Muslim fundamentalists. Thus, the temptation is great for Westerners to consider Islam ahistorically, as lacking any kind of distinctive history or any record of cultural progress. It is easy during these times of media clichés and religious oversimplifications for Westerners to dismiss Islam as just another backward, authoritarian religion bent mainly on resisting democracies and establishing, in the near term, theocratic states throughout the Middle East; and, in the far term, exercising hegemony throughout the world. Nothing could be further from the chronicle of Islam's history.

Briefly, Islam's religious, political, and cultural legacy to the world has been enormous. Among its distinctions are the following: Muslims have built some of the most beautiful mosques and tombs in the world. The Taj Mahal is an excellent example, a synthesis of Hindu and Muslim architecture. So, too, the Sulaimaniye in Istanbul has few peers anywhere as a majestic holy dwelling.

Furthermore, Islam was one of the first religious worldviews that emphasized the equality of all peoples, regardless of religion, race, or birth. All people are equal in the eyes of Allah. Whether rich or poor, literate or illiterate, what matters the most is whether Muslims, like the Prophet, strive to live God's message every single day of their lives. Unlike the Persian, Byzantine, and Roman empires of old, where class hierarchy and sectarian privilege and prejudice were rampant, Islamic countries emphasized only goodness and piety as criteria for full membership in the *ummah.*

During the first 700-year history of Islamic dynasties, cultural achievements soared. Renowned scholars and artists dazzled the then-known world with their brilliance. Islamic science, astronomy, geography, and philosophy greatly influenced Western thinking via Muslim Spain. In reference to the latter, Muslim Spain in medieval Europe was a model of a sophisticated and civil, political, and religious state. Intermarriage was common, even encouraged. Muslims fought alongside Christians in the wars of the time. Religious and ethnic tolerance was the modus operandi of the day. At the time, Muslim literature in Spain was the envy of the cultured world.

The Christian Crusades, fought from the 11th to the 13th centuries, effectively wiped out much of Muslim culture throughout Europe and the Middle East, although certainly not all. Muslims have a habit throughout history of disappearing in one place, only to resurface elsewhere. For example, European Christian Crusaders, trying to win back the city of Jerusalem from Muslims, slaughtered Muslim inhabitants (estimated by historians of the Crusades to be between 70,000–100,000 people, along with the hundreds of Jews burned alive in their synagogues), refusing to spare even women and children. Christians also defiled Muslim holy places. In spite of this barbaric slaughter of Muslims in Jerusalem, however, there were a number of great Islamic empires that surfaced afterward, particularly the non-Arabic Ottoman Empire (circa 1300–1900 C.E.) that survived in glory for several hundred years.

At the present time, there are two major Islamic sects, the Sunni ("orthodox") and the Shiite ("follower," "faction"). Each of these sects, in turn, has a number of subsects. The main reason why Islam split off into these two groups was because of succession and religious authority issues. Sunni trace their authority back to the venerable friend of the Prophet and the first Caliph, Abu Bakr; while Shia trace their authority directly back to Ali, a son-in-law of the Prophet. Although this division might appear obscure, even trivial to many Westerners, it has resulted in violence between the groups, in countries such as Pakistan, where both live.

The Sunni constitute almost 90 percent of all the Muslims in the world. While Sunnis are orthodox, they are not narrowly doctrinal or dogmatic. They are culturally and religiously pluralistic, and they base their theology on a broad framework of Islamic principles, as well as on the believer's direct relationship with Allah. Sunnis have no structured religious hierarchy. They rely instead on an Imam, a holy person who is very knowledgeable but not infallible about the Qur'an and Islamic rituals and ceremonies. Sunni Imams strive to be compassionate, tolerant, and politically pragmatic.

Shiites tend to be more outwardly political in their beliefs, because they originated in the 7th century as a political, not a religious, faction. Shia Islam is the official state religion of Iran. Shia is also the main type of Islamic worship in a number of smaller religious communities in India, Pakistan, and Iraq. Shiite Imams are invested by their communities with an almost Papal authority when it comes to religious matters. They are respected as infallible interpreters of all Islamic doctrine and ritual, and Shiites are obligated to follow their leadership.

Shiites believe that they represent the authentic Islam of the Prophet, and extremist Shiites are bent on converting nonbelievers throughout the world to Islam. Much Islamic revivalism and revolutionary fervor depicted today in the Western media is Shia inspired, particularly in a country like Iran. In contrast, in Egypt and Pakistan, two countries dominated by Sunnis, scenes of revolutionary Islamic revivalism are a lot less likely to occur on the television news. The Western media err whenever they attempt to make global generalizations about Islamic revolutionary fervor, based only on sensationalistic images coming from countries like Lebanon and Iran. Journalists must work harder than they do to understand the major historical, political, and theological differences between Sunna and Shia approaches to Islam.

Islam does include a mystical strain in its narrative called Sufism (a robe made of "wool," signifying asceticism, a life of simplicity and poverty), dating back to the end of the 8th century and reaching its peak in the 13th century. Today, Sufism has found many converts in the Western world because it answers the strong emotional needs of mystically-inclined personalities. It also preaches a message of universal love and peace (*sulh'i'kul*).

There are Sufis who prefer to follow their own "personal spiritual path (*tariqa*)." Some remain loyal to the basic principles of Islam; some disconnect to greater or lesser degree; and some others leave the orthodox faith entirely. Some Sufis live their spirituality by completely rejecting creature comforts. Others work actively to restore the purity of the Prophet's original message. And some engage in ecstatic spiritual experiences such as meditating, chanting, and whirling about, as a way to induce spiritual trances and experience oneness with Allah.

Sufism is an important counterweight to the legalism of Shari'ah law. It focuses less on the strictures of doctrine and ritual and more on the transcendent life of the inner spirit. For this reason, throughout history, Sufis have been persecuted by some Muslim leaders who refuse to give up their decadent and extravagant lifestyles. Also, some conservative Muslims consider Sufism to be heretical because it deviates from the "true path" by attempting to create a personal relationship with Allah.

Today, the presence of Islam is evident in every culture in the world. Despite periods of decline and advance, Islam survives. Sometimes, extremist sects within Islam resort to terrorism, assassination, and riots as a reaction to the creeping Western, secular influence in the Islamic world and also to the occupation of Islamic lands and holy sites by soldiers from the West. This is the Islam that makes the headlines. But there is another Islam that does not. And it is the Islamic narrative that we recount here.

The Doctrinal Dimension

Islamic doctrine begins and ends with the teachings of the Qur'an ("reading," "recitation," "discourse"). The Qur'an consists of 120,000 words, divided into 114 suras (chapters), and 6,000 verses, covering a vast range of content from metaphysics and ethics to legal teachings and sacred history. (Amazingly, some aspiring imams, at a very young age, have memorized every single word of the Qur'an.) Although it is true that the Prophet's thousands of traditional *hadiths* serve as rich commentary on the Qur'an, the first, major element of Islamic doctrine can be explained simply. To be a Muslim is to be willing to live in peace with others and in complete submission to Allah (an Arabic phrase meaning "a God"). To be truly human, therefore, is to submit to God in everything, without question, and to allow oneself to be guided always by God's Will.

The second element of Islamic doctrine is the *shahada* ("I bear witness"): *La 'ila 'illa Allah, wa Muhammad rusuul Allah* ("There is no God but God, and Muhammad is the Messenger of God"). Another Qur'anic Sura (57:3) says, "There is only one God who does not beget or is begotten . . . and there is like unto him no one." And one other: "He is the First and the Last and the Outward and the Inward and He knows infinitely all things" (Sura 52:3). For Muslims, the Christian concept of a Son of God is blasphemous.

The third element of Islamic doctrine concerns the Book of Deeds containing duties that every Muslim must attend to while alive. These duties are known as the *Five Pillars* of Islam. Briefly, these are:

- ▪ *Shahada* (the profession of faith, mentioned above). Unlike Judaism and Christianity, there are no complex conversion rituals or ceremonies (such as Baptism) in Islam. To make a simple declaration of faith in one God, Allah, and to testify that Muhammad is God's chief prophet is enough to become a Muslim, regardless of a person's race, geography, nationality, social class, gender, or political affiliation. However, the profession of faith must be accompanied by a profound change of heart and a commitment to serve Allah faithfully for the rest of one's life. The shahada is also pronounced at births, deaths, and before going to sleep and after awakening.

■ *Salat* (prayer), the primary, compulsory duty of each and every Muslim. Prayer for Muslims, like meditation for Buddhists, purifies the heart, bestows a sense of peace and tranquility, equalizes all social classes, develops self-discipline, soothes the passions, and brings people closer to a transcendent reality. Muslims pray five times a day, at specific times throughout the day, facing Mecca. Surah 2:110 says "be steadfast in prayer." Some go to the mosque, others pray wherever possible. Women pray at home or at the mosque. Imams (leaders of a congregation) lead prayer at the mosque. There are ritual washings before prayer, appropriate clothing to be worn, and most Muslims pray on a prayer mat or carpet. Some use a string of 99 beads reciting the 99 names of Allah over and over again. All Muslims, however, are enjoined to attend the mosque for midday prayer on Fridays. Regarding the importance of prayer to Muslims, a famous *hadith* records this: "I asked the Messenger of Allah . . . 'Which of all deeds is the most pleasing to God?' He replied: 'To offer the obligatory prayers at their due times.'"

■ *Zakat* (almsgiving, to purify), the voluntary contribution of money for the poor in order to show compassion for all of God's creatures. For a Muslim, everything belongs to God and everything returns to God. The Zukat is a "purification tax" on property and personal wealth, fixed at about 2½ percent of one's financial worth. Almsgiving, charity, and service are ways for Muslims to purify themselves of greed and to recognize their social responsibilities to others. Zakat is also a very effective way to equalize great differences in financial resources and to redistribute wealth in the community. Here are some representative Surahs advocating a regular, sacrificial giving on the part of all Muslims: "By no means will you attain to righteousness until you spend out of that which you cherish most" (Surah 3:91). "Those who are saved from their own greed shall be the successful" (Surah 14:91). "Spend your wealth for the cause of Allah, and do not be cast to ruin by your own hands; do good! Lo! Allah loves the generous"

(Surah 2:195). (By the way, the Qur'an urges all Muslims to give secretly so that the poor are not embarrassed.)

▪ *Sawm* (fasting) occurs during Ramadan, the ninth month of the Islamic calendar (the month when Allah revealed the Qur'an to Muhammad) between dawn and dusk. In some ways, fasting serves the same purposes as almsgiving. *Sawm* teaches Muslims to be compassionate, self-disciplined, and reflective. Fasting reminds Muslims of the afterlife, encourages a deeper spirituality, and shakes up routines. Fasting also flattens out differences because it is a communal activity. After all, every Muslim needs to fast at the same time, regardless of social class distinction. Sawm is ascetic in the sense that it exacts great personal sacrifice. In addition to refraining from food and alcohol, a Muslim must also abstain from sexual intercourse, gossiping, smoking, lying, cheating, breaking promises, and, most difficult for those who live in desert climates, drinking water during the day. Only two meals are permitted each day; a light meal before daybreak and a full meal after sunset. Here is a typical Surah regarding the importance of fasting: "O believers, you must fast so that you may learn self-restraint. Fasting is prescribed for you during a fixed number of days, so that you may safeguard yourselves against moral and spiritual ills" (2:183–184).

▪ *Hajj* ("to set out with a definite purpose") is an obligatory pilgrimage to the holy city of Mecca to visit the "House of God." *Hajj* is required of all Muslims before they die, but only if this is financially and physically possible. Surah 3:91 states that "It is the duty of all believers towards God to come to the House a pilgrim, if able to make their way there." The *hajj* occurs during the 12th Islamic month, and 2 million Muslims from all over the world gather in Mecca each year at this time. The *hajj* lasts 5 days, and each day is filled with traditional rituals, including circling the sacred shrine of Ka'aba (a cube-shaped building, the template of which is supposed to have been built by Adam). The pilgrimage ends with a festival of animal sacrifice, commemorating the prophet Abraham's willingness to sacrifice his son, Isaac, in response to God's request (which God later rescinded). The religious purpose of *hajj* is that Allah forgives the sins of those who make a pilgrimage to Mecca, the sacred center of the Islamic universe. It was in Mecca where Islam began, and it is here where all good Muslims are called to visit at least once before they die.

The Ethical Dimension

In addressing the Muslim community, Allah says: "You are indeed the best community that has ever been brought forth for the good of mankind; you enjoin the doing of what is right and forbid the doing of what is wrong, and you believe in God" (Surah 3:110). Thus, from the beginning, Allah stipulates the importance of living an ethical life in total submission to His Will. God leads, His people follow. Allah knows what is good, and so, therefore, ought His people. After all, throughout the Qur'an, Allah is referred to as the "Beneficent and the Merciful." Those who follow His path are destined to be with Him forever in Paradise. Those who stray by doing evil will end up in an afterlife that is filled with pain and suffering.

Because Muhammad was as much a law-giver and ruler as he was a Prophet and holy man, Islamic ethics has a strong legal component. It is also very practical, as was the Prophet himself. Islamic ethics is embodied in the *Shari'ah* (the way of Islam, Divine Law). The Shari'ah is a combination of legal/moral teachings from the Qur'an and the *hadiths*, including the Five Pillars mentioned above. Thus, the Shari'ah lays out the commandments of God as laws that govern all aspects of life, including, among others, the family, worship, morality, and even warfare. Throughout the Qur'an, a Muslim can find moral injunctions to worship the One God, be kind to parents, treat women with respect, be generous to the poor and to strangers, be just in trade, be compassionate, and be humble.

In fact, few people in the West know that in 1981 a "Universal Islamic Declaration of Human Rights" was promulgated by an all-Islamic Council made up of important Muslim leaders from a number of Middle Eastern and South Asian Muslim countries. This statement, while not binding on all Muslims, at the very least puts Islam firmly on record as basing its central ethic on social justice, human rights, and equality.

Here are just some of the human rights that the Declaration endorses: freedom, fair trial, protection against abuse of power, freedom of belief, freedom of speech, freedom of religion, free association, economic order, worker dignity, social security, protection of the rights of married women, education, privacy, and freedom of residence. In 1990, the Organization of the Islamic Conference, made up of members from every single nation with majority Muslim populations, published its own charter of rights. Remarkably, the Islamic Conference supported the earlier Declaration of Human Rights; in fact, it went one step further in that it subsumed all these rights under the aegis of Shari'a.

While it is true that the Islamic reach in the area of morality and ethics has often exceeded its grasp, this is no different from any moral system in the world. Ideals often fall far short of reality. As in every major country on earth, political expedience often trumps moral idealism. Religious ideals, whether Christian, Jewish, or Muslim, can be weakened by political programs more concerned with pragmatism than with moral integrity. But notwithstanding the harsher realities when politics and pragmatism in the Muslim world clash with the Islamic moral code of life, the ethical principles of equality, brotherhood, and social justice are fully supported and enunciated in the Qur'an, *hadiths*, and codified in the Shari'ah.

Finally, Islam is a religion that emphasizes individual moral responsibility. While it is true that God is both omnipotent and omniscient, He does not predestine human beings to live one way over another. People are fully responsible for their moral behavior, as they are in Christianity and Judaism. There is always an element of free will. According to one prominent Muslim scholar (Ahmed, 2001), Allah is concerned with promoting the following moral values: faith, justice, forgiveness, compassion, mercy, sincerity, truth, generosity, humility, tolerance, modesty, chastity, patience and fortitude, responsibility, and courage. Allah, according to the same scholar, abhors the following vices: hypocrisy, cheating, backbiting and suspicion, lying, pride, envy, anger, divisiveness, and excess/extremism (pp. 12–51).

Allah lays down each of these moral principles as duties throughout the Qur'an. In fact, this scholar summarizes the whole of Shari'ah moral law with a particular passage from the Qur'an: "Goodness and Evil cannot be equal. Repay evil with what is better, then he who was your enemy will become your intimate friend" (Surah 41:34). And, in a passage reminiscent of Christian and Jewish morality, he quotes the following Islamic proverb: "You shall not enter Paradise until you have faith, and you cannot have faith until you love one another. Have compassion on those you can see, and He Whom you cannot see will have compassion on you."

The Ritual Dimension

For Muslims, *niyya* (being deliberately aware of the meaning and intention of a ritual) must always precede the performance of each religious act and observance. This deliberate awareness focuses on the true meaning of ritualistic activities and ensures what Muslims call the "presence of the heart" in every act of devotion. (Buddhists, Christians, and Hindus, among others, have their own "centering' exercises.) For the Muslim, therefore, rituals signify something more than oft-repeated, mindless "habits." Rather, they are meant to underscore the dramatic importance of each sacred event in Islam. What follows are brief descriptions of a few key Islamic worship, holy day, and life cycle rituals. (We have already talked about the centrality of prayer rituals in a previous section.)

Holy Day Rituals

Ramadan occurs during the 9th month of the Islamic lunar calendar, usually 10 days earlier than the Christian solar calendar. Many Muslims try to read the entire Qur'an during Ramadan. Ramadan is a time for purification, reflection, fasting, atonement, spiritual discipline, and gratitude. There are, also, a number of other holy days in the Islamic calendar, but Ramadan is the most widely observed. These other holy days celebrate such events as the ending of Ramadan, the faithfulness of Abraham, the Prophet's journey from Mecca to Medina, and the birth of Muhammad.

Initiating and Welcoming Rituals

The *birth* ceremony is called *akikah,* and it is not universally practiced by Muslims. In fact, birthdays are not recognized and celebrated in the Islamic lunar calendar. Circumcisions (*khitan*) are performed on boys, but age and ritual circumstances vary according to region and local custom. For girls, there is no corresponding initiating event.

The *initiation into the faith* ceremony (*shahada*) marks the young person's entry into Islam, usually during the middle teen years. The ceremony can be held either at home or in a mosque. The youngster must repeat in Arabic the Islamic profession of faith mentioned in a previous section: *Ashshadu an la ilaha illallahu wa Muhammadur rasulullah* ("There is no God but Allah, and Muhammad is His chief prophet").

Marriage, while central to the Islamic faith, is not celebrated as a sacrament or a mystical union as it is in the Judeo-Christian West. It is, instead, a social contract that stresses rights and obligations, along with mutual respect, justice, and caring. In some parts of the Islamic world, marriages are arranged. Compared to Western marriage ceremonies, the Muslim ritual seems informal and brief. Witnesses simply observe the groom's formal proposal of marriage, and the dowry (money, animals, goods, etc.) that accompanies it. Sometimes an officiant presents a short talk on the meaning of marriage, but no elaborate and expensive ceremony is required. Occasionally, a reception (*waleemah*) takes place, but it is kept simple, with some dancing and music, and strictly nonalcoholic.

Funerals, like marriage, are known for their simplicity and directness, lasting about 30–60 minutes or so. A person of the same sex washes the body in water, and buries it on its right side, always facing Mecca. Before the burial, mourners gather, either in a mosque or in front of the deceased's house, to pray *Allahu akbar* ("God is Supreme") four times. This prayer signifies that, in the end, the Muslim surrenders all to God, even loved ones. Only God's grandeur remains. All human beings must return to their

Creator for judgment after having undergone the tests and challenges of earthly life (Surah 671–2). Although the Qur'an gives graphic descriptions of the joys of paradise and the miseries of hell, individual Muslims, as well as different sects, hold a broad range of opinion as to whether such passages should be taken literally or figuratively. Mourning is restricted to 40 days, and during this time, social activities are curtailed.

Islam Resources for Teachers: A Brief Bibliographic Essay

In our opinion, the single most helpful resource on Islam for teachers and students is Akbar S. Ahmed's *Islam Today: A Short Introduction to the Muslim World* (New York: I. B. Tauris, 2001). Ahmed is a Pakistani Muslim, an academic, and a resident of the United States. His presentation of Islam is as balanced and up-to-date as anything we have read on this religion. He is also a writer whose prose is clear and lucid, and almost totally devoid of special pleading and academic jargon.

Three other background resources that we found very useful for our purposes in this chapter are Karen Armstrong, *Muhammad: A Biography of the Prophet* (New York: HarperCollins, 1992); John Renard, *Responses to 101 Questions on Islam* (Mahwah, NJ: Paulist Press, 1998); and Malise Ruthven, *Islam in the World* (New York: Oxford University Press, 2000). What we especially appreciate about these three texts is that their authors write for a lay audience that has had no previous knowledge of Islam.

For a straightforward, informational overview of Islam, with its emphasis less on interpretation and advocacy and more on clarification of main concepts, events, and figures, we recommend Ruqaiyyah Maqsood's *Islam.* This overview, like others in the "Teach Yourself World Faiths" series, cited in another chapter, is crystal clear and no-nonsense in its approach.

Andrew Harvey's *Teachings of Rumi* (Boston: Shambhala, 1999) is a wonderful collection of Jalal-Ud-Din Rumi's poetry. Rumi was born in Afghanistan on September 30, 1207, and died in Konya, Southern Turkey, on December 17, 1273, and is generally considered to be the leading Muslim mystic. Harvey's Introduction effectively captures the profound mysticism and rich spirituality of Sufism.

The English edition of the Qur'an that we use throughout this chapter was given to us by a local, Arabic-speaking Imam. He called *The Glorious Qur'an Translation* (Elmhurst, NY: Takrike Tarsile Qur'an, 2000) the "best English translation available today."

5

The Narrative of Hinduism

Case Study #4: "Isn't it Illegal to Teach Yoga in Public Schools?"

At this afternoon's faculty meeting, all the teachers had shared their plans for the first 4-week round of electives they planned to offer students. Writers' Workshop, Forensic Science, Hiking, Community Garden—the ideas were all interesting, and Annalise had felt the general sense of excitement rise in the room as teachers talked about their passions. When Annalise's turn came, she explained, "I'm planning on offering a yoga class to help our students find a positive outlet for stress."

When her colleague, Henry, who was a devout Christian, turned red-faced and started sputtering, "We can't allow that!" it was entirely unexpected. She and Henry had always gotten along, but, frankly, they had never talked about religion with one another. Annalise turned to him, dumb-struck with surprise.

"But Henry, our students are much more stressed than we were when we were their age. They are faced daily with difficult choices about drug

Teaching Adolescents Religious Literacy in a Post-9/11 World, pages 77–92
Copyright © 2010 by Information Age Publishing

use. Many are working and acting as the adult in the family, taking care of younger siblings. A few of our eighth-graders are even parents themselves. And that's not to mention the stress they feel about applying and getting into the charter school of their choice in this city! Yoga can be a great way to de-stress. The physical . . ."

Annalise's voice trailed off as Henry abruptly interrupted. "I agree that the kids are stressed, but I can't endorse their learning any practice that teaches them to worship zillions of gods, that sanctions the caste system, that teaches them they will be reincarnated over and over again, with new chances to pay for whatever karma came their way during the last life. It's ridiculous. That's just irresponsible of us, and frankly, probably also illegal, given that it's teaching religion in the public school. Yoga comes right out of Eastern religions, you know."

"I know the origins of yoga, Henry," Annalise snapped, deeply offended. "I wasn't planning on teaching the students the religious beliefs, just the opportunity to clear their minds and strengthen their bodies." Annalise had been practicing yoga since college and had found it to be a valuable outlet for de-stressing. She didn't plan on backing down from her chosen elective, yet she also didn't want to provoke any strife among the faculty. By the end of the meeting the two teachers had agreed to talk together with their building administrator for direction. But tonight, as she drove home, Annalise wondered how they could possibly arrive at a mutually satisfying compromise.

Stereotyping Eastern Religions

For Westerners like Henry, brought up and rooted in a Judeo-Christian tradition, Eastern religions such as Hinduism can seem virtually incomprehensible. Religious stereotypes about the East abound in the United States, and, unashamedly, Henry utters many of them in his contretemps with Annalise. For him, yoga exercises are bound to lead students through the back door into a religion that is polytheistic and, probably, pagan. After all, everyone knows that Hinduism is totally different from Christianity, and, therefore, it is out of the mainstream, dangerous, and maybe even illegal to teach about it. Right?

To the Henrys in public schools across the United States, as well as to most Western adolescents, Hinduism, as well as other Eastern religions, will make little or no sense. This, we believe, is all the more reason for adolescents and their teachers to become literate about a religio-spiritual worldview that is every bit as dominant in major sections of the world as the Western religious worldview is here.

An opportunity for adolescents to study Hinduism could serve as an important gateway into the Eastern mindset. For example, Hinduism was a major influence on the development of Buddhism. More significantly, however, such a study would bring home to adolescents the genuine meaning of religious pluralism. In Hinduism, and in other Eastern religions as well, there is such an incredible diversity of beliefs and practices <u>within</u> the religions themselves that adolescents would get a dramatic, firsthand taste of the genuine richness, and complexity, of religious difference.

There are many additional reasons for teaching adolescents the basics about a religion like Hinduism. Hinduism is the major religion of India, comprising a membership of anywhere from 800 million to 1 billion adherents. Also, Hinduism has flourished in Southeast Asia for over 1,500 years. Moreover, at the present time, there is a growing Hindu religious influence in every major country in the world, exacerbated by a Hindu diaspora to the United States, as well as migrations to several countries throughout Western Europe.

Another reason for studying Hinduism is that India, fast approaching a population numbering a staggering 1.5 billion people, is a strong, international ally of the United States. Thus, it behooves us in the West, in an interconnected global community, to understand the rudiments of such a powerful world religion—in order to get a sense of its meaning for a billion-plus people. Hinduism and India are so inextricably linked throughout their history that to understand the latter requires a comprehensive understanding of the former.

Furthermore, to remain illiterate about Hinduism is to miss an opportunity to understand the Eastern perspective on what makes human beings tick. Hinduism's vast sacred literature, art, music, rituals, and traditions are jewels to be cherished, both here and throughout the world. Hinduism's unique spiritual wisdom, guidance, and inspiration are there for the taking, if only adolescents are given an opportunity in public school classrooms to encounter the oldest religious tradition on the face of the earth. Here is a compelling example of how a religious provincialism in the West could keep us from ever achieving a cosmopolitan—hence pluralistic—perspective toward religious narratives unlike our own.

There is an important caveat in all of this, however. To refer to Hinduism as one, homogeneous religion is inaccurate, as there are actually as many Hinduisms as there are local sects of Hindus. Numerical estimates range anywhere from the hundreds to the thousands of Hindu sects and subsects throughout India alone. Additionally, at the present time, because of the worldwide Indian diaspora, there is a growing Hindu influence in every major country in the world, including the United States and in several countries throughout Western Europe. Here, too, diversity of Hindu beliefs and practices is the rule not the exception.

Hinduism is also the world's oldest religion, having evolved for over 3,000 years, perhaps even for as long as 5,000 years, according to some estimates. Hinduism comes in every shape and size, as various in culture, geography, philosophy, theology, social class, and ritual as any religion ever practiced by human beings. A fitting motto for describing Hinduism's incredible internal diversity might very well be "out of one, many" (*e unum plures*).

Perhaps in their meeting together with the building administrator, Annalise and Henry can work out their differences. It would help, though, if Annalise could construct a case not just for exposing her students to yoga practices in an isolated elective course, but also to help them to become more religiously literate than they are. Depending on the openmindedness of the building administrator, Annalise has a wonderful opportunity to promote the expansion of the multicultural mission in her school to include teaching about the realities of religious pluralism. She could even broaden the conversation to talk about how much she would love offering an elective course in comparative religions and cultures, emphasizing particular religions such as Hinduism.

She could cite some statistics about the growing number of students from such countries as India, China, and Japan who attend their middle school, as well as other schools in their district. She could also point out how the odds are strong that many of these students are probably practicing such religions as Hinduism and Buddhism in their communities. Will any of this convince Henry to change his mind? Maybe, maybe not. But these facts and statistics could be an important way to get the ball rolling on creating an important curriculum innovation in Annalise's school system.

Core Beliefs and Practices in the Hindu Narrative

The Narrative Dimension

Here, in the fewest words possible, is the story of Hinduism:

"Once upon a long time ago, a world-famous religion came into being with no specific founder, no known starting date, and no dramatic historical event. Some believers think that this religion always was and always will be. Over time, this religion grew by leaps and bounds without any systematic planning or direction, until, presently, it is one of the five largest religions in the world.

"This religion features all kinds of Gods, and all types of worship. Some adherents sacrifice animals, some venerate shrines and statues, some sing and dance, some write and read, some become priests and teachers, and some become contemplative mystics. Some are very secular.

"There is no centralized authority, no Pope/Prophet/Imam-like leader, in this religion. There is no single, infallible, inerrant scripture or divinely inspired, sacred book. Adherents do not believe in a Heaven or Hell. Instead, believers hold that a succession of rebirths is necessary until adherents get it 'right,' no matter how long it takes. Believers also hold that people pretty much get what they deserve until they get it 'right.' There are no non-negotiable doctrines or commandments in this religion. This religion values sensual, as well as spiritual, pleasures; wealth as well as poverty; and worldliness as well as otherworldliness.

"Finally, this religion rarely, if ever, speaks of a God or a Divine Creator. Nevertheless, few religions today are as suffused with a sense of the mystery of 'Infinite Being.' For adherents of this religion, it is impossible to name this Infinite Being, but, without an acute sense of its presence, finite being remains forever incomplete. By the same token, without a full experience of finite being, a comprehension of this Infinite Being is impossible."

Picture what the reaction of adolescents might be as teachers introduce the narrative of Hinduism for the first time, especially in its thumbnail form that we used to introduce this section. For starters, Hinduism had no specific beginning like the three monotheistic religions. It simply grew by accretion through several millennia, or more colloquially, it grew over time like Topsy. Its influence spread in all directions in a completely unplanned and, yet, cumulative manner.

Hinduism's ancient roots lie in India, in the Indus valley, Saraswati River civilization. The word, "Hindu," derives from *Sindhu*, meaning the Indus river. Thus, Hinduism refers to the various religions of the Indus river people. No historian has been able to pin down the exact time of Hinduism's origins, because there have been so many local communities throughout early history that have contributed to the formation of Hinduism. And each indigenous community had its own endemic faith and belief systems, practices and rituals, and philosophies and deities.

Moreover, there is no central figure, or prophet, in Hinduism as there is in each of the three monotheistic religions. Hinduism is absent its signature Moses, Jesus, or Muhammad, although many great, and memorable, Hindu sages have appeared throughout history, right up to, and including, the 20th century. A list of more recent Hindu sages would include the names of Sri Ramakrishna (a 19th century mystic who preached the love of God and the importance of multiple approaches to the Truth, and who said, "Different creeds are only different paths to the Almighty"), Mahatma ("great soul") Gandhi, Swami Prabhupada (founder of the Hare Krishna movement), Indira Gandhi (former Prime Minister of India), Maharishi Mahesh Yogi (founder of the Transcendental Meditation Movement), and renowned spiritual leader J. Krishnamurti, who died in 1986.

Also, Hinduism's sacred texts did not take shape as inerrant Bibles or Testaments dictated or inspired by a single, all-powerful and all-knowing God. Instead, what emerged through time were collections of *Vedas*, a Sanskrit word for "knowledge" or "wisdom," most often conveyed through the performing arts and oral stories in an age when there were no books. In time, during the years 1500 to 800 B.C.E., the *Vedas* were inscribed in manuals of poetry, rituals, and philosophy.

There are two types of Hindu texts: *shruti* and *smriti*. Shruti texts constitute the eternal knowledge given to Hindu seers, and passed down through time to brahmin priests. Smriti texts contain traditional knowledge as described in some of the great Indian literature. Shruti texts include the *Vedas*, the *Brahmanas*, the *Upanishads*, and the *Aranyakas*. Smriti texts feature the Epics, the Code of Manu, and the Puranas. The four major Veda collections are the *Rig-Veda* (probably the world's oldest, most sacred text), the *Sama-Veda*, the *Yajur-Veda*, and the *Atharva-Veda*. The <u>Vedas</u> consist of over 1,000 hymns, chants, sacrificial rituals, magical spells, and incantations.

The world-famous *Upanishads* ("sitting at the feet of a master"), written in Sanskrit between 800 and 400 B.C.E., were a collection of spiritual treatises, numbering around 112, about the length of the Bible. The various writers of the Upanishads were thinkers and poets. One of the sayings in the Upanishads is "words are weariness," in the sense that while words are important ways to capture the meaning of an ineffable or higher Reality, in the end one needs to feel and to live this Reality if one is to truly understand and experience it. There comes a time when all words fail to name the unfathomable and, hence, the unnamable.

Equally famous is the Hindu classic *Bhagavad Gita* (often referred to in their writings by the American Transcendentalists Ralph Waldo Emerson and Henry David Thoreau). The *Bhagavad Gita* ("The Song of the Blessed One"), written around the 5th century B.C.E. (a debatable date among scholars), is a part of India's national epic, the *Mahabbarata*, a long epic poem eight times the size of the *Iliad* and the *Odyssey* combined. In a conversation just before a major battle, Arjuna (representing anyone who seeks guidance) asks Krishna (an incarnation of the God, Vishnu) whether any war can be just when so many lives will be lost.

The major religious theme of the *Bhagavad Gita* emerges during a long conversation between Arjuna and Krishna: If one is fighting for righteousness (*dharma*), and if one is willing to spend a lifetime reaching for God through devotion, renunciation, knowledge, and selfess action, then war is justified. Along the way, Krishna also teaches Arjuna the meaning of such key Hindu concepts as soul, karma, reincarnation, liberation, and justice.

Finally, imagine trying to convey to Western adolescents the sum and substance of Hinduism as a growing, global religion. Many will scratch their heads over the vast differences between Hinduism and the Western monotheistic faith-narratives, which they have lived in all their young lives. For most Western adolescents, Judeo-Christian notions of One Almighty God/Jehovah ruling the universe are in the religio-spiritual air they breathe and, hence, beyond question. What, then, will adolescents do when they learn about the existence of a dizzying profusion of deities and subdeities in the narrative of Hinduism?

In Western cultures where quantification, and scientific reductionism, are considered to be the most valid ways to depict and measure reality, what sense will adolescents make of this verse from the Vedic tradition?

"What is whole? This is whole. What has come out of the whole is also whole. When the whole is taken out of the whole, the whole still remains whole." (quoted in Levinson, 1996, p. 85)

We are confident that adolescents will, indeed, understand the narrative of Hinduism, if they are given a serious opportunity to study it. As educators, we believe in the amazing power of diverse worldview knowledge to produce insight, empathy, and, at times, even personal transformation. The human brain needs to know, and the human heart needs to feel. We have confidence, nurtured by years of teaching and learning, that an enhanced religious literacy is capable of producing both knowledge and feeling, wisdom and empathy.

Moreover, it is our hope that studying Eastern religious narratives such as Hinduism will help adolescents to find at least a modicum of overlap between Western and Eastern images of God, faith, and spirituality. For one, we believe that there is a basic, theological agreement between monotheistic and polytheistic religions. What is this common ground? *The Infinite, Absolute, Unchanging Reality is impossible to quantify, or to reduce in size, once and for all.* Thus, all religions agree, at some level, that whenever humans attempt to do this, they run the very real risk of committing idolatry. God becomes nothing more than a false idol, a shrunken-down version of an ersatz Divinity, taking on the qualities of some comic book or video game superhero.

The Doctrinal Dimension

To speak of a "doctrinal" dimension to Hinduism is to court disbelief, if not outright laughter, among Eastern religion experts. If it can be said of any religion that it is truly doctrine-free in the traditional sense, it is Hinduism. So, we will be using the term "doctrine" in the most elastic way possible. Henceforth, in this section, "doctrine" will mean a particular philosophy of life and spirituality that has been worked out through thousands of years, but a philosophy that does not represent infallible teachings authoritatively ordained as True and Indisputable.

In a nutshell, and living very dangerously, we paraphrase the words of a contemporary Hindu teacher, Swami Tathagatananda, when he was asked to summarize the Hindu belief system: God is one and indivisible, but people are only able to worship this God in different forms. In some respects, humanity itself is one and indivisible, and its essential nature is divine.

Hinduism, therefore, is about encouraging people throughout the world to realize their divinity, and, in the process, to inch closer to an understanding of a mysterious, one-and-indivisible God. There are an infinite number of ways to understand and realize this divinity, and these are called *yogas*—exercises that teach personal, physical, and spiritual self-discipline.

In order to elaborate further on the above, we unpack some key terms in Hinduism and add brief explanations:

■ *Brahman, Brahma, and Brahmin.* Although at first glance, the three terms look interchangeable, they actually have different meanings for Hindus. *Brahman* represents One Ultimate Reality, or the Creative aspect of Being. Brahman is a concept similar to what Westerners might call God or a Supreme Being, but what Hindus think of as the Being behind all being—without which being has no meaning. Brahman is an ultimate reality that is changeless; an eternity with no beginning or no ending. It is both impersonal and personal, and manifested in an endless array of symbolic shapes and forms—no single one of which captures the entirety of its true essence. To complicate matters even further, some Hindu sages would also ask: Just what is the Being behind Brahman Being that gives Brahman Being meaning? Even the question causes headaches, but it is a typical Hindu, philosophical query. *Brahma* represents a particular Creator God, a concept that is somewhat out of fashion in contemporary Hindu philosophy and theology. And Brahmin names a representative of a prestigious priestly class (caste) based in India. There are Brahmins in India today, though, who are not priests, but who do have the authority to read from the Vedas. Nonpriest Brahmins hold prestigious leadership positions in India, and are considered to be of very high status.

- *Atman,* Sanskrit for "breath," is the individual soul or life-force (the breath of life) that dwells within everything human and nonhuman. It is eternal and indestructible. It is pure being, pure consciousness, and pure bliss. It is what connects human beings to ultimate reality, because both phenomena have *atman* in common. It is a life force that is both immanent and transcendent. Only the eternal and blissful in us is able to reach to the eternal and blissful in Brahman. When the sage in the *Upanishads* is asked to define the nature of the Godhead, he says "*Neti, neti* ("Not this, not this"). When pressed to be more positive, he says "*tat tvam asi*" ("Thou art that"). This is to say that what is best in us is Brahman or the Godhead itself . . . and vice versa.

- *Vedas* ("true knowledge") are the traditional holy books of Hinduism, written in Sanskrit and dating from the second and first millennia B.C.E. The Brahmin, or members of the priestly class, have taught the knowledge in these books for over two millennia. If it is possible to say there is any orthodoxy in Hinduism, then it lies in the traditional wisdom of these handed-down texts. Collectively, the *Vedas* include philosophical and metaphysical verses, commentary on these verses, esoteric teachings, and mystical texts. The four earliest Vedas are the *Rig Veda, Sama Veda, Yajur Veda,* and *Atharva Veda.* Both the *Upanishads* and the *Bhagavad Gita* are canonical, *Vedic* texts that reveal mysterious, eternal truths about the relationship of the finite to the infinite.

- *Karma,* is a Sanskrit word that means "action," "deed," "ritual," or "result." Within the context of Hindu metaphysics, and first appearing in the *Upanishads,* the word *karma* refers to the principle that one becomes good by doing good, and one becomes bad by doing bad. Karma has also taken on the meaning of cause-and-effect actions that can be used to explain or predict the past, present, and future. In brief, behavior in the past affects the present, which, in turn, affects the future. We pretty much get what we deserve, according to how we have lived our lives in the past. Here is what the *Upanishads* has to say about *karma*:

> According as a man acts and walks in the path of life, so he becomes. He that does good becomes good; he that does evil becomes evil. By pure actions he becomes pure; by evil actions he becomes evil. . . . Reaching the end of the journey begun by

> his works on earth, from that world a man returns to this world
> of human action. (Mascaro, 1965, p. 140)

Hindus, Buddhists, Sikhs, and Jains based their eschatologies
(teachings about the last things) on the principle of *karma*. The
concept of *karma* explains a person's present life condition and
future prospects because it puts suffering and good fortune in
perspective. The key to achieving release from suffering and misery in this life is to build a store of good deeds or *karma*.

- *Samsara*, a Sanskrit term meaning "flowing together," or, more
  loosely, "wandering from one lifetime to another," is closely associated with the doctrine of *karma*, particularly in Buddhism. Buddhists emphasize the importance of the renunciation of worldly
  desires as necessary for attaining release from a person's endless
  wandering through painful cycles of birth and rebirth.

- *Moksha*, or "liberation," is the ultimate goal for all Hindus in the
  samsara process. It is the final release from the repetitive cycle of
  birth and death. There are many "paths" (ritual action [*karma
  marga*], devotion [*bhakti marga*], and knowledge [*jnana marga*])
  to achieve *moksha*. (The *Bhagavad Gita* features a detailed description of these three paths.) Thus, by following the path of knowledge in order to reduce the bad effects of *karma*, a Hindu can
  practice selfless actions, meditation, and exercise, and be willing
  to surrender totally to the Divine Reality of Brahman. Here is
  what the *Upanishads* have to say about liberation:

  > He who in the mystery of life has found the *Atman*, the Spirit, and
  > has awakened to his light, to him as creator belongs the world of
  > the spirit, for he is this world.... When a man sees the Atman, the
  > Self in him, God himself, the Lord of what was and of what shall
  > be, he fears no more.... He has no bonds of attachment, for he
  > is free; and free from all bonds he is beyond suffering and fear.
  > (Mascaro, 1965, p. 141)

- *Yoga* ("yoking"), translating into words such as "effort," "technique,"
  and "joining," usually refers to acts of meditation, concentration,
  various bodily movements, and breath control activities. There are
  several systems of Yoga. One is Royal or Raja Yoga, which includes
  a series of pithy aphorisms (Yoga Sutras), developed by the sage
  Patanjali around the 2nd century B.C.E. What Westerners, today, understand yoga to be probably owes a lot to Patanjali who presented,
  in 195 succinct aphorisms, a variety of physical and mental exercises meant to yoke body and mind. The objective of all yoga activities
  is to liberate the soul in order to move it closer to a termination

of the samsara process. A related objective is to yoke or bond the self with the supreme spirit or universal soul. A yogi or yogin is one who practices yoga. *Hatha yoga* is more elaborate and esoteric than *Raja yoga*, and it requires a mastery of rigorous, complex physical techniques in order to bring the body under complete control. *Kundalini yoga* concentrates on freeing the latent spiritual power located at the base of the spine. Kundalini yoga occurs through a series of seven body centers called *chakras*. These are sources of spiritual and psychic energy.

The Ethical Dimension

It is important to say, at this point, that there are no extensive, formal treatises on ethics in Hinduism. Instead, norms of conduct have evolved over three millennia in a somewhat haphazard way, in bits and pieces. The major sources of Hindu ethics include countless moral sidebars, pieced together from selected passages in scriptural literature. Other sources are local practices and customs, the examples of saints and sages throughout the ages, and, most important, the good consciences of individual Hindu practitioners.

In Hinduism, the inner conscience of the religious person is regarded as the ultimate decision-maker in the realm of ethical behavior. In fact, Hindus think of life as a promising, moral training ground for learning how to make ethical decisions. Hindus know that they, alone, are responsible for building moral foundations for their lives. While it is true that the ethical sources mentioned above can offer guidance and support, Hindus understand that, in the end, it is the individual who must struggle alone to overcome the pride and cravings of the self.

It is up to the individual to let go and to let be. It is up to the individual to learn to renounce self-centeredness, and the selfish longings that accompany this state of mind, by embracing and loving all living beings. In this respect, here are the passionate words of Ramana Maharshi (quoted in Harvey, 1996):

> When you truly feel equal love for all beings, when your heart has expanded so much that it embraces the whole of creation, you will certainly not feel like giving up this or that. You will simply drop off from secular life as a ripe fruit drops from the branch of a tree. You will feel that the whole world is your home. (p. 51)

We have already referred to many of the aforementioned ethical sources in previous sections, so we will not repeat ourselves here. Suffice it to say that the following excerpt on ethics from the *Upanishads* pretty much sums up the Hindu perspective on morality (quoted in Coogan, 2005):

> Speak the truth. Follow the path of righteousness.... Having bought the wealth dear to your teacher, do not cut your ties. Do not neglect truth.... Do not neglect the well-being of your body. Do not neglect fortune and wealth. Do not neglect study and teaching of sacred texts. Do not neglect the rituals to honor gods and ancestors. Consider your mother and father, your teachers and guests, as Gods.... Do only those deeds that are without blame. Hold in esteem only the good that you have seen in others. Give with faith. Give in plenty, give with modesty, give with fear, give with full knowledge and compassion. (p. 66)

These words are well-known throughout the Hindu world, and are often recited at university graduation exercises in India. This excerpt captures the full spirit of the Hindu moral *dharma* ("duty, righteousness, ethics"), emphasizing the virtues of loyalty, hospitality, gratitude, compassion, modesty and humility, respect, nonjudgmentalism, nonviolence, affirmation of life's pleasures including wealth and sex, good health, generosity, faith, and knowledge.

More specifically, in the area of medical ethics, Hindus believe in, and practice, birth control, although poorer families have several children as a kind of hedge against the ravages of old age and a pensionless existence. Mercy-killing is forbidden, but opium use to control pain is acceptable, even if, ultimately, it ends up killing the patient. Hindus, also accept the practice of abortion as a legal and moral way to limit unwanted pregnancies.

So too, suicide is acceptable in Hindu society, although not if it is used simply to escape from the cycle of *samsara*. Drugs such as cannabis and hashish are generally approved ways to enhance spiritual awareness. Finally, it is rare for a Hindu to eat the flesh of a cow. Orthodox Hindus regard cattle as sacred incarnations of particular deities, and, therefore, they forbid the slaughter of these animals, as well as others.

In this respect, *ahimsa* (noninjury) is a universal Hindu ethic that holds all life, including human and animal, to be sacred. Thus, a majority of Hindus adopt a policy of nonviolence toward living creatures, which has led to the growth of vegetarianism throughout India. Albert Schweitzer (1875–1965), a famous medical missionary and theologian who lived and worked in Africa, based his philosophy of "reverence for life" on the Hindu principle of *ahimsa*. Reverend Martin Luther King, Jr., preached a philosophy of nonviolence and pacifism as a way to bring about racial equality in the United States, as a result of his admiration for Mahatma Gandhi's teachings on *ahimsa*.

In Chapter 7, we speak on the ethical implications of Hinduism's treatment of women, as well as the existence of a caste system.

The Ritual Dimension

It is important to remember, before reading this section, that not all Hindus observe festival seasons, holy days, or public rituals. Hinduism is a truly pluralistic religion with many ways of worshipping. In fact, some Hindus do not engage in worship rituals at all. A sometimes insurmountable "anomaly" for Westerners is that formal *group* worship, devotions, and celebrations in public places such as churches or temples are fairly rare in Hinduism. Usually, during their private, family worship times, Hindus pray to their favorite Gods, eat special sacramental foods (*prasad*), engage in sacred readings, and even chant, either individually or collectively.

There is no single holy day in the Hindu calendar equivalent to the Sabbath in the West. Thousands of sites, days, and seasons in India are considered sacred among Hindus. "Sacred" sites include mountains, caves, groves, rivers, towns, cities, and forests. Bathing (*yatra*) in a sacred river, for example, can be enough to gain liberation, and this can occur anytime, not just on a particular day of the week.

Still, there are many magnificent Hindu temples, spread throughout the south Asian subcontinent, dedicated to particular gods such as Shiva and Vishnu, as well as to several goddesses. These temples (seen as sacred extensions of heaven on earth) have become epicenters of piety and influence throughout the Hindu world. Millions of Hindus make pilgrimages to some of the most sacred temples (the richest and largest is the temple of Tirumala-Tirupati in Andhra Pradesh) throughout the lunar year. It is in these sacred temples (many located near bodies of water like the Ganges river) where Hindus can "cross over" (*tirtha*) from life to death. Bathing in these holy waters is one way for Hindus to purify their souls.

Temple worship, however, has its Hindu detractors, who believe that each and every Hindu is a "temple of the supreme being." For them, the body is divine, not the building or shrine. Listen to the words of the 8th-century C.E. Hindu poet Periyalvar: "Build a temple in your heart. Install the lord called Krishna in. Offer him the flower of love."

Also, websites on the Internet have taken the place of temple worship for millions of Hindu devotees (sometimes these sites are called "electronic ashrams"). In an instant, Internet surfers can see representations of deities, gurus, and saints; hear sacred music; and read the holy books. But downloading images on these websites is forbidden, because it is considered disrespectful.

What follows are some key holy periods in Hinduism:

- The Festival of Navarati ("Nine Nights") is celebrated in the lunar month spanning mid-September to mid-October. This is the time that Hindus celebrate several goddesses, but especially Sarasvati, the patron goddess of learning and music. Hindus ask Sarasvati to bless the "tools" they use for their arts, crafts, and trades.

- The Festival of Dipavali ("Necklace of Lights") is one of the most popular festivals in India, occurring between mid-October and mid-November, mostly in people's homes. The festival is a way of thanking the particular Gods (*puja* or "ritual worship") who are important to the families. Hindus decorate their homes with lights, set off fireworks, and sport new clothes. Some exchange presents and prepare festive meals.

- Other holy days include *Duhsehra/Durga Puja*, celebrated in early autumn in recognition of the triumph of good over evil. *Rama Navami* is a springtime ritual that celebrates the God Rama. *Krishna Janmashtami* is the birthday of Krishna, occurring in late summer. And *Shiva Ratri* takes place in the last days of winter as a celebration of the God Shiva.

Observances of certain life-cycle rituals (*samskaras*) often play a key role in Hinduism:

- The Infant Naming Ceremony (*namakarana*) happens on the 12th day after birth, because the mother is considered to be in a state of ritual pollution for 10 days. This ceremony can take place either in the home or in a hall. Boys' names, according to some scriptures, are two to four syllables, and girls' names are one, three, or five syllables.

- The Rite of the First Solid Food, occurring 6–8 months after birth, celebrates the first time that a child consumes solid food such as rice. This "rice-eating ceremony" is usually celebrated in the child's home during a family gathering. At pre- and post-receptions, traditional Indian food is served, minus alcoholic beverages. *Prasad*, or food offered to a deity, is given to the child before the guests are fed. Sometimes a *swamiji* (monk) or a *panditji* (priest) is available to officiate.

- Marriage is the most sacred family affair in Hinduism. It is also the major rite of passage for both the bride and the groom. Marriages are often arranged by the parents or guardians of the bride and groom. (In India, arranged marriages are the rule, and not the exception, among Sikhs, Jains, Muslims, and Christians as well.) While some Westernized married couples arrange their own marriages (often called "love marriages"), they still must seek the permission of both sets of parents. Hindu marriages, taking place after sunset, feature seven separate ceremonies: the verbal contract between the fathers of the bridge and groom; the giving away of the daughter to the groom by her father; welcoming the bride and groom; holding hands; a walking ritual; creation of a holy fire that the bride and groom walk around four times; and the placement of red vermillion on the forehead and the furrow of the bride's parted hair. Mantras from the sacred *Vedas* are recited in Sanskrit at strategic religious times during the ceremony, which usually lasts about 3 hours. This time includes a lavish wedding feast.

■ Funerals center on the cremation (*mukhagni*) rite. The nearest male relative of the deceased usually arranges the funeral, after the death notice is signed by a local doctor or a subsidized medical practitioner (a paramedic). There are no "funeral homes" in Hinduism, so the body remains at home until it is taken to the site of cremation, 24 hours after death. The *shraddha* (bereavement ceremony) occurs either 10 or 30 days afer the funeral, depending on the deceased's caste position. This ceremony functions to liberate the soul of the deceased for its ascent to heaven.

Hinduism Resources for Teachers: A Brief Bibliographic Essay

The most concise and engagingly written resource on the five major Eastern religions (Hinduism, Buddhism, Taoism, Confucianism, and Shinto) that we recommend highly to both teachers and adolescents is *Eastern Religions: Origins, Beliefs, Practices, Holy Texts, Sacred Places*, edited by Michael Coogan (New York: Oxford University Press, 2005). This book contains dozens of dazzling photographs that are bound to catch the eye of aesthetically curious adolescents.

Once again, the *Teach Yourself Books* on Hinduism is a handy reference for teachers looking for a simple presentation of key definitions, translations of words, dates, names, and events.

The following primary source translations of the Vedas that we recommend highly are:

The Upanishads, translated by Juan Mascaro (New York: Penguin Books, 1965). The Introduction alone is worth the price of the book. *Bhagavad*

Gita, translated by Stephen Mitchell (New York: Three Rivers Press, 2000). Once again, the Introduction is a lyrical rendering of the major themes and meanings of this classic Hindu Veda. We also highly recommend a Veda almost completely overlooked outside India, and now available in English for the first time. *The Uddhava Gita: The Final Teaching of Krishna*, translated by Swami Ambikananda Saraswati (Berkeley, CA: Ulysses Press, 2002), written centuries apart from the *Bhagavad Gita*, is rich with philosophy, poetry, and practical advice.

Finally, a book that we consulted often on the differences and similarities between Asian and Western philosophical and spiritual thinking is J. J. Clarke's *Oriental Enlightenment: The Encounter Between Asian and Western Thought* (New York: Routledge, 1997).

6

The Narrative of Buddhism

Case Study #5: "Aren't Buddhists Atheists who Hate Life?"

On a bright spring Monday, tenth-graders at a small high school in the Northeast sauntered into their World Cultures class in ones and twos. The recent warm weather had instilled a sense of restlessness in much of the school community, and students were eager to get outside after the long winter. "Class outside today, Mr. D.?" several asked hopefully as they entered the room. Their teacher, Mr. Delorme, smiled and shook his head. The students laughed, elbowing and regaling each other with tales of how distracted they had been the last time they had class outside, during the previous fall.

As the students gradually settled into their seats, the large circle of desks began to close, filling up with growing bodies and long legs spilling into the center of the circle. Mr. Delorme called for their attention and asked students how they had spent their weekends. Several shared about a movie they had seen; others talked about attending the regional marching band competition.

Teaching Adolescents Religious Literacy in a Post-9/11 World, pages 93–107
Copyright © 2010 by Information Age Publishing
All rights of reproduction in any form reserved.

Mr. Delorme then stood near the front of the room, by the white board, on which was written "The Noble Eightfold Path Toward Righteous Living." He asked them how last week's assignment had turned out. Part of the curriculum in this World Cultures class was a focus on several of the world religions. Last week they had focused on Buddhism. Mr. Delorme had instructed students to keep a log of their actions all week, doing what they would normally do, but noting when they believed they had aligned with the Noble Eightfold Path and when they felt detoured from it.

Having taught this class for almost two decades, Mr. Delorme prided himself on making the concepts relevant and accessible to the adolescents in his school. One of the best ways he had found to do this was to help students put themselves in the shoes of others. It was not uncommon for him to ask students to "try on" an aspect of a religion or culture under study as a way to make a personal link to the learning.

"So, how did it go last week on your Eightfold Paths?" he queried, smiling. "What did you learn?" Several students talked eagerly about their experience, sharing the connections they made to their speech and actions over the course of the week. One student, however, was uncharacteristically quiet throughout the discussion. Noting this, Mr. Delorme called on him to share his perspective on the matter.

"Jared, do you care to share with us what observations you made last week?" Mr. Delorme asked. "Not really, Mr. D. I wasn't able to complete the assignment. I mean, I started to keep a log of my actions, but my parents were upset about this assignment. They didn't want me to meditate. My church, you see, prohibits meditation. I could get locked in a trance and then that would open me up to the temptations of Satan. Also, Buddhists are atheists, and so they don't meditate on God. What's worse, they don't even pray. I read somewhere that Buddhists worship Buddah, who was just a guy, not a God.

"And when they meditate, they only concentrate on themselves. They just don't care about God or other people. In fact, my dad said that he thinks Buddhists really hate life, because they claim there's so much pain and misery around. Mr. D., I don't want to hurt your feelings, but my family and I believe in the Ten Commandments, not the 'Noble Eightfold Path.' I really don't see the reason for studying this pagan religion."

Publicly, Mr. Delorme assured him that there was no expectation that students do anything beyond their normal activities, rather merely to note their similarity to, or difference from, a Buddhist way of life. Privately, however, Mr. Delorme was perplexed. He was always careful to explain the assignment in writing, and ensure that students brought it home to their families for precisely this reason. This semester had been no exception. He did not want parents to perceive this as promoting any particular religion or as discounting any of their own beliefs or practices.

Yet, regardless of this sensitivity, one student had felt he was unable to complete the assignment and therefore had not had the opportunity to fully realize the concepts in the unit. Moreover, he seemed to completely misunderstand the facts behind Buddhism. Mr. D. wondered how he might have changed the assignment or communicated more effectively with families in order to ensure Jared's feelings of success.

Can the East Ever Meet the West in a Public School Classroom?

Mr. Delorme is beginning to doubt himself again, as he always seems to do whenever he introduces his students to the Eastern religions. He wonders for the nth time whether the Eastern religious perspective is so much in conflict with the Western religious perspective that most of his students will just never get it. Jared is one of his best students. He is on the honor roll, a school leader, and a great community-service activist, but when it comes to religious narratives like Buddhism he, like others his age, has no way to relate his own Christian experience to the Eastern spiritual experience.

It is as if Christians and Buddhists live in two separate worlds, destined never to find a common ground. For Mr. D., at times, it all appears so futile, but he resolves to press on anyway in his determination to introduce his high school students to other perspectives on religion and spirituality. After all, Buddhism is a powerful religious influence in several countries, ranging from India and Afghanistan to China, Korea, Ceylon, and Japan in the East; and, in Southeast Asia, from Burma (Myanmar) to the Indonesian islands of Java and Bali.

Today, Buddhism is still the main religion in Tibet (even though the Chinese government controls the country), Sri Lanka, and Thailand. It also has a strong presence in Cambodia and Vietnam. Estimates vary, but Buddhists can claim upward of one-half billion adherents throughout the world, including the United Kingdom, Canada, and the United States.

Mr. D. reasons that, as a culture studies/social studies teacher, he has a professional responsibility to enlarge the conventional Judeo-Christian worldview of his middle-class American students. For sure, he will take great pains not to negate or minimize this worldview; rather, he will strive to deepen and enrich it by showing where it overlaps with and differs from other religious worldviews. This, he believes, with all his heart, is what is necessary in order for his students to become true global citizens, knowledgeable about differences instead of being fearful of them.

Perhaps Mr. D. thinks his greatest challenge will continue to be to expose his students to a unitary way of thinking, a both–and view of the world instead of an either–or. But is this radical change in perspective doable, especially for adolescents? Mr. D., who is not a Buddhist but a Christian, knows that it has only been in recent years, after lots of personal reflection, meditation, and reading Eastern forms of spirituality and metaphysics, that he himself has been able to rid much of his own Western-conditioned thinking of artificial dualisms and false splits.

Yet, because he has been socialized and trained in the Western mindset all his life, he still struggles daily to open up his thinking to alternative perspectives. How, then, he worries, will he be able to help his students to get the most out of such a brief introduction to the Eastern worldview? Won't they be forced to forget the lessons of nondualistic thinking he is trying to teach them once they leave the classroom and have to engage the workplace *and* the marketplace on their own terms—if they are to be successful?

Core Beliefs and Practices in the Buddhist Narrative

The Narrative Dimension

Buddhism is some 550 years older than Christianity, and 1,200 years older than Islam. Ironically, the Buddha himself predicted that his teachings would only survive his death by 500 years at the most. He was wrong. His teachings have stood the test of time for over 2,500 years, and they are still going strong. Each new generation of adherents, of course, tweaks the Buddhist narrative to fit its particular historical time and place, but the essential practices and beliefs remain stable. For a religio-spiritual narrative to survive and prosper as long as Buddhism has, the general storyline (and message) must be a compelling one. And it is.

The Buddha lived around the years 566–486 B.C.E. His own personal story of spiritual discovery mirrors the central teachings of Buddhism in a remarkably dramatic way. Siddhartha Gautama, who eventually became the Buddha, started life as a wealthy nobleman in Nepal—a youthful Indian prince and a member of the warrior class (kshatriya)—whose early life was filled with great privilege and pleasure. Gradually, however, his disillusionment with this way of life took shape as he started to venture further and further from the comfortable confines of his sheltered existence. It was during these travels away from his palace, at age 29 and married with one son, that Siddhartha observed four events (the "Four Sights") that would eventually change his life.

Legend has it that the first time he left the palace with his charioteer, Khanna, he saw a hobbling elderly man who was bent, frail, toothless, and wrinkled. Barely upright, the man, with trembling hand, reached out to Siddhartha for help. "Why," Siddhartha asked his charioteer, "is this wretched, hurting, old man in such a terrible state?" The answer, that this is the general fate of all human beings, including himself, shocked him.

On a second excursion from the palace, Siddhartha saw a person afflicted with a disease and suffering terribly. The man had also soiled himself, because he was in such great pain. On a third excursion, Siddhartha observed a corpse being carried to a cremation ground, and later, as was the tradition in India, he saw it burned in full public view. And during his fourth trip outside the walls, Siddhartha saw a holy man (*sadhu*), a wandering ascetic who mortified his flesh by extreme acts of self-denial, trudging along the streets with his alms bowl. Siddhartha was stunned with the dawning realization that all of these experiences were the universal lot of humanity. Nobody escaped them, including, most of all, himself.

The fourth sight hit Siddhartha particularly hard because it presented him with what today we might call the existential dilemma of becoming aware of one's inevitable human finitude: Should he give up his wealth and luxury, as well as his career, family, wife, and son, in order to pursue the life of a *sadhu*? After all, he reasoned, if aging, suffering, pain, and death are the eventual fate of every human being and if the pleasures of life, at best, are nothing more than ephemeral and transient diversions—inevitably giving way to the harsher realities of human finitude—then, in the end, joy and happiness are really nothing more than a cruel illusion.

So what is left after all is said and done that gives life meaning is the question that haunted Siddhartha. Would he ever be able to find permanent release from the endless cycle of suffering and torment? No longer did his wealth, power, and the presence of countless dancing girls and courtesans in the palace give his life any lasting purpose. It all became stale, and he grew to be jaded. In his early texts, Siddhartha, later the Buddha, would say to his monks:

> The ignorant, ordinary person, who is himself subject to aging, suffering, and dying, feels when he sees an old man, and is himself not yet old, uneasiness, shame, disgust, for he applies what he sees to himself. . . . As I considered these matters, all joy in my youth vanished utterly from me. (Schoeps, 1968, p. 174)

The Buddha believed that three types of vanity plagued all human beings: vanity of youth, vanity of health, and vanity of life. These vanities prevent most of us, at a very early age, and on through adulthood, from remembering that there is no escape from aging, sickness, poverty of the spirit and flesh, suffering, and death. Much later in life, after reaching his own enlightenment and becoming a Buddha, Siddhartha would make the following assertion: "Within this fathom-long body is found all of the teachings, is found suffering, the cause of suffering, and the end of suffering."

Unlike Christianity, Judaism, and Islam, in Buddhism, there is no transcendental redemption from suffering. There is no God Who will eventually make things right in an afterlife, Who will soothe us in the present, and Who will, in the end, provide a reason for the suffering, if only we will be patient and trust Him and obey His commandments. For the Buddhist, only the human being can extinguish suffering by radically transforming a previously unenlightened way of life. Only the human being can awaken to the here and now, and respond to what *is*, not to what *was* or *will be*. And so, Siddhartha Guatama decided to leave his comfortable surroundings (the "Great Going Forth"), shaved his head and beard, donned modest yellow garments, and became a homeless beggar.

He fasted, mortified his flesh for six years, got little sleep, neither bathed nor wore clothes for long periods of time, and surrounded himself with a group of disciples and companions. But, despite all of this self-sacrifice, he still remained restless and unfulfilled. Acts of extreme austerity just did not deliver any lasting truths to him, and so he gave them up.

Reaching a point of near-hopelessness and desperation, Siddhartha found a spot beside a river in northern Central India, under a large pipal (fig) tree (today known as a Bodhi [enlightenment] tree), and he resolved to stay there until he had reached enlightenment. In his own words: "...even though my flesh may wither away, my blood dry up, I shall not move from this seat until I gain enlightenment" (Schoeps, 1968, p. 174). And he literally did not move, sitting motionless in a deep meditative state for long periods at a time.

Eventually, after much temptation, resolve, and skill, Siddhartha achieved what is called by Buddhists his "Great Awakening." At that point, he became the Buddha, which literally means, "The Awakened One." During his long, meditative state, Siddhartha discovered what would later constitute the basic teachings of Buddhism (the *dharma*). (Buddhists refer to this period as "Setting in Motion the Wheel of Truth.")

And later, after 49 days of complete stillness and contemplation, he made the decision to travel throughout northern India with his disciples and friends, preaching his message to others and establishing monastic communities (*sangha*). He did this for 45 years, dying at the age of 80, after having achieved his "final nirvana," his "perfect enlightenment" (*parinirvana*). His disciples (*arhats*) continued to preach throughout India, spreading the Buddha's teachings about compassion, peace of mind, and *dharma* truth.

The Buddhist tradition has undergone multiple permutations during its 2,500-year history. Unlike the three major monotheistic religions, there is no supreme being in Buddhism. The Buddha himself was only a man, someone who sought truth in order to understand the meaning of suffering and death. He was charismatic enough to be able to convey his truth to others in such a way as to create a sense of the sacred without fostering a belief in a creator God or a reliance on infallible, sacred scriptures. In the centuries following Buddha's death, a number of rival Buddhist schools and sects emerged, finding homes in such countries as Sri Lanka, Indonesia, China, Korea, Japan, and Tibet, where Buddhism remains a potent religious force, right up to the present time.

The Doctrinal Dimension

Before we begin examining the specifics of the doctrinal dimension of Buddhism, we first need to say a few words about the historical interrelationship of Hinduism and Buddhism. Hinduism exerted an enormous influence on the development of Buddhism, and, for over 2,500 years, both have managed to coexist together in relative peace. (There have been serious exceptions, however, as in present-day Sri Lanka where, for the past half century, Buddhist Sinhalese and Hindu Tamils have lived in violent religious and ethnic conflict with one another.) In fact, Buddhism, in recent centuries, has had a reciprocal impact on the development of Hindu thinking and practice. Religious studies scholars call this intermingling of pieces of religious systems "syncretism." We prefer to call it "narrative overlap."

Sometimes in the history of religion, this overlap is intentional, sometimes it is not. Sometimes religions get swallowed up by other religions, and total assimilation is the result. But, in the case of Hinduism and Buddhism, each of these religious narratives has managed to retain its basic uniqueness. Hinduism and Buddhism have remained religiously independent of one another for over two-and-one-half millennia, even though they share a common history and, in part, even a similar philosophy and metaphysic.

Both religious movements began in India, for example, but Buddhism arose as a reaction to certain tendencies in Hinduism, which we talked about in the previous chapter. For example, the Buddha rejected Hinduism's emphasis on the supernatural, the absolute theological authority of the brahmins, the elaborate Vedic rites and rituals, fatalistic notions of karma, and the caste system. He also challenged what he thought was Hinduism's excessive reliance on tradition and scriptures.

By the same token, however, the Buddha held on to general Hindu notions of reincarnation and karma, albeit in a much more nuanced and modified way. And the Buddha also maintained the Hindu belief in nirvana and personal liberation, as well as in *samsara* and the sanctity of all life.

What is it that Buddhists believe, then, if they possess no creation theology, authoritative scriptures and traditions, priestly castes, and recite no official creeds? While Buddhism is essentially nondoctrinal in the sense of being nondogmatic, there is an identifiable core of beliefs that most Buddhists hold to be true. This common, philosophical core begins and ends with many of the issues that the Buddha himself struggled with before his enlightenment. Thus, the heart and soul of Buddhism are embodied in the "Four Noble Truths" and the "Middle Way." These are the *dharma*, the self-evident truths and teachings of the Buddha.

The First Noble Truth

Life is suffering (*dukkha*), disease, and inadequacy. The Sanskrit meaning of *dukkha* is a "wheel out of kilter." It is not that life is always bleak and hopeless, but that our lives are imperfect and our happinesses (*sukkha*) and successes are fleeting. All too often our reach for peace and contentment exceeds our grasp and our joys are short-lived. We are rarely, if ever, fully satisfied. The lingering, subliminal awareness that each and every one of us will someday die, that it will all end forever, brings home the *dharmic* truth of impermanence, and puts our lives in perspective.

Change and decay are an endless process, touching everything that is. There is no exception to this *dukkha* truth. The Buddha recognized that human beings have great difficulty coming to grips with this truth, because it is so frightening. The reality of impermanence, or human finitude, always is. He said: "It is difficult to take a hair split a hundredfold, and with an arrow, shot from a great distance, strike and pierce a single, split hair strand. But it is even more difficult to attain to the insight that all life is suffering" (quoted in Schoeps, 1968, p. 177).

The Second Noble Truth

Dukkha is caused by *tanha* (thirst), the desire or craving to hold on tightly to things, ideas, and people as surefire ways to satisfy all our needs. For Buddhists, this is an impossible mission, because these cravings are endless and insistent, and they enslave us. They produce only unhappiness and frustration. The truth is that no achievement, possession, or relationship will ever satisfy all our needs. We are driven, restless creatures always on the move to experience some new sensual desire, intellectual insight, or avocational pleasure. But alas, in the end, it all comes to naught, because we are enslaved by our needs to want more and more. Nothing is ever enough.

As long as we cling and crave, grasp and grope, we will suffer. *Tanha* is a no-win game. We can never hold on tightly to anything, because everything is a process that is constantly changing and impermanent. It is like trying to hold on securely to steam, a cloud, or to water. The message inherent in the Buddha's teaching of *dukkha*, and expressed in colloquial language familiar to most of us, is simply this: "Pain is inevitable, but suffering is optional." It all depends on our perspective, says the Buddha, our willingness to embrace our pain and be open to what it might teach us by way of compassion and interdependence.

Thich Nhat Hanh, a Buddhist priest and a Vietnamese peace activist, puts it this way: "The Buddha called suffering a 'Holy Truth,' because our suffering has the capacity of showing us the path to liberation. Embrace your suffering, therefore, and let it reveal to you the way to peace." Or as Geoffrey Shugen Arnold says: "When we see into the emptiness or illusory nature of things, of life and death, of sickness and health, of youth and old age, then we're master of all things. We are free to be healthy, we're free to be sick, we're free to grow old." (both of these quotations are taken from the *2005 Zen-Page-A-Day Online Calendar* at www.pageaday.com).

The Third Noble Truth

The way to inner peace is through personal liberation, and this means eliminating *tanha* by achieving *nirvana*. Nirvana is not an afterlife of eternal paradise. Rather, it entails the cessation of all selfish desires and forgetting the self in the here and now. Nirvana means letting go of the need to possess, to hang on, to crave, and to control. Nirvana literally means to "blow out" the fires of longing, yearning, and hungering. These fires are the "fuel" of *samsara*, a concept in Buddhism that refers to the endless cycle of birth, craving, and death that each of us must experience until we learn to extinguish the fires that perpetuate our suffering.

A related term, *karma*, a word that means "action," is grossly misunderstood by Westerners. It actually has little to do with fate, luck, or with a previous life whose mistakes have to be worked out in a present life for as long as it takes for a person to get it right. Regarding the latter concept, many non-Tibetan Buddhists throughout history have rejected the Hindu notion of an endless series of "reincarnations or rebirths," preferring instead to think of the *dharma* as a moving wheel in which a condition constantly shifts and changes.

The Buddha taught that *karma* is a practical way of understanding how the law of cause and effect can point us in the direction of stopping those behaviors that cause our suffering and pain in the first place. We need to know that our unenlightened behaviors have a cumulative effect on our unhappiness: Their result is to fuel the fires of misery that torment us. Somewhere, somehow, sometime, each of us is fully responsible for stopping those behaviors. Hence, *karma*—knowing how what came before affects what happens now and what will happen later.

The Fourth Noble Truth

The Noble Way is an Eightfold Path (see the next section) that leads to the achievement of *nirvana*. This Eightfold Path is, in part, a collection of practices meant to curb self-destructive cravings. Yoga exercises, breathing control, meditation, fasting, and a variety of mystical activities help Buddhists to subdue the grasping self and quiet the "chattering monkeys" of the cognitive intellect.

It is important for Westerners to note that Buddhists refuse to separate these practical exercises from what they call *sankhya*. This means knowing how to differentiate between the excesses and deficiencies of asceticism and worldly activity. For Buddhists, the Noble Eightfold Path is learning how to live a life with balance, harmony, moderation, and peace.

The Ethical Dimension

In addition to certain prescribed practices, the Eightfold Path also encompasses a series of moral precepts: Right Understanding, Right Intention, Right Speech, Right Conduct, Right Occupation, Right Endeavor, Right Contemplation, and Right Concentration. It is essential to understand, however, that for Buddhists the term "right" (*samma*) has little to do with "good" or "bad," "right" or "wrong," as we in the West understand the word. Rather, the word has strong pragmatic overtones in Buddhism such as "this works," "this fits," or "this is appropriate given the reality I live in or the reality I would like to live in." In other words, the ethical meaning of "right" is doing what is conducive to personal enlightenment, to achieving a personal awakening.

There are two main schools, or traditions, in Buddhism that go about achieving a moral awakening in different ways. *Theravada* Buddhism dominates in Sri Lanka and Southeast Asia. *Mahayana* Buddhism survives in Japan, Korea, Mongolia, and China. There are, also, a number of other

Buddhist sects including Zen, the Pure Land School, and Nichiren Buddhism. And each of these includes several different denominations and traditions.

The Theravada ("School of the Elders") tradition traces itself directly back to the sacred teachings of the Buddha. It stresses asceticism, solitude, monastic life, and total withdrawal from society. The ideal is to attain the status of the *arhat* (worthy) monk, who lives a rigorous and scholarly life of self-denial in a monastic sangha. The Theravadan sacred scriptures, the *Tipitaka* (Three Baskets), feature strict monastic regulations, sayings of the Buddha, and theoretical commentaries. Also, the Theravadan *dhammapada* is a summary of the Buddha's *sutras* (collected sayings).

The Mahayana or "Great Vehicle" movement in India, around 100 C.E., introduced a new corpus of Buddhist scriptures, and placed more emphasis on the active, community role of laypeople (nonmonks). Also, Mahayana Buddhists, in the lands of north and east Asia, introduced the notion of the *bodhisattva* (one who is enlightened), a spiritually advanced person who works in the world in order to help others to achieve nirvana. Mahayana Buddhists emphasize compassion and service in their moral mission.

Whether Theravada or Mahayana, however, all Buddhists agree essentially on the ethical significance of the Eightfold Path. This can be summed up in three basic principles: no harmful actions (*shila*); cultivate a disciplined, meditative mind (*samadhi*); and understand (*prajna*, wisdom) the ever-changing, no-self nature of consciousness that possesses no permanent identity. Additionally, the Five Moral Precepts stipulate: no killing, no stealing, no abusive sex, no lying, and no intoxicating beverages.

All Buddhists, too, would agree that the highest ideal of Buddhist ethics, reflected in the spirit of the Eightfold Path, is *metta*, "loving kindness," and exercising a benevolence and empathy toward all without calling attention to itself. In the *dhammapada*, one hymn says: "Enmity does not subside through enmity, but only through amity does emnity subside. Overcome anger by not growing angry; overcome evil with good; overcome the miserly by giving; overcome the liar by truth."

What follows, in brief outline, are the ethical implications of the Eightfold Path for "right" living in the world:

- ▪ *Right view or right understanding.* Everything in the world is interconnected and in constant flux and flow. This is the Buddhist view of how things actually are. Also, right understanding is the insight that comes from reflecting on the Four Noble Truths. Therefore, understand that once you take an inflexible moral view on something, you bump up against another's moral view. Respect the views of others, at least at the outset.

■ *Right intention.* Personal insight and truth come only through strong resolve, effort, and hard work. A Buddhist understands that the only way to reach enlightenment is, in the words of a popular advertisement, to "just do it!" In the Western vernacular: "Walk the walk, don't just talk the talk."

■ *Right speech.* Always speak in such a way that you respect others. Also, avoid gossip, which is cruel, and idle chatter, which is a waste of time. Avoid lying, because it is a major distraction in pursuing enlightenment. It forces the mind to keep track of the lies rather than keeping the mind in meditative focus. In addition, crude speech cheapens the speaker.

■ *Right conduct or action.* This is what Western ethicists call the principle of "nonmaleficence": Do no harm. Stealing, committing adultery, using intoxicants, hurting others, and so on, are harmful.

■ *Right occupation or livelihood.* Avoid work that might place you in compromising ethical positions, or that might keep you from "awakening." Work that is consistent with *dharma* moral teachings encourages honesty, compassion, peace, and balance.

■ *Right endeavor or effort.* Always keep your eye on the ultimate prize: enlightenment and nirvana. Mindfulness (being fully present in the moment, being watchful and ready, being calmly observant) requires that you cultivate the qualities of patience, positive outlook on life, and avoidance of negativism in everything you do and with everyone you meet. Be mindful always of doing good for others. In the words of the Buddha, "Go forth on your journey, for the profit of the many, out of compassion for the world, and for the welfare and bliss of humankind."

■ *Right contemplation and right concentration.* Maintain an inner calm and learn how to become focused, centered, and fully conscious. The purpose of right contemplation and concentration is to become aware of the impact of our own thinking on the pain and misery (*dukkha*) that we experience in the world. Nobody else is to blame. We are. Adopt the perspective that only you can control your own mind, your own consciousness, your own joy and happiness.

We close this section on the ethical dimension in Buddhism with a short prayer that a present-day, enlightened *bodhisattva*, Tenzin Gyatso, the

14th Dalai Lama, utters every single day upon waking (Dalai Lama, 1999). It aptly captures the sum and substance of Buddhist ethics, which translates to compassion at all times toward self and others:

> May I become at all times, both now and forever
> A protector for those without protection
> A guide for those who have lost their way
> A ship for those with oceans to cross
> A bridge for those with rivers to cross
> A sanctuary for those in danger
> A lamp for those without light
> A place of refuge for those who lack shelter
> And a servant to all in need. (p. 237)

The Ritual Dimension

The primary purpose of ritual in Buddhism is to honor, not venerate or adore, the *Buddha*—the central events in his life, as well as his *dharma* teachings and the founding of his monastic orders (*sangha*). Buddhists call these the "Three Jewels" and the "Three Refuges." Secondary events calling for ritual activity usually include celebrating planting and harvesting seasons, as well as initiation and life cycle rites, and these take on the particular character of the different cultures in which they occur. Thus, Buddhist rituals are both universal in their sacred significance and local in the specific forms of celebration they take.

The three major holiday events celebrated by all Buddhist traditions are Nirvana Day (February 15), commemorating the death of the Buddha; Hanamatsuri Day (April 8), celebrating the birth of the Buddha; and Bodhi Day (December 8), observing the day that Siddhartha Gautama made the vow to meditate under the Bodhi Tree until achieving enlightenment. During each of these ceremonies, and depending on the culture, there can be retreats; colorful processions; festivals; displaying, and, in some cases, bathing Buddha images and relics; special *pujas* (devotions); meditations; recognition of great bodhisattvas; gift giving; as well as a whole host of additional activities.

Individual life cycle events are very important in Buddhism because they serve to bond individuals to the community, thus enriching the social fabric. As important, however, these rites of passage join individuals and communities to the eternal patterns of the cosmos. This latter is significant because it assures everyone that no turning point in an individual's life will ever destroy the interdependence of all things. All is one, and one is all, and life unfolds in a series of repetitive cycles.

While individual life cycle events are universal in Buddhism, ritualistic celebrations of them are highly eclectic, and are unique to different cultural backgrounds and belief systems. Central individual life cycle events include the following:

- *Birth and adolescence.* Depending on the particular culture, birth may or may not be recognized by formal, ritual ceremonies. In Buddhism, at least in theory, there is no doctrinal distinction between birth, death, and rebirth. All are intimately linked in a Wheel of Becoming (*kalachakra*). In some Buddhist cultures, however, there can be ceremonies celebrating pregnancy, birth, head washing, hair shaving, cradle placing, naming, the first dressing, first rice feeding, ear boring for girls, hair tying for boys, initiation into the faith for boys and girls, as well as into a formal monastic life, including priestly ordination for boys, and for girls who get ordained as Buddhist nuns. These rituals occur between birth and age 13, except for ordination, which can occur as late as age 70. Ordination rituals reenact the Buddha's renouncing of the world, celebrate social maturation, and dramatize the rite of passage from childhood to adulthood.

- *Marriage.* Marriage ceremonies may be very informal or formal, religious or secular, once again depending on local customs. A Buddhist monk does not have to perform the ceremony. Throughout Buddhist Asia, as a pre-marriage preparation, priests consult horoscopes to determine marriage suitability, chant scriptural texts, and guide the married couple as they recite publicly the Three Refuges and the Five Precepts. This recitation of "faith" is optional, however.

- *Old age and death.* Often the 60th birthday calls for a religious ceremony, sometimes called a "life extension" ritual in a country such as Thailand. The 60th birthday, the completion of the fifth astrological cycle for Buddhists, is a special marker of the gradual physical decline of the human body. Death rites are universal throughout the Buddhist landscape. Death signals a release from suffering, and for those Buddhists who believe in reincarnation, it represents the chance for rebirth and karmic justice. Elaborate funeral rites occur in all Buddhist cultures, and some feature chanting, expelling death demons, sutra recitations, processions, and readings from the Tibetan Book of the Dead.

Buddhism Resources for Teachers:
A Brief Bibliographic Essay

The *Teach Yourself World Faiths* resource on Buddhism, by Clive Erricker, is a very serviceable introduction to what Buddhists think, what they do, and how they live their lives.

Teachers and students will appreciate the simplicity and inspiration of two books by Steve Hagen, a contemporary Zen priest and teacher for more than 30 years. *Buddhism Plain & Simple* (New York: Random House, 1997) and *Buddhism Is Not What You Think* (New York: HarperCollins, 2003) are vintage Hagen. Everything that teachers and students need to know about the Buddhist worldview, philosophy of life, ethos, and mood is in these extremely practical books. As much self-help, in the best sense, as scholarly investigation, these two volumes probe the most essential and enduring existential questions facing adolescents and adults. They also offer good advice to Westerners.

Another contemporary volume, this one by Vicki Mackenzie, *Why Buddhism?: Westerners in Search of Wisdom* (New York: HarperCollins, 2003), contains the speculations of 15 contemporary Westerners in search of Buddhist wisdom. All of these interviewees are thoughtful, practical, and of diverse social class backgrounds and professions. What they all have in common, however, is their search for a more joyful and compassionate way to live. Each has turned to Buddhism for answers.

One of the most popular books ever assigned to one of our courses is Thich Nhat Hanh's *Living Buddha, Living Christ* (New York: Riverhead Books, 1995). Hanh is a Vietnamese Buddhist monk who was once nominated by Martin Luther King Jr., for the Nobel Peace Prize. No writer on Buddhism that we know has made such a remarkable effort to show the similarities between Buddhism and Christianity, between Eastern and Western thinking. So, too, The Dalai Lama's *Ethics for the New Millennium* (New York: Penguin Putnam, 1999) has been a huge hit with graduate students in the author's applied ethics course.

The primary source that we frequently consulted on Buddhism is *Buddhist Scriptures*, edited by Donald S. Lopez, Jr. (New York: Penguin, 2004). This is an anthology that brings together many historical texts never before gathered together and published in English.

7

Religious Controversies and Misconceptions

Red Flags for Teachers

Currently, several misconceptions, stereotypes, and controversies are fueling religious unrest and conflict throughout the world. It is important for teachers to understand what these internal and external tensions are all about, and what they might mean for the future of religious pluralism on a global scale. In this chapter, we briefly examine several of what we think are the most important internal and external conflicts and challenges today confronting the world's five major religious traditions. One of the best ways that teachers can break down the barriers of ignorance and bigotry regarding religious difference is to be acutely aware of the wide array of misconceptions, myths, and stereotypes that continue to riddle most media coverage of the world's religions.

We hope that what follows comes across not as a critique of or an apology for any of the five religions but, rather, as an honest, unflinching look at a number of controversial issues that continues to fuel media distortion. We want to deal head-on with the very difficult challenges and misrepresentations facing the major religious traditions throughout the world at the

Teaching Adolescents Religious Literacy in a Post-9/11 World, pages 109–132
Copyright © 2010 by Information Age Publishing

present time. We do this in order to equip teachers with the information they will need to expose students from a variety of faith communities to a pivotal insight: all religious communities, regardless of their differences, face similar challenges, conflicts, and misunderstandings.

It is our contention that what religions have in common by way of their special challenges is at least as significant as the doctrinal differences that divide them. The universality of these internal religious controversies and misconceptions, each played out in their own distinctive ways, has the wonderful potential of *binding us together* (the Latin root of the word *religion*) instead of tearing us apart. Why? Because we are less likely to designate the religious beliefs and practices of our neighbors as "other" if we realize that their problems are also our problems, and their successes are also our successes. All the religions, each in their own unique fashion, are in the process of helping people make meaning. Moreover, all the religions must do this while dealing with their own types of internal and external controversies and misconceptions.

Controversies and Challenges in Judaism

1. *The failure of Judaism, a nonmissionary religion, to expand its religious membership worldwide, thereby posing a threat to its long-term viability as a major religious presence in the world.*

The number of Jews worldwide has remained relatively stable for decades, numbering anywhere between 20 and 25 million people. Jews represent only a tiny portion of the world's population of 7 billion people, even though their disproportionate influence on national and world cultures has been vast. It can be said that the Jews have been, and are, an amazingly resilient, creative, and productive people.

However, the number of Jews who actually practice Judaism has remained less than stable. There are many reasons for this. Intermarriage is a big problem in that, currently in the United States and England, over 50% of Jews now marry non-Jews. At the very least, marrying out of the faith means, in general, a less intense commitment on the part of both the parents to perpetuate the beliefs and rituals of the Jewish family, community, and especially, its faith dimensions.

Here are some other alarming statistics. Only a decade ago, the annual Jewish birthrate was roughly two-thirds the death rate. In the early years of the 21st century, it is now slightly under two-thirds. Also, a third of Jewish marriages end in divorce, and this number is rising. Moreover, only half the Jews who marry do so in a synagogue.

A much larger percentage of Jewish men marry *out of* the religion of their youth. And while a small percentage of non-Jewish women do choose to convert to Judaism before marriage, very few do after marriage. These statistics do not bode well for the importance of raising an observant Jewish family, an experience that is utterly crucial for the continuation of Judaism as a family-centered, community-based, tradition-grounded religio-spiritual narrative.

Finally, because Christianity is still the dominant religious narrative in the United States and also because Evangelical/Fundamentalist/Pentecostal forms of Christianity are experiencing such rapid growth throughout North America, the future viability of Judaism in this country, even to maintain its current, relatively small religious presence, is very much up in the air. Movements such as "Jews for Jesus" are ominous indicators of the subtractive effect the Evangelical Christian outreach movement could have on Jews throughout the West. This type of active Christian proselytizing is even more intense in Europe and South America.

2. *The threat of widespread, anti-Jewish stereotyping to the future survival and growth of Judaism.*

It goes without saying that Christian stereotyping of Jews as "Jesus killers" gives serious pause to a younger generation of Jewish parents who are thinking of raising their children to be openly observant practitioners of their faith. Who, after all, wants to expose their children to the threat of physical or psychological violence precipitated by a groundless charge of deicide? It was not the Jews who crucified and killed Jesus; it was the Romans. Fortunately, during the 1960s Second Vatican Council, and even though it happened very late in its 2,000-year history, the Roman Catholic Church came out and vigorously denounced claims accusing the Jews of being God killers.

A terrible fact of life in the 21st century is that some people continue to hate Jews because they are a very visible minority who are sometimes labeled "non-Christians." This is often a code-word, or a synonym, for "strange" or even "inferior." In some extremist cases, the synonym is likely to be "bad" or "evil." Until the reality and worth of religious pluralism is understood and accepted in this country, then those people who believe and worship differently from the dominant, Christian ethos will continue to be persecuted.

It is also important that adolescents understand that not all religious Jews are Zionists. Zionism is a political movement to establish and develop a Jewish national homeland in the land of Israel. Often, however, commentators in the media who disapprove of the policies of the Israeli government against the Palestinians paint all Jews, including Jewish believers, to be pro-Israel, anti-Arab, political zealots. This is inaccurate.

Some Jewish believers support the national state of Israel, some do not, and some have no opinion. Noam Chomsky, for example, is an outspoken Jewish critic of Zionism. Unfortunately, the damage is done in the minds of much of the public. Sadly, if the mass culture stereotype is true for many people that *all* Jews are Zionists, then, for them, all Jews, whether they are religious or not, really have only one major agenda—strengthening the homeland of Israel, regardless of who is harmed along the way.

3. *Major theological discrepancies between Christianity and Judaism that create the unlikelihood of ever reaching a mutual détente between the two faith systems.*

There is such a large theological discrepancy between the precepts and practices of Judaism and Christianity that the differences seem virtually irreconcilable. For example, the doctrines of the Christian Trinity, the Incarnation, and the Atonement have no parallel in Judaism. Conversely, such ritual Jewish practices as circumcision, extensive fasting, and strict dietary restrictions, as well as such beliefs as the "doctrine of election," fail to resonate much for Christians.

Furthermore, each of the two religio-spiritual communities marches to the beat of entirely different, biblical drummers. Even the depiction of the Jewish and Christian Gods in the scriptures could not be more dissimilar. Their Godly temperaments, purposes, and characterizations often conflict in serious ways with one another.

Also, Jewish and Christian politico-religious histories and traditions bear little, if any, resemblance to one another. In fact, it is no exaggeration to say that many adherents of Judaism today deeply resent the tendency of some Christians to conflate Judaism and Christianity into a pat, catch-all term like *Judeo-Christianity.* For these Jews, Judaism is unique, and it is neither the precursor nor the co-partner of Christianity. Judaism has survived for the better part of 3,000 years, and, so, in one sense, some Jews see Christianity to be a relative newcomer to the religious scene.

4. *The future of Judaism as a major world religion.*

Some ask the questions: Will the faith survive in its present forms, or will it even survive at all? Will the subdivisions of Orthodoxy, Conservatism, and Reform Judaism pump new life into Judaism because of their cafeteria-like variety, perhaps offering something for everyone? The *upside* of splintering into a number of different subnarratives is that some faith systems can be revitalized and enriched. Judaism is a richly textured and diverse faith narrative, and, like most worldviews, it needs to continually rediscover and update itself if it is to survive.

In fact, most recently, there is another school within Judaism called "Reconstructionism," created in the 20th century by Mordecai Kaplan. This movement attempts to be responsive to the reality of constant change in Jewish life. It thinks of Judaism as primarily social and cultural and not religious. Thus, it emphasizes the values of democracy, social action, and Jewish continuity over strictly theological matters.

Reconstructionism even rejects some core Jewish religious ideas, such as the belief that the Bible is the word of God. Kaplan taught that God is neither supernatural nor transcendent. In contrast, God is immanent, located within the believer and the social order. Kaplan also rejected the notion of Jews as God's chosen people, thinking this claim to be arrogant and exclusivist.

The *downside* of multiplying intramural religious narratives within Judaism, however, is that these various subdivisions could prevent (maybe even fatally inhibit) the further growth of Judaism. The concern that comes to mind is whether these various schools of Judaism, based on significant theological differences, will become more and more specialized in their emphases, and, hence, more and more cut off from one another. Is it possible that Judaism might experience its own version of the "Protestant Reformation," whereby one or another group could break from "Rome," thereby forming an independent religious sect?

There are no easy answers to these questions, of course, and other religions face many of the same problems. For example, a growing tide of secularism throughout the world is a threat to *all* religio-spiritual narratives. In fact, an evolving secularization has become a coherent worldview of its own, rivaling religious worldviews in almost every country in the Western world. Ironically, it has not been lost on religious studies scholars that Jewish nonbelievers actually form the majority membership in a variety of secular humanism movements. These run the gamut from Ethical Culture, to Jewish Socialism, to the American Civil Liberties Union, to Secular Zionism, and to Humanistic Judaism.

At the very least, secularism dilutes the strength and consistency of most religious commitments, whether these be to Judaism, Christianity, or Islam. At the most, it threatens to make religious worldviews obsolete. Roughly one-third of the world's population currently identifies as "nonbeliever." And another one-third identifies as either "spiritual," "eclectic," or "noninstitutional" in religious inclination. This leaves approximately one-third of the world's people solidly committed to a specific faith tradition. And if majority support in the United States for such secular causes as abortion, birth control, divorce, same-sex unions, and pornography is any indication, then a secular perspective has infiltrated most, if not all, of the United States' religious denominations.

Controversies and Challenges in Christianity

1. *The unprecedented growth of Evangelical, Fundamentalist, and Pentecostal church communities. We will call this the "EFP narrative."*

Evangelicals emphasize the spreading of the "good news" in the Gospels through overt missionary activity. For them, eternal salvation is won mainly by faith and not by good works or through the sacraments alone. Fundamentalists believe in a literal interpretation of the Bible, particularly as this applies to matters of faith and morals. And Pentecostals stress direct inspiration from the Holy Spirit as the key to God's Kingdom.

Obviously, making EFP a single Christian entity has its reductive hazards, as each separate entity has its own religious variations and permutations. However, the exponential explosion of growth in this more conservative Christian narrative is evident throughout the world today. In the Western hemisphere alone, one out of every three adult Christians currently identifies as either E, F, or P. In another 10 years it will be one out of every two. By the year 2050, it could well be 100%. This will drastically change the face of the Christian church throughout the world, and it is already beginning to do so.

What is the growing appeal of EFP Christianity to its adherents? This is a complicated question, but, in brief, EFPs are looking for a Christianity that is intentionally evangelical in spreading its message of good news throughout the world. They strive for an understanding of Christianity that is based strictly on the literal word of God as written in the Bible. And they insist on preaching and practicing an emotional, rather than a doctrinal, faith—one that reflects the joy and enthusiasm of the Holy Spirit. EFPs, whatever their internecine religious differences, are united in their attempts to revolutionize the Christian message by returning believers to its roots, as located in the Bible.

This is a movement that is far less church based than more traditional forms of institutional Christianity. It is individualistic more than it is collectivistic. It is a movement that eschews formal religious dogma and doctrines, authoritative teaching magisteria, normative codes of ethics, prescribed church liturgies and rituals, and "dead" church narratives that fail to capture the genuine excitement of the "Kingdom Already" as well as the "Kingdom Not Yet."

Just how much the EFP global revolution will further dilute, and Balkanize, the Christian church remains to be seen. Whether or not the EFP revolution will empty the mainline churches for good and render clerical hierarchies an anachronism is anyone's guess. But to many Christians, the United States and South America are very close to achieving what Martin Luther advocated in the 16th century: a genuine priesthood of individual believers, absent a hierarchical priestly caste and church.

2. *The increasing popularity of a strictly literal (sometimes called "fundamentalist") interpretation of the Bible.*

Closely related to the EFP explosion in growth is the increasing popularity among many conservative and traditional Christians of an absolute and literal understanding of the Bible. This tendency toward biblical literalism in America, and also in some other Western nations, is fueled by what many Christians see as a total abdication of moral responsibility by the more mainline churches, parents, and educators. Conservative Christians of all denominations look around, and everywhere they see the moral detritus of a creeping secular humanism in the larger society. As a result, they conclude that the United States has become a nation of sexual permissiveness, moral relativism, and scientific skepticism.

All of this signals, for a majority of Christian conservatives, the need for God's people to return to permanent biblical truths and morals. In this regard, today many conservative Christians lobby for the public display of the Ten Commandments in state buildings, and for open expressions of prayer and Bible reading in the public schools.

They also encourage the teaching of creationism and intelligent design as an antidote to and alongside the "theory" of evolution, which they consider to be a Godless theory of the origins of the universe. Christian conservatives also vehemently object when the public schools presume to teach such subject matter as sex education, health and spiritual development, and a variety of academic disciplines that foster only liberal and secular points of view. For conservative believers, the social sciences, humanities, and natural sciences appear to be the major culprits in this area.

As an antidote to what they consider to be a runaway secular humanism, many Christians look to locate the truth elsewhere, and this is in God's Divine word, as recorded in the Holy Bible. The conservative Christian view holds that the Bible is inerrant (completely without error) in its teachings of faith and morals. Among these inerrant teachings are that the only way to God and eternal salvation is through his Son, Jesus Christ; someday the world will end in total disaster, but not before Jesus Christ will return to Earth to issue a final dispensation of guilt or innocence to sinners; and all those who repudiate the Bible's inerrant teachings on faith and morals will be lost to God's Kingdom forever. In order to forestall America's precipitous moral decline, then all of us need to cleave to the absolute standards of Scripture, and exercise what some Christian conservatives think of as an unyielding "biblical obedience."

One of the major controversies surrounding this current embrace of biblical literalness and absolute truth among so many Christians today is that it tends to pit conservatives against liberals in politics, and traditionalists against progressives in the schools and colleges. Within Christianity itself, scores of moderate, mainline churchgoers are leaving their liberal churches in droves in order to join biblically-based religious communities that pledge uncompromising fidelity to teaching the inerrant truths of the gospel. The extent to which both conservative and liberal Christians can find a way to reconcile their theological differences, wherein everyone feels safe and needed, respected and cherished, poses a challenge of the first order.

3. *The paradox of religious pluralism.*

The paradox of religious pluralism worldwide is now upon Christians with a vengeance, particularly after 9/11. What the bombings of the World Trade Center and the Pentagon brought home with a thud to Americans is the daunting reality of religious and political pluralism. This is to say that one of the significant post-9/11 lessons for Christians is that non-Christians can believe as fervently as Christians in the "irrefutable" truths of their own religions. More important however, and tragically so, extremists in those religions, as well as in Christianity, can inflict terrible harm and destruction on others—in the name of their God.

This is not to say that all religions are born equal, or that their teachings are morally equivalent, or that all religious extremists are equally evil. Rather, it is to pose a very difficult question that comes up for all religions: How is it possible, in the name of religious and cultural pluralism, to tolerate, and even to respect, different religions' claims to truth when some of these religions, especially their extremist wings, are intolerant of the very principle of tolerance?

Moreover, if Christians truly believe that they alone possess God's truth as located in the Holy Bible, and that the way to the Father is through the Son only, how, then, can it be logically consistent for these same Christians to tolerate, let alone respect, the "untruths" of opposing religious claims to God's truths? Thus, the paradox of pluralism: learning how to tolerate those who, if they were to prevail, would attack and destroy the very principle of tolerance itself.

Religious extremists notwithstanding, today we face the fact of a world brimming over with religious differences, both inside and outside the various Christian churches and denominations. How Christians should orient themselves to this reality will be a challenge in the years ahead. Should they try to convert the world to Christianity? Or should they instead concentrate on their own personal relationships with God, and leave others to work out their own beliefs?

Or should they attempt to forge some kind of active relationship with other religious believers, based not only on a polite respect and tolerance for differences, but a genuine attempt to learn from them? This latter experience is sometimes called "interfaith dialogue," and we believe it is a necessity for educators to promote; this, especially, at a time when representatives of all the major (and many minor) faith traditions often live together in the same countries.

Controversies and Challenges in Islam

1. *The Western misconception, fueled by the media and special-interest, right-wing politics, that Islam is a violent, fanatical religion that resorts to acts of terror, such as suicide bombings, in order to impose a particular religious ideology on the world. This stereotype continues to put all Muslims in the West on the defensive, and, in some cases, even endangers their lives.*

The suicide bombers of 9/11, like the majority of terrorists throughout the world today, were not Muslims in the most traditional sense. They were members of a Wahhabi-Saudi group (founded by Abd al-Wahhab during the 18th century) of extremists who are often referred to by moderate Muslims as a "death cult." This is the same group that claims Osama bin Laden as one of its leaders. These extremists are dedicated to policies of separatism, supremacism, and aggression.

Thus, Wahhabi-Saudi extremists are to Islam what members of the radical, militant Christian Identity Movements are to Christianity. Think of Timothy McVeigh, the Oklahoma City bomber who destroyed a federal building, killing 168 civilians, in order to bring down a "Zionist-occupied" government and replace it with a Christian one. In other words, Muslim and Christian extremists are dangerous, heretical fringe members of two world religions that actually teach peace, mercy, compassion, hope, and love, and not their opposites.

Also, there is not a single passage in the Qur'an that equates the term *jihad* with "holy war" or "terrorism." These are gross distortions of the word. *Jihad* actually means "effort, excellence, and exertion" in behalf of an individual's becoming stronger in Islamic spirituality and moral behavior. Muslims are urged by their sacred scriptures to wage *jihad* with the Qur'an, not with weapons of destruction, mass or otherwise (except in self-defense and fighting against oppression, much like just war theory in Christianity). A genuine Muslim jihadist works on himself first and foremost.

Moreover, a growing number of scholars are conducting empirical studies of every single act of terrorism occurring in the last 25 years (see, e.g., Bloom, 2005; Pape, 2005). The results of these studies show that upward of 90% of all terrorist acts in the Middle East, including suicide bombings, have little or nothing to do with the religion of Islam. In actuality, the world's leading terrorists today are not Muslims. They are the Tamil Tigers in Sri Lanka, a secular, Marxist–Leninist group with Hindu roots. Also, savage acts of terrorism have occurred in Northern Ireland for decades, committed by Catholic and Protestant Christians against one another. Ironically, very few paramilitary, non-Islamic terrorist groups throughout the world are so readily identified by their religious affiliations the way that Muslims are.

These same scholars also make the case that acts of terrorism did not originate with Muslims. Rather, they have a long history dating back to the Christian Crusades. In fact, at one time or another, all the world's major religions resorted to acts of terrorism whenever their leaders felt called by "God" to convert nonbelievers, to protect their special, religio-political interests, and to advance their "divinely inspired," imperialistic agendas. For example, more than 3,000 Japanese Kamikaze pilots, during World War II, flew their planes into fully loaded aircraft carriers in complete dedication to the Emperor Hirohito, whom they considered to be divine. They were later lionized as "holy martyrs" by the Japanese people. And Baruch Goldstein, a Zionist Jew who wanted to expel Muslims from Israel, embarked on a deadly suicide mission in 1994, resulting in the massacre of innocent Arab worshippers in the al Ibrahimi Mosque in Hebron.

Moreover, acts of terrorism originating in Muslim territories have a secular and political, not a religious, objective: to remove U.S. military troops from Arabic homelands. Even Al-Qaeda (the "cell"), led by Osama bin Laden, is driven, first, by nationalism. Al-Qaeda's primary objective is to expel United States troops from the Persian Gulf region, and, only second, to restore Islamic rule to Arabic countries.

Obviously, when it is in the interests of terrorists, they will justify their aggression by appealing to specific religious passages in their holy scriptures. Most of these passages are taken completely out of context, and interpreted in such a way that God is on the side of terrorists who then become "holy warriors," or even religious "freedom fighters." In reality, however, it is governments that fund and sanction terrorism throughout the world, not religions. Whether innocent victims die in New York City, Washington D.C., Saudi Arabia, Jerusalem, Palestine, Lebanon, Kurdistan, Afghanistan, or in Chechnya, it is legally constituted governments that sanction, and support, these barbaric horrors. Distorted, self-serving, and highly selective scriptural passages are merely frosting on the cake.

2. *The general Western misperception that Islam is an Arabic religion, and, therefore, only Arabs are Muslims. Moreover, Islam has little or no place in Judeo-Christian countries because its way of life and value system are thought to be totally antithetical to democracy and human rights.*

The fact is that not all Muslims are Arabs or people living in the Middle East. Currently, there are approximately 10 million Muslims living peacefully and productively in the United States, who think of themselves as proud and loyal American citizens. In this country alone, there are more than 1,400 mosques. (A little known fact is that while approximately 40% of all Muslims in the United States are African American, contrary to media-generated sensationalism only a tiny percentage of these follow Louis Farrakhan's Nation of Islam.) Clearly, Islam is here in America to stay, as are millions of Muslims of all colors and backgrounds.

So, too, there is a growth explosion of Muslims throughout the United Kingdom, France, Canada, and Western Europe, in addition to Africa, India, the Middle East, and even in South America. Also, by the year 2025, if current conversion trends in the West along with an escalating population growth in the Islamic world continue, then Islam could very well become the largest religious community in the world, easily surpassing 2 billion committed and practicing—not nominal—believers. This is roughly one-third of the world's population.

And, like Christianity, the coming Islamic global community will be pluralistic not monistic, just as it is today. It will feature a number of Islamic subgroups distinguished as much by their particular ethnicities, cultures, nationalities, politics, traditions, and histories as by their common religious beliefs and practices.

Contrary to popular opinion in this country, throughout the Qur'an, and throughout Muhammad's *hadiths* (six major collections of the Prophet's sayings) as well, there is a palpable and strong defense of human rights. Among the many human rights championed by the Qur'an, and by Muhammad in his *hadiths*, are the following (Maqsood, 1994): the right to die; the right to equality; the right to freedom; the right to justice; the right to equality before the Law; the right to the basic necessities of life; the right to marriage; the right to privacy; and the right to education. One important example regarding Islam's advocacy of the right to religious freedom is the oft-quoted Surah 2:256 in the Qur'an: "Let there be no compulsion in religion."

3. *The stereotype that Islam subjugates and oppresses women.*

One misconception that continues to plague Muslims in the United States and elsewhere has to do with women's rights. Many people in the Western nations believe that Muslim women are completely subjugated and subordinated in the name of a "misogynistic" religion that confers all power on men. For example, some anti-Islamic, Western commentators claim that Islam encourages the mutilation of a woman's clitoris. In actuality, excision, infibulation, and female genital mutilation have nothing whatever to do with Islam. (Clitoridectomy is a practice common in some African tribes, especially in Somalia.) The Qur'an neither sanctions nor encourages any of these practices. In fact, it frowns upon them.

Progressive Muslims are the first to admit that greater improvement in the area of women's rights is always desirable in Islamic countries, as they are in the United States when women only in recent history won the right to vote, but still have not yet won an Equal Rights Amendment, or been elected to the Presidency. Some Muslim scholars actually argue that, in many ways, women's rights are respected more in the Muslim world than in parts of the Christian world.

For example, Islamic doctrine teaches that men and women were created equally, from the same single "soul" (Surah 4:1). Thus, their rights and responsibilities are equal to men's. Both men *and* women can initiate divorce proceedings in most Islamic countries. Furthermore, women, even female orphans, are granted strong financial rights in divorce and inheritance settlements everywhere. Muslim women are able to own property, accumulate financial wealth, and be fully self-supporting, if they so choose. Muhammad's first wife, Khadijah, was a successful and wealthy business woman, who was actually Muhammad's employer before they married.

In fact, there is almost no exploitation of women in the workforce in Islamic countries because of the clear injunction throughout the Qur'an to respect the rights and integrity of women. Because the Qur'an speaks so highly and respectfully of women in a number of Surahs, and by Muhammad as well in his *hadiths*, sexual harassment is virtually nonexistent in the Arabic workplace, unlike in the United States. On those very rare occasions when it does occur in Islamic countries, the abuser is quickly called to account. Usually, his employment is immediately terminated.

Moreover, women are paid fairly, and they have a right to decent working conditions at all times. While there are undoubtedly male chauvinists in Arabic countries who mistreat women, so too there are male chauvinists, regardless of their religious beliefs, in all countries throughout the world. Mistreatment of women is a global universal, sometimes inspired and justified by religion, sometimes not.

Contrary to Western opinion, Muslim women in most countries are never forced to seclude themselves (*purdah*), unlike upper-class Hindus, Persians, Byzantines, Ultra-Orthodox Jews, and even some women who belong to conservative Christian sects. Neither are they forced to wear clothes (*burqa*) that cover every part of their bodies, including the customary veil (*hijab*). It is important to understand that in the vast majority of Muslim countries, how a woman dresses, behaves, and interacts with others, including men, is entirely the woman's choice. And this is becoming even more widespread in the more conservative Islamic countries, due to better education and employment opportunities.

On those occasions when some Muslim women do choose to wear more conservative clothing, they make the choice without apology. Why, they question, should women who are Muslims be forced to adopt the modernist dress styles of the West? Why should they be coerced to separate their religious beliefs from their secular lives? For many Muslim women, Islam is everything, and it touches all of life, not just a portion of it.

Moreover, in those rare instances in Arabic countries where polygamy is practiced (one study [Ahmed, 1980] says that less than 0.02% of Muslim men are polygamous), those women who freely choose polygamy over monogamy do it, in part, as a protest against Western forms of women's liberation. Why, they challenge, should a Judeo-Christian, Anglo-Saxon ideal of marriage—one man, one woman—be imposed on every man and woman on the face of the earth? Is not this just another example of Western imperialism at its worst? Some Muslim women believe that with the soaring divorce rate in the Western secular democracies, in reality, it is serial monogamy and assorted extramarital affairs that have become the actual templates for Christian marriages. Why, they ask, is this better, on its face, than polygamy?

4. *The overall misperception that Islam is a cruel, unforgiving religion, with a concept of criminal justice that seems barbaric, and a theological mission hellbent on worldwide "coerced conversions."*

It is true that graphic images of beheadings, cutting-off of hands, public beatings, and stonings in Islamic countries are becoming more common in the Western media. The stereotype that Islamic punishment of criminals is severe and barbaric hangs in the Western air. In actuality, the Qur'an does, indeed, make a strong case for corporal punishment regarding the most reprehensible crimes committed against human beings. In those few states (Saudi Arabia is one of the most publicized by Western media) where such heinous punishments do occur, theft, burglary, mugging, rape, and murder are rare to nonexistent.

Most important, however, is that these types of corporal punishments are rarely practiced in the majority of Muslim countries, and never in South Asia. The Qur'an teaches that compassion, mercy, and kindness must always be the first and last resort in dealing with criminals. In fact, in most cases, a bereaved family of the victim can forgive a murderer, and this will be taken into account in sentencing by the courts.

It is also important to note that, on their part, Muslims are shocked at the cruelty of gassing, electrocuting, and lethally injecting human beings—punishments that they see as the United States' only solution to capital crimes. Many Muslims are quick to note that with the number of violent and deadly crimes on the rise in the West, capital punishment hardly acts as a deterrent.

Finally, contrary to popular opinion in the West, Islam does not advocate hunting down unbelievers and then torturing and killing them unless they either recant or convert. The passage usually taken out of its full, historical context (and mistranslated) in the Qur'an (9:5) and often used to justify this stereotype is: "Slay the unbelievers wherever you find them, and take them captives and besiege them and lie in wait for them in every ambush."

The Arabic word for "unbelievers" is more accurately translated as "idolaters." Thus, the entire passage (9:1–6) goes on to explain that the idolaters are actually a group of pagan warriors who violated a peace treaty with the Muslims. It is a specific instruction for Muslims, subject to all the rules for just war, who find themselves unfairly attacked by an enemy. The passage commands that a 4-month warning period be given to the enemy before war commences. And it allows the military opponent to renounce the fight and seek help, with no precondition requiring a conversion to Islam.

Controversies and Challenges in Hinduism

1. *The widespread belief that Hinduism discriminates on the basis of social class, which ends up in an exploitative caste (jati) system.*

Any discussion of the caste system in India must begin with an understanding of Hindu religious and philosophical cosmology (the nature and structure of the universe). Here is a quotation from the *Rig Veda* that sets the historical stage for the establishment of four social classes in Hinduism, based on the elaboration of duties assigned by the "lustrous one" (the "Lord"):

> To protect this whole creation, the lustrous one made separate innate activities for those born of his mouth, arms, thighs, and feet. For Brahmans, He ordained teaching and learning the Veda, sacrificing for themselves and sacrificing for others, giving and receiving.... For a Kshatriya, he ordained... protecting his subjects... giving to the Brahmans, having sacrifices performed, studying the Veda, and remaining unaddicted to the sensory objects.... For a Viashya he ordained protecting livestock, giving, having sacrifices performed, studying, trading, lending money, and farming the land.... The Lord assigned only one activity to a Shudra: serving these other classes without resentment. (Coogan, 2005, pp. 102–103)

Thus, from the earliest of times, Brahmans and Kshatriyas were considered the ruling classes in Hindu India. The Brahmans, in fact, were the ones who decided whether a king's actions conformed with the Hindu *dharma*. Both the Brahmans and Kshatriyas ruled over the Vaishyas and Shudras, but it is the first three classes who are the "twice-born," those who receive a "second-birth," as a result of learning the Veda. Shudra servants are excluded from all of these activities. The Brahman is the "lord of the cosmos." The Skhatriya is "master over the earth." The Vaishya is "lord of the more limited domains" of domestic wealth and livestock. The Shudra are granted mastery over their own bodies, and, frequently, not even this.

From this religiously constructed hierarchy, established thousands of years ago, the social caste system of India emerged. Through the millennia, pecking order distinctions were made between "pure" and "impure" social classes, touchables and "untouchables." Over time, thousands of intermingled castes subsequently evolved, each with its own occupational specialty and class standing. For example, there were hunter castes, charioteer castes, and "half-breed" castes.

Many Hindu scholars claim that reducing Hinduism, and Indian society in general, to simplistic caste-depictions is really the product of a prejudicial, Western Orientalism (e.g., Clarke, 1997). Orientalism is the view that the United States constructed a fictional narrative of so-called "Oriental" beliefs and practices in order to justify their imperialism in the Middle East and in Southeast Asia. These scholars point out that castes in large, urban sectors of Indian society are actually breaking down. These same scholars also remind us that, in time, "caste" as an institution in India will become more of a historical anomaly and an embarrassing curiosity, much as the institution of slavery has become in the United States.

Other scholars believe that, even though discriminatory and exploitative caste systems are diminishing throughout India, as they properly should, hierarchical arrangements of human societies can sometimes be justified as noble goals. This, after all, is what Plato attempted to do in *The Republic*. His society was, in theory, a perfect balancing of ruling class, warrior class, and commercial class, based on people's unique, innate talents, temperaments, and training.

Whether or not one agrees with Plato's, or with the *Rig Veda's*, idealistic ordering of human society, utopians through the ages have extolled the benefits of living in a mutually beneficial social order. Throughout history, great thinkers have longed for a society that exists in perfect harmony. This is a social order where people are asked to do only what they do best, and where everyone gains and no one loses. This is a society where wars of oppression have become archaic, because, now, they are seen as being nothing more than an outmoded means for achieving peace and harmony—both within and beyond nations.

Despite the dreams of utopians, however, more progressive Hindus, such as Arya Samaj, Gandhi, and Ambhedkar, repudiated the principle of caste discrimination in India, based on a person's *varna* (color), which is a social, not a religious, category. Later, Gandhi's India Constitution outlawed it. The "untouchables" (*dalits*) were those human beings who were considered inferior because of their color, birth, and occupation. To this day, some discrimination still exists against these men and women, even though Gandhi described this prejudice as a "crime against humanity."

Among some sectors in India, especially where a new spirit of Hindu fundamentalism and Indian nationalism is emerging, the old bigotries die hard, just as they do throughout the Western world and, particularly, in the United States. In fact, there is strong evidence that, in India, the political forces of secularism and democracy are on a collision course with the religious forces of a more militant, fundamentalist Hinduism. This brings to mind the increasing animosity, and eventual violence, that has occurred between Muslims and Hindus ever since the partition of the country on August 15, 1947, into two nations—India and Pakistan.

2. *The widespread belief that Hinduism discriminates against women.*

It is true that the treatment of women in Hinduism through the millennia has been checkered at best. In the early period, Hindu women were granted the privilege of studying the *Vedas* with gurus. In the middle period, however, women were suppressed. Nunneries largely disappeared. Girls were given in marriage against their will, and their education was no longer taken seriously. Also, ritual pollution, the belief that women are tainted because of menstruation, caused men to treat them as "impure."

This mistreatment of women has its foundations in the theology of the early Hindu *Vedas*. According to *vedic* teachings, fewer women than men belong to the Brahmin, Kshatriya, and Vaisha *varnas* (social classes). Thus, most women are held back from ever gaining final release (*moksha*) from the cycle of *samsara*, based on their lower social class and caste affiliations. In the *vedic* literature, despite some notable exceptions, women are treated as spiritually, politically, and domestically inferior to men.

For example, on a mundane, day-to-day level, it is only senior males who are heads of the family. Women do all the cooking and cleaning in Hindu households, and are responsible for the ritual purity of the kitchen. Also, there are increasing newspaper accounts that amniocentesis in the cities is a medical technique being used to abort female fetuses. Patrilineal succession (passing through the male line) of property and land make male offspring a highly desirable commodity in Hindu families.

Despite the persistence of these and other inequities, in modern times, particularly among the educated classes, there have been changes for the better in the status of women. Women are able to hold prestigious jobs in business and education, especially in urban areas. They have separate bank accounts, and they own land and property. Although women cannot be Hindu priests, they can assist in the performance of religious rituals along with the husband. Improved education has taken place at every level of schooling, child marriage has almost disappeared, and women once again are taking part in *vedic* reading and in politics.

But in spite of these improvements for women from the upper classes, most progressive Hindus believe there is still a long way to go in India before *all* women, rich and poor, educated and uneducated, are able to achieve full human rights.

3. *The widespread belief that Hindus are polytheists.*

By some counts, Hindus are said to believe in hundreds of thousands of Gods. Never mind that for Hindus, there is, in theory, an infinity of possible representations of the Divine. No, for a majority of Westerners who might be prone to stereotypes based on misinformation and/or ignorance, this just proves that Hindus must be polytheists. In response, most Hindus would assert that the Divine just cannot be pinned down, because the Ultimate Godhead is beyond gender, number, or human comprehension. Thus, an endless array of manifestations of this God are necessary. There are, throughout India, thousands of unique temples and shrines, as well as countless public and private sites, which display colorful and imaginative icons representing a multiplicity of deities.

Hindus, however, in contrast to Western stereotypes, do tend to believe in One Ultimate Godhead, but they also believe there are innumerable ways of depicting this Divinity. This variety of manifestations of pan-Hindu gods and goddesses springs from a profound sense of respect and awe, as well as from an awareness that naming the ineffable always ends up distorting and limiting the eternal mystery of the Divine Being. Hindus, unlike the vast majority of Western believers, know their limitations when dealing with a Supreme Being. Therefore, they seek a variety of indirect relationships, via a plethora of deities and subdeities, with the Ultimate Godhead.

For example, to mention but one of these representations of God, Hindus consider Shri (or Lakshmi) to be the mother of all creation. She is the goddess of wealth and good fortune, and her picture, often symbolized as a lotus flower, can be found everywhere that daily commerce occurs in India. Just a glance at her image is said to bring good business luck to the observer. (Most local villages actually feature a number of goddesses or *Kali.*) A few other important deities are Krishna, Rama, and Shakti.

Some Hindu devotees from earlier periods tried to reduce all Gods to a kind of Holy Trinity. Thus, Brahma (the creator), Vishnu (the preserver), and Shiva (the destroyer) were said to have represented the three most important aspects of the One Divine Godhead, and these gods in turn spawned thousands of subgods. At the present time, however, few Hindus accept this triune reductionism.

They prefer, instead, to venerate the Brahma (one personification of the Absolute) by creating rituals that convey the infinite complexity and bewildering paradoxes of the Godhead's profusion of roles. For Hindus, there is no contradiction here. They believe in One Absolute Grounding Reality that manifests itself in millions, possibly billions, of shapes and forms.

We maintain that adolescents in the West are eminently teachable regarding the significance of the panoply of deities in the Hindu tradition. We are confident that they are able to understand the spiritual difficulties of trying to relate the finite to the infinite, the secular to the sacred, the ordinary to the extraordinary, the simple to the complex, the one to the many, in ways that ultimately make sense to them.

Judaism, as we have seen, has no Incarnate Being. Christianity has but one Divine Incarnation—Jesus. Islam has none. Hinduism, in contrast, has hundreds of millions of Divine manifestations. According to many scholars, post–Generation X and millennial adolescents are quite comfortable with multiple interpretations, as well as a variety of colorful, alternative images, of the Supreme Being. In fact, for many adolescents, these different approaches and paradigms actually function as faith strengtheners rather than faith weakeners.

Controversies and Challenges in Buddhism

1. *The concern among many monotheists in the West that Eastern and Western religious worldviews are essentially incompatible, and thus never will the East be able to meet the West on any common ground.*

It is true that these worldview disconnects can be pretty mystifying to Western adolescents, and also to adults who belong to one or another of the traditional, monotheistic religions. For example, one Christian scholar (Schoeps, 1968) maintains that what separates Buddhism from Judaism, Christianity, and Islam is that Buddhism believes in extinction and the monotheistic religions believe in salvation; Eastern religions believe in suffering, and Western religions believe in guilt. For this scholar, therefore, religious cross-fertilization between East and West is impossible.

To some extent, of course, these divisions do hold true, but whether or not they are irreversible remains to be seen. Just what are the essential differences between Buddhism and the monotheistic religions? Even though, as in Christianity and Judaism, there actually exist <u>many</u> Buddhisms, there are, nevertheless, some core beliefs that cut across the different Buddhist schools and sects. It is these non-Western beliefs that make Buddhism look esoteric, strange, or even threatening to many Western believers.

For example, Buddhism is not an institutionally-based religion. It is concerned more with daily, spiritual practices than with church doctrines. It is as much a philosophical worldview as it is a religious system. It is more self-reflective and contemplative. It emphasizes meditation more than praying, mindfulness more than worship.

Buddhism's view of human suffering is more stoical and less redemptive. It is this-worldly, not other-worldly. Its eschatology (study of the last things, including death, immortality, and resurrection) is rooted in a belief in reincarnation (successive rebirths until enlightenment is reached) and ultimate nirvana (the cessation of all human desires and ultimate peace), and not in an afterlife of eternal reward or eternal damnation.

Buddhism emphasizes the notions of impermanence, nothingness, and an egoless self instead of their opposites. It stresses that there is no intrinsic meaning to existence in contrast to the Western religious belief in a divine cosmic purpose that guides, and confers meaning on, everything in life.

There is no creator god in Buddhism as there is in the three major monotheistic religions. Existence always was and always will be. Moreover, what matters most is that existence just "is."

For Buddhists, divinity exists within each and every one of us and is not reserved exclusively for a god or gods. Divinity is imminent, not transcendent, internal, and not external, to the person. Intellect alone is not enough to know this reality. Letting go of worldly attachments and suffering and achieving a calm, inner peace (*samatha*) are necessary as well.

And, finally, Buddhism rejects dualistic thinking. All is one, and one is all. According to such popular Buddhists as the world-renowned, current Dalai Lama, the sharp dichotomies between spirit and matter, and ego and egolessness, in Western thought often result in a fractured view of the world, one that emphasizes materialism, individualism, competition, and warfare at the expense of spirituality, community, cooperation, and peace.

False Western dualisms, according to Buddhism, often pit the self against itself; the self against others; divisiveness against unity; and anger and cruelty against compassion and pacifism. It is this essential disparity, or disconnection, between the Eastern and the Western religio-spiritual worldviews that often pits one against the other in the West, and ends up in mistaken, or even downright cruel, caricatures of Buddhism.

In truth, however, there is much that binds together Buddhism and the three monotheistic religions. For starters, the three worldviews, at least in theory, emphasize compassion, love, service to others, and forgiveness. The worldviews recognize that suffering is an unavoidable fact of life, and that, when approached with the right mindset, it offers great spiritual benefits. The three religious traditions feature saints and saviors, sacred rituals and ceremonies. They believe in living each and every day mindfully and respectfully.

None of the monotheistic religions would, in principle, reject the basic ethical truths contained in the Eightfold Path. Neither would they dismiss outright the wisdom of the Five Moral Precepts (abstention from harming, stealing, sexual misconduct, lying, and drugs). The three religious worldviews believe in holding people accountable for their actions. And, they believe that greed, anger, prejudice, and ignorance can be overcome by their opposites, if there is a will to do so. Finally, the concept of "awakening" for the Buddhist is similar to the concept of "metanoia" (change, or conversion, of heart and mind) for the Christian, Jewish, and Islamic monotheists.

2. *All Buddhists are atheists.*

This is one of those mistaken, and potentially dangerous, caricatures of Buddhism. Because most students and adults in the West have had little opportunity to study comparative religions and philosophical worldviews in schools, misunderstandings about Buddhism abound. Some of these are harmless, but this one, in particular, is misleading, possibly even dangerous, because it is simply incorrect.

It is based on sheer ignorance of Buddhism. For example, Jared, the Christian student in Mr. D.'s class, in the case that introduces Chapter 6, claims that Buddhists do not believe in a God. This is perhaps the most persistent myth about Buddhism that continues to circulate in the Western world. This is alarming because, in the West, to call someone an atheist is to raise the fearful spectre of someone who is theophobic (hater of God), immoral, secular humanistic, relativistic, nihilistic, and, in the United States, even unpatriotic (because patriotism is understood to be both the love of God *and* country).

The fact is that some Buddhists are atheists, and some are not. Theravadins, for example, insist to this day that the Buddha is not a God, and that there are no deities in Buddhism. All attempts to honor the Buddha, therefore, are never meant to be acts of divine worship. Instead, they function to remind the believer that the Buddha had virtues worth emulating, and these are necessary in order to gain enlightenment. For some Theravadins, honoring the Buddha might even help them to gain release from the repetitive karmic cycle of birth, death, and rebirth.

Mahayanans, on the other hand, teach that those who are enlightened, and thus released from the cycle of reincarnation, can be treated as deities. These are "celestial bodhisattvas" or "celestial Buddhas." They work miracles, and they intervene in the affairs of the world. One of the famous Mahayanan Gods is Avalokiteshvara ("Lord Who Looks Down on Us"). In actuality, there are a number of celestial Buddhas in the Mahayana tradition. Another well-known celestial Buddha is Amitabha ("Infinite Light") who is said to have created a paradise for enlightened Buddhists after their deaths.

Whether or not Buddhists are atheists or theists depends on their membership in particular sects in particular parts of the world. The fact is that there have always been Buddhists who revere local deities and spirits. And there have always been others who do not. It is important to note, however, that few Eastern Buddhists would ever call themselves "atheists." This is a Western term, and it is largely beside the point.

Buddhists think of "atheist" as a fighting word (so, too, "theism," but for different reasons), someone who denies, often dogmatically, the existence of a God; someone, ironically, whose purpose in life is as much God-centered, and driven, as a theist's. The only difference, from the Buddhist's perspective, is that the former spends inordinate amounts of time *denying* God's existence, while the latter spends inordinate amounts of time *affirming* God's existence.

In contrast, in the East, belief in a god or gods is secondary to how one actually goes about seeking release from the endless cycle of suffering. For Buddhists everywhere, the major purpose of their religio-spirituality is to grow in wisdom and compassion in order to gain surcease from an all-pervasive suffering that is the human lot. If deities help in this regard, then this is fine. If not, then this is appropriate as well. Regardless, though, growth in wisdom and compassion happens mainly through an individual's total commitment to the "Three Jewels," the Buddha, *dharma*, and *sangha*, and this entails strenuous self-discipline and consistent personal effort.

3. *Buddhists have a disdain for life. Therefore, some Western monotheists believe that Buddhism is pessimistic, negative, and even downright depressing.*

The fact is that Buddhists love life, but in different ways and for different reasons (although some ways and reasons do overlap) from the monotheistic religions. This Western misperception that Buddhists hate life begins, and ends, with a grave misunderstanding of the Buddhist teachings of impermanence (*annica*) and no-self (*anatman*).

As we have seen in earlier sections, *impermanence*, for the Buddhist, refers to the inescapable, changing, and passing nature of all of life. The Buddha put it this way:

> Thus, shall ye think of all this fleeting world:
>
> A star at dawn, a bubble in a stream, a flash of lightning in a summer cloud, a flickering lamp, a phantom, and a dream. (Harvey, 1996, p. 72)

Nothing remains the same or lasts forever. Stars have long been extinguished by the time we see them from our vantage point on earth. Bubbles in a stream evaporate even as the water passes. A flash of lightning is momentary, and then it disappears forever. A flickering lamp eventually dims and dies. So, too, our individual lives pass away, as do all our evanescent dreams.

But does the Buddhist emphasis on impermanence and suffering, therefore, translate to a hatred for living and a love for suffering and dying? Not at all. What is ultimately perishable must be cherished and loved while it lasts. For the Buddhist, the fact that our lives are finite and short, like the flickering lamp, ought to motivate us to be more mindful of the present moment, to wring as much joy and happiness out of our passing lives as we can. As in suffering, an awareness of our impermanence has the potential to make life sweeter.

To this purpose, Zen Buddhists, among others, practice mindfulness, the ability to be here and now, and to observe everything that happens in the moment. Mindfulness entails remaining positive at all times. It means ridding the mind of negativism and striving for equilibrium. It means being tuned in to our own propensity to continue to crave and grasp, the ultimate cause of all our suffering. Above all, however, it means that we need to respect all of life and to engage it compassionately and tenderly. And, on a personal level, it urges us to embrace and kiss our joys as they fly, even as we experience the inevitability of our suffering and dying.

The belief in *no-self* is a complex, epistemological aspect of Buddhism, and, perhaps for some monotheists, one of the main reasons why it appears impossible for East ever to meet West on a religious level. But a belief in no-self does not necessarily mean that a Buddhist hates life. In fact, just the opposite occurs.

The doctrine of no-self is closely related to the Buddhist belief in impermanence. If everything changes and passes away, Buddhists believe, then to speak of a stable, permanent identity (an essence) to anything makes no sense. Modern physics and biology have corroborated the fact of shifting identities in all living things. The study of evolution, for example, confirms for scientists the truth that all species must undergo constant, adaptive changes if they are to survive.

So, the Buddhist reasons, if human beings are constantly changing, what sense does the concept of an "unchanging self" make? What makes the "self" in the present the same "self" as in the past? Perhaps the concept of "multiple selves" within the same human container would be a more accurate designation. But even this "same human container" is subject to change. Our bodies are not the same today as they were yesterday, and they will not be the same tomorrow, either at the subatomic or phenotypical level.

The Buddha taught that understanding, loving, and getting fully into the activity of life required neither a notion of self or no-self. This split, too, he thought was an unfortunate dualism. A better metaphor for the Buddha was "stream." We are not unchanging "bubbles" in the stream, the Buddha taught, because, eventually, these bubbles cease to exist, some pop quickly, some slowly. But, for all the bubbles, the end is the same.

In fact, everything in the stream, including the stream itself, will someday cease to exist. We are each, instead, process, movement, fluidity, flow, a continual coming and going. Change is the only constant. We are not "I," we are "stream." It is not the "I" that exists, it is the flow, the ongoing stream that exists. And, likewise, my consciousness of the ongoing stream is always in flux.

But does this Buddhist belief in the doctrine of a no-self ipso facto lead to a hatred of life, or worse, a hatred of those religions that believe in the permanent and eternal existence of a self or soul? Of course not. In fact, the Buddha taught that this makes each and every experience in our lives even more precious; as it does each and every stream of consciousness, including the religious.

No longer do we need to obsess over our ever-changing, ever-suffering, ever-decaying selves, or over the impermanence of our pet theories, or over the ultimate uncertainty of our philosophical/religious/political beliefs. Instead, now we can see the permanent self, or absolute ideology, as an illusion, and begin to experience fully every single aspect of our lives—and this includes all our concepts—as in constant flux and movement. Everything is part of everything else, and everything affects everything else.

For the Buddhist, the truth is that there is no self or other. There is only direct and immediate perception based on what is. Dualisms and concepts disappear. Everything is linked, interdependent, and changing. This is the human condition. We are all alike in the sense that we are all streams. Therefore, we share a common humanity. No more, the Buddha reasoned, will human beings need to slay one another because of their difference, their otherness. Now it is possible to get about the process of living and loving rather than dissecting, or perseverating over, these states of being.

8

The Religious Literacy Toolbox
Practical Tips for Teachers

In the opening chapter, we created a rationale for the need to teach about religious difference in the nation's public schools. Following that, we devoted several chapters to a detailed description of the central facets of each of the world's five largest religious traditions. In the preceding chapter, we pointed out some of the controversies and stereotypes that continue to swirl about each of these religions. We did this in order to alert teachers to the oversimplifications and distortions of the popular media, as well as by adherents of competing faith systems. In this chapter, we create a toolbox of concrete pedagogical strategies for those middle and high school teachers who seek practical help in educating adolescents to become religiously literate. We focus our teacher's toolbox on several constructivist strategies, including creating a safe classroom climate; emphasizing student-centered learning; making meaningful interdisciplinary connections; and connecting the past with the present.

Teaching Adolescents Religious Literacy in a Post-9/11 World, pages 133–154
Copyright © 2010 by Information Age Publishing

Constructivism in a Nutshell

Regarding our take on constructivism, we are grateful especially to Brooks and Brooks (1993) and Rachel Kessler (2000) for their work with public school teachers on behalf of constructivist teaching and learning. Stated succinctly, we believe that students do not merely passively receive, but in fact actively construct the knowledge they study. Cognitive scientists and brain researchers have documented the constructivist insight that "believing is seeing." Students are not simply cameras and tape recorders. About 85% of their perceptions of the so-called "factual world" is determined by their mental models, their cognitive screens, built out of their prior experiences and anchored in their preexisting assumptions and values. Each of us, and this includes our students as well, experiences and reacts to the world in our own unique ways.

Constructivist teaching and learning, therefore, responds to adolescents' fundamental need to learn who they are in relation to the world around them by drawing on their past experiences, and by drawing out what different students believe about the various worlds they live in. To this end, therefore, constructivist teaching–learning goes beyond simple knowledge retention and the cultivation of specific skill sets. It is interdisciplinary. It is integrative. It is heart, head, and hand based. It encourages honest self-examination, and a continual reexamination of what is important and what is not in adolescents' ongoing search for self-understanding. It is both emotional and cognitive, speculative and practical, spiritual and material, religious and secular, theoretical and experiential.

Constructivist teaching–learning requires both service to the self and service to others—in equal proportion. It entails a series of interdisciplinary offerings, featuring the common theme of self-discovery, that cuts across several of the humanities—including psychology, philosophy, religious studies, history, literature, art, music, and theater, as well as the social sciences and natural sciences. In short, the great Socratic dictum "Know thyself" is the necessary fulcrum for all constructivist education.

John Dewey, and later Jerome Bruner (1990), set the stage for this current generation of educators to understand that students bring a wealth of prior knowledge and experience to their learning. Education, therefore, is more about helping students to make meaning of those prior experiences than it is about filling empty buckets or writing on blank slates. Constructivist educators strive to give students permission to dig deeply into their own evolving senses of self and others, because they understand that there are many valid ways to teach and learn.

In fact, it can be said that the scientific theory of multiple intelligences requires a corresponding theory of multiple pedagogical techniques, strategies, and interdisciplinary content. The sad fact is that too many teachers and administrators in the nation's public schools, in spite of widespread lip service and positive rhetoric, lack substantive or applied knowledge (or understanding) of multiple intelligences. There are many reasons for this, of course, but most can be reduced to one explanation: The public school hierarchy rewards, and selects, those educators who possess one particular type of intelligence over all the others—what Gardner (2006) calls "linguistic and logical–mathematical" intelligence. This is the type of intelligence that reaps the most benefits in American society, as occupational reward systems are grounded in this particular type of intelligence. In contrast, we urge teachers of adolescents to learn how to educate a multiply intelligent student body, especially in the realm of educating for religious literacy.

Certainly linguistic and logical–mathematical intelligences are important in today's high-tech, results-driven, problem-plagued world. But we are also convinced that other intelligences confer survival benefits on all of us as well. These other intelligences are particularly suited for teaching adolescents religious literacy. These alternative intelligences, according to Gardner, are musical, spatial, kinesthetic, naturalistic, inter- and intrapersonal, and existential. In the realm of learning about religious pluralism and alternative forms of spirituality, it is obvious to us that inter- and intrapersonal, and existential, intelligences are key. We need teachers who are skilled interpersonally in working with people, who can communicate well across differences—particularly religious ones—and who have mastered the arts of evocation, inspiration, and clarification. Teaching for religious literacy also requires educators who have mastered particular knowledge and skill sets—which we describe below—and who have a natural penchant for raising, and then processing, the universal existential questions of meaning, purpose, faith, and belief.

Establish a Safe Classroom Culture

In Chapter 2, Gina Theodorakos faced a tremendous dilemma in her high school mathematics classroom: how to intervene appropriately in a heated conversation filled with stereotypes about Judaism. When confronted with the need to decide, she chose to shut the debate down rather than open it up. Certainly, in many ways such a response is easier. Yet as Gina's case depicted, her choice did not promote any global understanding on the part of students, nor did it foster a multicultural view of respect for difference;

on the contrary, it resulted in further stereotyping and a hate crime of demeaning and offensive graffiti in her school.

We are sympathetic to Gina's situation. We know it is not easy to tackle such controversial topics in the classroom, especially when one worries about inflaming an already fiery debate or inviting parental and administrative concerns. Moreover, it is challenging to take time to address such content in a math class, especially in an era of high-stakes testing and accountability. Yet we are also convinced of the importance of grappling with such concepts head-on. How, then, can a teacher create a classroom climate conducive to the exploration of deep-seated beliefs and the consideration of opposing ideas? And how can one justify doing so in a mathematics classroom?

A critical first step toward talking about religion in public schools is creating a classroom culture in which students feel safe to take intellectual and personal risks. To do so, teachers first must build a space that models intellectual integrity; honors and encourages grappling with challenging ideas; and acknowledges the ordinariness of failure and the right to try again.

Classroom as Community

One way to do this is to define the classroom as a community, and to engage learners in conversation about what that means. Establishing class norms together can be a powerful way to heighten student acceptance of the rights and responsibilities that accompany such a community. What makes a 'community'? How will we act together in this room? How will we talk with one another when we disagree? How will we recognize our commonalities and celebrate our differences? Such questions are fruitful beginnings to set the stage for the later, larger considerations of religious belief.

Imagine the shift in Gina's classroom if that group of learners had constructed a foundation for respectful dialogue earlier in the year. When hearing such stereotypical and demeaning remarks, Gina could have stopped the action in the classroom to revisit their notion of community, inviting the students to consider, "Is this how we've agreed to celebrate our differences? No? Then how do we? And, most importantly, what can we learn from, and about, one another along the way?" Even though she did not possess substantial knowledge about religion, Gina would have had a helpful tool at her disposal to address the issue of religious difference, through the lens of their agreed-upon norms and their community.

Posting the norms in a visible spot and ensuring that all members of the class receive a copy can facilitate revisiting the norms regularly to make certain they accurately describe the classroom climate. If they do not, a thoughtful conversation can help the class get back on track. While many classrooms begin with good intentions about group norms, too many never return to these community agreements as the year progresses. Such revisiting is a crucial step toward making the norms a living document, rather than one that sits gathering dust on the shelf.

Of course, defining the classroom as a community with norms is not enough. Teachers must also help students come to know one another personally. Laughter is a remarkably helpful element of a close and respectful community, prior to delving into sensitive material. Developmentally appropriate community-building tasks, those that promote cooperation and collaboration over competition, can help students find connections between themselves and peers and often have a good time along the way.

If Susan's tormentors had had meaningful opportunities to connect with her and other classmates on a *personal* level prior to the work of mathematics that spanned the year, they might have seen from these experiences connections and commonalities, rather than the "us versus them" dichotomy that spurred their feelings of inequity. Initial, joyful, and personal connections serve as bonds to strengthen adolescents' capacity for more challenging dialogue with one another later.

Furthermore, teachers become an important part of that community when they plan for classroom discussions that are free of advocacy. Public school teachers are required by the First Amendment to teach about religion fairly and objectively, ensuring that they refrain from both promotion and denigration of any particular belief system. One helpful way to avoid the interjection of one's personal religious values is by attributing the concept or perspective appropriately (e.g., "Many Jews believe..." or "According to the Torah..."). Such attribution ensures a dialogue that is free of the teacher's endorsement or disapproval, therefore liberating students to speak freely about their own beliefs without fear of a "wrong" answer.

Moral Conversation

Introducing students to what Nash (1997, 2008) has coined the "moral conversation" can also help establish a safe classroom culture that makes tackling difficult topics easier in middle and secondary schools. The goal of the moral conversation is to establish a safe and invigorating space for examining controversial issues. These spaces include both classrooms and journals; both teacher–student and student–student dialogue. Teaching students a few important ground rules to the moral conversation can be a fruitful beginning.

First, every single person deserves a presumptive respect for the views he or she expresses. Each person holds a responsibility, in Nash's words, to "find the truth in what they oppose and the error in what they espouse."

Second, people engaged in moral conversation display empathy and understanding for others at all times. They attempt to find common ground rather than critical dichotomies. Replay Gina's classroom, for example, with her students' working toward finding common ground instead of disagreeing about differences. The outcome would be dramatically altered.

To make this type of classroom conversation meaningful for young adolescents, it is helpful to present a metaphor to explain it. Think of moral conversation as more like a good, old-fashioned barn-raising where people work together in order to construct something, rather than as an academic boxing match where the last one left standing is the victor. And, third, moral conversation requires that people attribute the best, not the worst motives. The ideal end of a moral conversation is to reach a mutually acceptable agreement; at the very least, all participants in the dialogue must be able to leave the conversation with dignity intact.

Here are a few brief constructivist recommendations for engaging students in conversation about religious difference: (1) create a welcoming conversational space with students that features maximum psychological safety and invites maximum participation; (2) encourage conversation at all times by asking probing, open-ended questions; (3) spend time one-on-one with students whenever possible, which is one effective way to initiate candid moral conversation with adolescents about religion, because it underplays status and power differentials; (4) attribute the best motive, and assume the best intentions, when talking with students about religious issues; and (5) show some humility and open-mindedness by first looking for the truth in what you oppose and the error in what you espouse.

Emphasize Student-Centered Learning

Student Choice

Those who teach in middle and secondary schools know about the extraordinary power of choice. Few pedagogical elements increase student motivation as effectively as the opportunity for students to have a voice both in *what* is studied and *how* it is explored. Those opportunities enhance the likelihood that students will find personal relevance in the curriculum, something they often seek and all too rarely find. In Chapter 5 Annalise and Henry are fortunate in that their school already has a structure enabling students to choose what they study through elective offerings. Extending this program to include chances for students to voice what they are interested in, and allowing for student-led electives, would be a powerful next step.

One high school teacher was reminded of the importance of following students' questions and empowering them with choice and ownership over the curriculum while studying the Protestant Reformation. In the middle of the class discussion, one student blurted out, "Wait, what are the *huge* differences that caused this split? They don't seem like that big of a deal." The discussion moved from his specific question to larger questions, including "What separates religions?" and "What is the connection between religion and power?"

These students were eager to continue the conversation and to comprehend why religion is such a powerful force in the world. As a result, the students, along with their teacher, hosted a Philosophical Dinner. They invited a number of people from outside of the school and as a result 25 philosophers sat together over dinner, grappling with the question: What is religion? Students talked about how they understood religion and how their personal belief systems emerged as they connected to ethics and morals. In the months that followed, students continued to bring their teacher readings about religion that connected to their dialogue.

The Philosophical Dinner is a magnificent example of what can happen when students are empowered with choice about the direction of the curriculum. Although the reality of contemporary schooling presents educators with the challenge of addressing local, state, and national standards, we are convinced that thoughtful study of religion can be embedded in most curricula. To those who remain reluctant to see connections between religious literacy and their content areas, we suggest another look at the standards that guide one's practice.

Asking pertinent questions, reading primary sources, evaluating media, interpreting information, summarizing, comparing and contrasting, analyzing patterns and trends, organizing and displaying data, estimating theoretical probability, connecting past with present, analyzing and interpreting elements of text, grouping historical events, demonstrating cause and effect, identifying and debating issues—these are but a few rich opportunities to embed the study of religious concepts into one's curriculum, and surely the myriad possible connections warrant a book unto themselves.

One teacher explained to us, "When 'religion' has come up, it is not as part of The (official) Curriculum, but as what comes up 'naturally' as part of the exploration of a topic. Embedding it in what we are exploring makes it more real and connected. It is *not* 'let's look at religion'; it is 'let's look at life in a connected way.'"

We have seen students gain tremendous understanding in classes that have followed the religious questions naturally as they've emerged. We also have observed educators successfully teaching for religious literacy by creating lessons, units, and classes that focus explicitly on religion. In both situations, what renders the experience effective is not the overall approach but rather the educator in the classroom who is deeply committed to empowering adolescents in the 21st century with knowledge and understanding of religious diversity. Such teachers, approaching the task from a multicultural perspective, are willing to follow a question wherever it leads, to acknowledge they may not know the answers, and to take the work of religious literacy seriously as they work with students to find the multiple truths that exist.

From Teacher-Talk to Student-Talk

Also in keeping with a constructivist approach, teachers should aim to maximize student talk in the dialogue for religious pluralism, while limiting their own. While, of course, teachers play an important role in enhancing the learning at hand, offering guiding questions, redirecting, ensuring the accuracy of information, and using a respectful tone, students learn the most when they are grappling with the ideas firsthand themselves.

One innovative approach that we have observed involved a middle school classroom hosting a professional storyteller as an artist-in-residence. Teaching students the techniques of effective oral narrative, the storyteller invited students to tell religious stories or folktales to the whole group. After a week's preparation studying their particular stories and oral technique, students taught their classmates various narratives in an engaging manner. While the speaker internalized the meaning of the story, the audience was captivated in a new way.

While whole-group activity and dialogue are important, so too is the opportunity for students to break into smaller groups or pairs to investigate the concepts at hand. Particularly with sensitive topics such as religion, smaller groups can be a helpful means of trying out one's ideas on a smaller scale prior to "going public" with them in the larger classroom venue. Free-write responses to a teacher prompt that students then share in pairs give students the chance first to reflect independently, and then to move to expressing his or her ideas with another person in a safe way. Such scaffolding of dialogue can build a quieter student's courage to ultimately voice opinions in a larger realm.

Moving from teacher-talk to student-talk maximizes students' opportunities to be active and respectful members of the ongoing conversation, which is a primary goal in teaching for religious pluralism. By adopting a constructivist and facilitative approach, educators can invite meaningful questions as the basis of curriculum, questions that enable a learning community to make sense of the vast religious diversity of our global community.

Student Questions

When Ricardo and Rosa in Chapter 3 raised their questions about Christianity in Mr. Gutierrez's sixth-grade classroom, they introduced moral conversation about religious difference into their learning community. Although fostering such a conversation was not Mr. Gutierrez's original goal, his students, like so many others before them, presented him with a powerful teachable moment. To his credit, he viewed their questions as a learning opportunity and embraced them as curriculum. Indeed, following student questions is at the very heart of teaching for religious literacy. But how can educators follow student questions when they themselves may not hold the answers? And how does one foster such questions in the classroom?

So often we, as teachers, stick to the relatively safe material of our particular disciplines, yet adolescence is a time when the essential existential questions begin to emerge. Where did we come from? Why are we here? What happens after we die? Few students feel they have a safe place to go with such internal ponderings, and questions about religion and spirituality are often at the very heart of these thoughts.

Instead of remaining close to a harmless curriculum, teachers need to pose authentic questions and create a space for their consideration. These need not be add-ons or extras; rather, integrating such questions into the curriculum enables teachers to explore the material they feel is important, yet with greater student relevance. For example, utilizing a piece of fiction set within a background of Christianity, C.S. Lewis's *The Screwtape Letters* (1982) helps educators of adolescents not only to teach plot or character development but also to confront moral dilemmas within a Christian context. Such literature also invites students to ask questions about Christian themes such as pride, ambition, redemption, mortality, sin, and the existence and function of devils and angels.

Of course, the most meaningful questions about religion stem from the students themselves. Learning about religion by basing the curriculum on student questions immediately heightens the relevance of the subject matter. We encourage teachers to begin the study of religion by inviting students' own questions. In public school classrooms, as Ricardo demonstrated in Chapter 3, students are filled with genuine questions about the religious world that surrounds them.

Their questions range from the concrete (e.g., Why do some people wear hats to pray? What is a mosque?) to the more abstract (e.g., Is there a God? If there is, why would this God allow such suffering? Why do some people in non-Christian countries hate us?). When students pose such questions, they become more invested in discovering the answers and in conversing with others to hear diverse perspectives toward that end. Such questions are fruitful beginnings to any unit of study on religion.

In keeping with honoring students' questions, teaching adolescents about religious pluralism requires adopting many features of a constructivist approach to instruction. In constructivist classrooms, learners apply their prior knowledge to construct a personally meaningful understanding of new information. In particular, teachers find their role shifting from expert to facilitator. In traditional instruction, the teacher is viewed as the content expert, one who selects a body of content for students to learn. The teacher typically relies heavily upon lecture, and employs assessment and evaluation techniques that are often thought of as objective, with one correct answer to a given question.

When exploring religious pluralism in particular, this approach can be value-laden. In a facilitative role, on the other hand, teachers expect students to construct meaning and acquire understanding through their own experiences. The teacher then becomes a guide, assisting students in exploring a wide range of perspectives within a new body of knowledge. Within this framework, the learning is less reliant on what the teacher knows, and more reliant on students actively seeking answers and making meaningful connections to prior learning.

Mr. Gutierrez modeled this particular pedagogy through his willingness to momentarily abandon his preconceived plan for the morning and follow the students' questions into an immediate investigation of Christian symbolism. In so doing, he made space not only for the racial, ethnic, and cultural diversity that was a regular part of his multicultural approach, he also embraced religious difference and knowledge as worthwhile subject matter in his public school.

Teaching from a constructivist approach is challenging for many, as it requires relinquishing substantial control in the classroom: control of discussion, of the direction of the new learning, and of parts of the curriculum. Teachers also face the challenge of anticipating and mediating a vast array of unanticipated student responses. However, when teachers empower students with such opportunities, as Mr. Gutierrez did with Ricardo, Rosa, and their classmates, they enable them to struggle with the inexact nature of religious pluralism and the world, struggles upon which new understanding is formed.

Make Interdisciplinary Connections

For the purposes of teaching about religion in middle and secondary schools, it is helpful not to envision religion as a singular subject, but rather as a field with myriad interdisciplinary connections. At its best, the study of religion is a rich interdisciplinary task; at the least, we hope teaching for religious pluralism is multidisciplinary. Although it is tempting to relegate the teaching of religion solely to Social Studies departments in high schools, who might then address the concepts in World Cultures or World History courses, we believe that every middle and secondary teacher has a right, and a responsibility, to draw upon the world's belief systems wherever meaningful curriculum connections can be made. Furthermore, the inherently interdisciplinary nature of the study of religion is an excellent match for the contemporary middle school, as teaching teams are designed specifically to approach concepts and themes in an integrated manner.

Mathematics and Sciences

Of all disciplines, mathematics may very well be the one that causes the greatest numbers of raised eyebrows when we propose promoting religious literacy in the classroom. How in the world, some ask, are we supposed to address *religion* in *math* class? Some of the most passionate and effective teachers we know approach their content from a multicultural perspective, which is one answer to the question. When one considers religion as an essential component of multiculturalism, attending to a culturally diverse curriculum calls for the integration of religious differences as well.

One middle school math class studied proportionality by tracking, via the media and Web-based modeling software, both reports of religious discrimination and the relative increase of racial profiling incidents since 9/11. Students' awareness both of mathematical *and* religious concepts increased as a result. A high school math teacher we know worked from a multicultural perspective when she invited students to examine and project the world's growth of major and minor religions while learning statistics and probability concepts.

These two mathematics classrooms are fine examples of teachers recognizing the interdisciplinary potential in the study of religion and capitalizing on that within their own subject area, by teaching from a social justice perspective. If Gina's mathematics curriculum in Chapter 2 had been centered on issues of multiculturalism, for example, students could have experienced consistent, embedded opportunities to explore their own religious differences, while at the same time mastering mathematical skills and concepts.

The sciences, as the intelligent design/evolution case in our opening chapter portrays, present unique challenges to the teaching for religious literacy, as so often science and religion, faith and reason, are considered to be in conflict. We believe that a wonderful teaching opportunity lies within conflict, however. Rich questions such as the following emerge from the study of competing forces: What scientific discoveries have been made in the past centuries, and how have different religions reacted to these discoveries? Why? Which basic tenets did such discoveries threaten? Which did they support? Utilizing Galileo not only to teach about astronomy and the earth's rotation but also to help students comprehend historical and religious traditions results in a well-rounded citizenry who understands both the scientific and the religious world in which we live. Math and science are too often viewed as separate entities from the humanities, holding few disciplinary concepts in common. We encourage those committed to teaching about religion to cross these perceived boundaries consciously and intentionally.

Literature

A wide array of texts provides rich resources to those who believe, as we do, that teaching for religious pluralism is vitally important. First and foremost are the sacred texts themselves. In Jim's case in Chapter 4, selections from the Qur'an could provide his students with an account of the predominant concepts, stories, figures, and ideals relevant to Muslims. Of course, the Torah, the Bible, and other texts serve similar purposes when studying other religions. One high school teacher shared with us her plans for the upcoming school year to compare and contrast quotes from the Qur'an that are often criticized as calling for "holy war" with quotes from other religious texts. We agree that such side-by-side consideration of sacred texts can provide a powerful lens into religious commonalities and differences.

Although religious texts are an integral part of learning about religions, many genres of writing may prove useful to exploring such belief systems. One helpful approach is the incorporation of historical fiction as a means to comprehend the experiences and motivations of others. Certainly for Jim, the integration of historical fiction enabled his students to draw meaningful connections to contemporary life. Exploring choices made by protagonists or antagonists also can be a helpful method of examining central religious tenets.

Furthermore, memoir and poetry can illustrate powerfully the role religion has played in others' lives. One middle school teacher we know uses "wisdom tales" from various religions, inviting her students to read and analyze them for the religious values they embody. In a similar vein, another teacher in the same school introduces folktales of each religion, expecting his students to read them, to identify the values depicted in each, and to draw visuals representing those values for each religion.

Songs and song lyrics, both historical and contemporary, also offer insights into religious tradition. Chants, hymns, or otherwise, the rhythm, sound, and feel of a song can convey to adolescents the deep sense of religio-spirituality embodied by the tradition.

Furthermore, film as a teaching resource has the added advantage of being a medium many adolescents enjoy, yet at the same time it can convey a powerful message. One teacher we know used excerpts from the film *Gandhi* and analyzed it in terms of the impact religious values had on his life, on his work, and on other religions. Other films, such as *Malcolm X*, can provide equally relevant insights into lifestyles, beliefs, and traditions that are helpful to the less verbal learner.

Of course, just as students can learn from studying others' work, so too do they learn by experimenting with various genres in their own writing or craft. We suggest that students examine the film, historical fiction, lyrics, or poetry both from a content viewpoint but also as a creative model. Students can write poetry or songs depicting the questions they have or a short story that illustrates religious conflict or commonality within a culture or family. Additionally, students can create their own podcasts, digital stories, or film documentaries about the vital role of religion in their own communities, to be unveiled at a community event.

Imagine, once more, Jim Marcel's classroom in Chapter 4, and the conversation about "people who look like the Taliban." Without a working knowledge of Islam, his students remained fearful and uncertain, ignorant of one of the world's major religious faiths. Now consider what one high school teacher recently described to us, regarding the change she's seen since integrating religious concepts into her Social Studies curriculum: "I've seen Muslim students in my class being comfortable sharing their own stories and being proud to be Muslim. There are a lot of students at our school who are Muslim and do not say anything about it. Being able to share your culture and be proud of it is something I am working on in all of my classes." Why teach about religion in public schools? This teacher's comments sit in stark contrast to the conversation ensuing in Jim's classroom. The students arrived in this very different intellectual place as a result of one teacher's willingness to tackle challenging curricular material, to take enormous intellectual risks, and to teach for religious literacy.

The Creative and Visual Arts

At the start of Chapter 5, Annalise and Henry are at a critical, and familiar, crossroads in the debate about teaching for religious literacy in public schools. It is not uncommon for a person to feel threatened by the introduction of an alternate belief system, particularly when it is perceived to be contrary to his or her own. Clearly, Henry viewed Annalise's interest in teaching yoga as a random, poorly conceived plan to engage students in a pagan ritual. Annalise, while well intentioned, planned only to focus on the physical and mental benefits of yoga, without including a consideration of the important religious traditions from which the practice stems.

In some ways, these two teachers are not as far apart ideologically as they think they are. Neither of them is promoting an exploration of religion in the classroom. In fact, in both of their cases, an understanding of what it means to teach for religious literacy could help them bridge their gap. They both need to recognize that when students learn about various religions, they come closer to understanding their own lives and the world that surrounds them. How can they do this effectively within their own context? Certainly examining dance, movement, and other artistic traditions within a faith is a great start. Similarly, their school's structure of elective offerings enables them to capitalize on that crucial factor in teaching adolescents: student choice.

Dance and movement are powerful opportunities to advance the exploration of religion. Religious dance often tells a story that is central to a religion's tenets and is therefore an evocative way to teach about a particular religious narrative. Students can learn about and attend performances of ritual dance. To help students make connections between their learning and the presentation at hand we suggest teachers pose questions that lead to reflective insights: What religious figures did you recognize on stage? What story is being portrayed here? What important message does this dance convey to its believers? When would this dance be performed? When would it not? Which members of the religion are allowed to perform it? Did it move you in any way? If so, how? If not, why not?

Whether or not a school is within proximity to such performances, dance and movement provide an important opportunity for learning. While we remain mindful that it is important to convey a sense of the religion without trivializing it through mimicry, where appropriate students can learn dance and movement approaches from those who practice or study the techniques. One helpful way to determine a dance's appropriateness is to ascertain its level of sanctity within the religion.

For example, is it a ceremonial dance or a sacred one? In Balinese culture within the Hindu tradition, sacred "Wali" dances may be performed only within the inner court of a temple. However, certain ceremonial "Bebali" dances are usually performed in the middle court of a temple, where others may view them. Taoist Tai Chi also offers both movement and a glimpse into another belief system, one renowned for its study of the arts of health and longevity. It is similarly worth discussing why some religions have dance and/or movement as a foundation for ritual and why other belief systems expressly forbid it.

In a school day too often filled with sitting, such occasions for physical movement provide both welcome kinesthetic opportunities and a chance to understand a religious practice on a more visceral level. As we explored briefly in the case of Annalise and Henry, yoga is one such practice stemming from Hinduism that provides students with an understanding of mental and physical focus and balance. Instead of removing yoga entirely from its historical, cultural, and religious contexts, Annalise might consider incorporating it into a richer study of religious belief systems, with clear objectives. Then, rather than stifling its roots, she could help students uncover yoga's rich meaning and reveal why it is worthwhile for them to understand the complexities of various religious traditions.

In addition to dance and movement, the visual arts are a particularly productive avenue for the exploration of religion. Regardless of one's subject orientation, a teacher or a team could adopt many of these practices in order to foster an interdisciplinary approach; that is, to help students make sense of religion by connecting the disciplines in meaningful ways.

Religion is a long-standing subject in art and can be a useful medium to guide students in their exploration of a religion's primary themes, historical evolution, and major figures. One helpful entry point, where possible, is to visit a museum's collection. While field trips to museums can often bring to mind visions of bedlam and chaos, teachers who equip their students with specific, focusing questions about the particular religion(s) under study provide clear direction to their learners and focus to the experience. Working closely ahead of time with museum docents to explain the learning objectives provides further focus to the exploration.

Teachers can encourage students to concentrate on connections between their new learnings from classroom study and the art they are viewing. They might ask, for example, which religious figures did you see portrayed in the paintings or sculpture? What stories were depicted and from which religious texts did they stem? What connections do you see between the time period of the artist's work and the way in which he or she portrays the subject? Is there a relationship between the artist's country and his or her portrayal? Between the artist's country and the chosen medium employed? Between the religion depicted and the medium employed? What religious symbols did you identify? How were familial roles depicted? Gender roles?

While we advocate that students come into contact with the actual artwork whenever possible, we also recognize the challenges inherent in such a goal. Those without access to art museums can take advantage of Web-based museum holdings, visiting works of art in a virtual manner and posing similar questions. Many major museums now offer virtual access to extensive collections. Logging onto these collections and projecting images through an LCD projector can bring a museum's holdings onto the walls, turning one's classroom into a museum.

Of course, in addition to studying artists' work, many students enjoy the opportunity to create their own art. One middle school teacher we know invited his learners to identify a piece of writing important to them and to apply the art of illumination while teaching about Christianity in the Middle Ages. Students chose poetry, song lyrics, and memoirs, among others, to illuminate with decorative and elaborate embellishments.

Social Studies

In Chapter 4, Jim Marcel's students were struggling to comprehend a timely, real-world issue: How can we live peacefully in a country that has been attacked by religious extremists? Indeed, how can his students proceed with their daily lives without feeling a sense of deep-seated concern, particularly when the messages they receive from their parents and the media caution them to be wary of certain types of people? As a result, Jim faced an extraordinary challenge as a public school teacher. How can he diffuse his students' growing prejudice? And how can he help the students make meaningful connections to history and to present-day life that will enable them to make better choices for our nation's and our world's future?

Certainly for many educators, parents, and students, it is easiest to envision the teaching of religious concepts and narratives within the field of social studies, like Jim's classroom. In fact, the limited teaching for religious literacy that exists in our nation's public schools occurs primarily in Social Studies department offerings: courses entitled World Cultures, World History, Contemporary Issues, and the like. We agree that the fields of history, geography, economics, and civics and government are well suited as backdrops for the study of religion. In this way, Jim Marcel had the distinct advantage of not feeling as though he needed to "sacrifice" one content area for the sake of another.

Regardless of the strong match with his content area, Jim, nevertheless, struggled to find an effective way to teach students the dangers of stereotyping a religious group. Religious difference is all too often overlooked or left unaddressed. While multicultural educators have worked diligently to abate racial and ethnic prejudice in our schools, much less attention has been paid to religious difference, perhaps because of the general reluctance to address religious issues in a public school setting. While some may find it easier to ignore such differences under the precepts of the separation of church and state, the situation unfolding in Jim's classroom illustrates how vital it is to attend to religious diversity.

As Chapter 4 illustrates, the Qur'an-based ideals of Islam as a faith tradition are a far cry from the extremist violence portrayed regularly by the media. Knowing more about Islamic traditions might have enabled Jim to move the class from fear and prejudice to informed understanding. Yet not knowing about Islam presents an opportunity as well. How might the case of Jim's classroom take a different trajectory if he accompanied the group in a focused exploration of Islam, as a result of the dialogue that had emerged? Following the learners' questions as the basis for curriculum presents an immediate opportunity for relevance.

One high school Social Studies teacher we know recognized the importance of teaching from a multicultural standpoint, while integrating religion as a primary component. Her class held a mock United Nations conference, with each student representing a country in the Middle East. The students were expected to arrive at a roundtable session with ideas for the future of Iraq from the perspective of "their" particular countries.

In order to prepare for that event, students first read about and discussed the war in Iraq. They next investigated their chosen countries' systems of government, geography, religious beliefs, economic systems, and cultural norms. Then they explored how various factions of their countries' population viewed the war and their accompanying government's stance on the conflict, utilizing readings and email correspondence to embassies and local college professors. The unit culminated with a guest presentation from a professor of Middle Eastern Studies, who joined the class to talk with students about their learning and to answer the foreign policy questions that had emerged. Finally, students synthesized their new understandings of the Middle East perspective with their own opinions on the war.

It is easy to envision the productive turn Jim's teaching would take next, given motivation and the license to follow his students' challenging questions about religious concepts and groups. This type of teaching, albeit time-consuming, is precisely what teaching for religious literacy in the social studies requires. It requires following students' questions where they lead. It requires adopting a multicultural view that seeks to foster in students the ability to understand and respect distinctly different ethnic, racial, cultural, and religious communities.

It requires examining complex relationships between religion and economics, civics and government; and power and control. And it requires a willingness to consider history from multiple perspectives and an expectation that "truth" will vary depending on the stakeholder. Such consideration of how various accounts of historical events differ by religion illuminates new historical *and* religious concepts.

Reflective Writing and Personal Narrative

While classroom dialogue is arguably most critical to attend to in order to promote a pluralistic view, teachers should also consider the rich inner dialogue that accompanies students' learning. Such inner dialogue can be fostered through reflective writing of many sorts. Journals are a potent way for students to consider compelling questions in a safe venue. Many of the questions posed by Sharon Daloz Parks (2000) lead effectively into learning about religious belief: "Do my actions make any real difference in the bigger scheme of things? Why is suffering so pervasive? What is my society, or life, or God asking of me? Anything? Is there a master plan? What constitutes meaningful work? What is my religion? My spirituality? Do I need either one? How, if at all, am I complicit in patterns of injustice? When do I feel most alive?"

Students can also use journals to play out various scenarios. Asking adolescents to compose a dialogue involving two people of different religions is a potent writing-to-learn activity through which students can both acquire a greater understanding of another's perspective and demonstrate their growing knowledge of others' belief systems. Similarly, teachers might ask students to consider in writing how one might react to various global issues (abortion, war, cloning, euthanasia, employment, women's education, marriage) based on differing religious backgrounds. Certainly, Mr. D.'s assignment (in our chapter on Buddhism) to record a log of one's actions was a beginning framework for fostering inner dialogue, as learners had the opportunity to reflect internally on their actions in relation to a set of beliefs.

We have also found letter writing to be an extraordinarily helpful learning tool. What some have come to call "epistolary pedagogy" can help students understand religious content through a real or imagined audience. Writing to a teacher, to a grandmother, to God, to a best friend, to a minister or rabbi—all are means through which students can learn to focus not solely on the content, but rather on the sense they are making of that content.

One middle school teacher described to us a culminating activity that exemplifies this type of epistolary pedagogy. He was teaching eighth-graders a health unit that explored conception, pregnancy, sexually transmitted diseases, and birth control, and had invited guest presenters of varying views to speak to the students about topics such as sexual activity, contraception, parenthood, and reproductive issues. Speakers included physicians, representatives from the local parent–child center, local religious leaders from various faiths, and members of a right-to-life group.

At the unit's end, he asked students to place themselves 30 or so years in the future and to write a letter to a potential child of theirs about these issues. Aside from having a list of "things" they needed to include for the assessment of content understanding, students were required to explain, from the perspective of a parent writing a child, why they were giving the advice they did. The work encouraged them to think about their own beliefs and others', and where pertinent how their own faith tradition's teachings impacted the decisions in their life.

Personal narrative writing gives students the opportunity to reflect *in story form* on what gives their lives a sense of meaning and purpose. This type of writing starts with the *student's* religious and spiritual questions and beliefs rather than with the lives, thoughts, and activities of *others*. It gives students permission to make sense of the raw material of their religious and spiritual journey—first from the inside-out before going from the outside-in—by telling their own stories of meaning-making. If nothing else, personal narrative writing sends the message to the student that vulnerability and questioning on matters of faith and spirituality count for something in the public school classroom. The best way for students to communicate vulnerability, honesty, and authenticity in their writing is to construct personal stories that make their points in a somewhat dramatic way.

Religion, like life, as every writer knows, is incongruous, complex, and paradoxical. It can bore us, soothe us, upset us, confound us, and anger us, sometimes all at once. Therefore, our personal writing instruction to students is to try always to be honest in telling their stories. We ask them to say what they mean and believe what they say. We remind them, however, in their personal narrative writing about religion and spirituality to leave room for the ellipsis dots that, in theory, can always end every sentence they write, and every story they tell, and every truth they proclaim. Why? Because the quest for religious meaning and understanding never ends; it only stops...for the time being. There will always be something else to add.

All stories of meaning evolve—given the passage of time, the changing of life's conditions, along with the natural growth of each and every student's quest for knowledge and understanding.

We have used a number of strategies, among others, to motivate students to express openly, in a very personal way, the rich inner dialogue they have in response to each of the religions and spiritualities we teach. Here are a few of the narrative genres we have recommended that our students might use in their writing: spiritual autobiographies; personal religious or spiritual credos (statements of belief); dramatic narrative vignettes of times when students might have experienced transformative religious and/or spiritual doubt, insight, and/or conviction; dramatic transformative scenarios in the form of narrative case studies or mini-plays; and, perhaps the most successful of all, getting high school students to compose Internet narrative blogs and Facebook entries in order to stimulate their peers to engage in interactive religious and spiritual storytelling.

Reflective writing and personal narratives are key characteristics of a pedagogy for religious pluralism. In his assignment exploring a central Buddhist practice, Mr. D. exemplified a clear commitment to support students in making authentic connections between their own life choices and the choices of others. Helping students to understand deeply the motivations and beliefs of others is challenging terrain indeed, and it is best accomplished by creating space and support for a rich inner life and offering multiple opportunities to explore in detail the faith traditions of others.

Teach from the Inside-Out

In Chapter 6, in his World Cultures class, Mr. Delorme is stumped. How could he have conveyed the assignment to compare one's actions with the Noble Eightfold Path to students and parents in a way that didn't threaten their own religious stance? Jared made it quite clear that he perceived the assignment as in direct conflict with his own beliefs. Yet, Mr. D. felt he was always careful not to promote any particular faith. In his efforts to make the learning relevant, Mr. D. has stumbled onto one of the greatest challenges we face in teaching about religion in public schools: how to make the faith "real" to learners without appearing to either promote or trivialize it.

One hallmark of a constructivist approach is the premise that new concepts and skills are most easily embedded in natural, spatial memory, suggesting that experiential learning is a promising route toward greater understanding. However, while experiential learning is often effective for adolescent learners, in the study of religion teachers need to consider the importance of maintaining the sanctity of particular religious beliefs. One of the greatest challenges in teaching about religion is helping students to understand the tenets of each religion deeply and at a visceral level, while not overstepping the boundaries of that religion.

Whereas role-playing can often be an effective way of conveying complex concepts to adolescents, such role-playing holds the potential for either belittling or promoting a religious group's beliefs. As one middle grades teacher recently remarked to us, "It's a challenge to come up with ideas that allow the students to get hands-on experience of the religion without 'cheapening' the actual practice."

Another teacher cautioned, "I think one needs to be very careful of anything that hints at 'be a Hindu for a day' or anything that experiential— we'd never want any perception of steering kids toward a particular religion." How, then, can teachers help students to experience the religion appropriately in order to understand it deeply? How can teachers help students to understand a religion from the inside-out?

One approach to helping students comprehend a religion's tenets is to guide students toward primary sources. Teachers might ask students to read portions from sacred texts as a means of understanding their message. Interacting with people of various faiths can also be powerful. Guest presenters provide a helpful means of hearing firsthand about religious beliefs. Relying on guests also avoids generalizing about a particular tradition by learning about religion as a personal experience rather than solely as a set of dogma.

If teachers use this method, it is crucial that the invited speakers possess the necessary skills to contribute to a scholarly and objective discussion and that they understand the First Amendment considerations involved in talking about religion in the classroom. Religious leaders in one's community can often be an excellent resource. Similarly, students can interview people of various faiths with a common set of questions, and return as a class to compare and contrast their learning. Imagine the learning that might have resulted in Mr. D's class if students had interviewed Buddhists about the challenges of adhering to the Noble Eightfold Path, and contrasted it with Jared's or other Christians' experiences living with the Ten Commandments.

Interviewing people is but one of many approaches to envisioning the potential for learning outside of the classroom walls. What resources exist in a community, or neighboring city, that might teach adolescents about various religions? To the extent possible, teachers can invite students to spend time within a religion's sacred space. We've known learners who have visited mosques, convents, and evangelical churches. Others have spent time with Buddhists, examined religious websites, and taken labyrinth walks.

Additionally, active, hands-on construction enables students to think deeply about new concepts, and can be particularly engaging for adolescents. One teacher we know taught the concepts of impermanence and meditation to students through the construction of Zen gardens while studying Buddhism. Through this opportunity, students relied on active construction as a means toward internalizing new understanding

9

Some Lesser Known Religious Narratives

Case Study #6: "Isn't There Something in This Proposal to Offend Everyone?"

Eileen Kaufmann gently set the proposal down on her desk and met the steady gaze of the two high school teachers who sat in her office. As principal of this Midwestern urban high school, Eileen was accustomed to entertaining the questions and concerns of her faculty, and she was well regarded by upper-level administrators, the school board, and parents. A veteran administrator of 20 years, she typically felt comfortable aligning various faculty requests with student needs. This time, however, she felt a general reluctance to respond immediately to the proposal at hand—a joint request by the English and Social Studies departments to construct and offer a college preparatory elective Religious Pluralism class in their building for the following school year.

"Well, Eileen? What do you think?" asked Rachel, the head of the Social Studies department, excitedly. "We've held several joint department meetings to discuss the importance of such a course, and we've reached consensus as a faculty that this course would fit in well with our current

---

Teaching Adolescents Religious Literacy in a Post-9/11 World, pages 155–178
Copyright © 2010 by Information Age Publishing
155

college preparatory offerings. There's no question that it's a relevant and timely topic. It would equip our students with a broader understanding of the world that surrounds them. Since 9/11, it's never been more important. Jake and I are prepared to team-teach the course."

"I just don't know, Rachel," Eileen admitted. "I appreciate the need to teach our students the rudiments of the world's *five* great wisdom traditions, as you and Jake are currently doing in our World Cultures course. But a separate course geared exclusively to religious difference, one that includes all these lesser-known religions you mention, this makes me very nervous. I can anticipate a problem with this new course proposal of yours. I fully understand the need to broaden the scope of such an offering because, as you both make clear, more and more immigrants from abroad are moving into our small city, and into our schools. And when they do, they bring with them a number of faith traditions that most of our students, and even our teachers, know nothing about.

"But, I can only imagine what our more traditional parents will say when they get wind of this proposal. Some will be concerned that we shouldn't be teaching about religion at all, as they were with your World Cultures course. Others will wonder why we're not emphasizing the dominant Judeo-Christian tradition in our country. And, many of our immigrant parents will be upset that we're opting to teach *some* immigrants' religions but not giving theirs equal coverage. I have to admit that I understand so little about these lesser-known religions that I honestly couldn't even guess what they might have in common, let alone know their differences.

"Anyway, it wouldn't be responsible of me to endorse a curricular change of this nature without at least testing the waters a bit. We need our community to support our school, and, after all, we serve this community. We're a public school. How will it be possible to make everyone happy? What religions would we teach? What ones would we leave out? Won't this proposal have something in it to offend just about everyone?

"I tell you what, Rachel," Eileen said. "I need some time to consider this further. I'm the one who's going to have to take the heat if this new course of yours bombs. Let me know what some of these lesser-known religions are that you'd like to include in your course, and I can get back to you. I can understand covering Judaism, Christianity, Islam, Hinduism, and Buddhism in a separate, up-front religious pluralism course, and this will be risky enough. But these other religions you're talking about—like Taoism, Confucianism, Shinto, Baha'i, Santeria, Sikhism, the African religions, Voudouism, even Neo-Paganism and Wiccan—all of this makes me really nervous. It sends up red flags all over the place.

"At least the World Cultures course doesn't call undue attention to the comparative religions piece in it. So, I'm going to ask you and Jake, in the next few weeks, to give me a proposal outlining some of these other religions you'd like to cover—what they are, what they might have in common and what they don't, and why you think they are important for our students to know. Then I can make my decision in a more intelligent way. Okay?"

Nothing Ventured, Nothing Gained

What follows is a dialogue that takes place between Rachel and Jake after they leave the principal's office:

Jake: "It's pretty obvious to me that once Eileen brings our proposal to the community it will die a certain death. Just look at how the science standards were taken to task. There is a very strong parents' group that wants intelligent design to be considered alongside, or really instead of, evolution in science classes, that I just know they will militantly oppose a course in religious pluralism. So, I say, let's just forge ahead, teach this course, and ask forgiveness from the community *after* the fact instead of trying to get permission *before* the fact. Why is Eileen being so timid about this?"

Rachel: "I think she's worried about covering her butt and ours as well. Actually, she's just being a good administrator. She wants to get at least a semblance of support from other principals in the city, along with central administration and the school board. She, and we, are breaking new ground here, and informed consent from all the relevant parties is vital if we want to pull this off."

Jake: "But should the school be in service to the dominant voices in the community, simply to perpetuate its religious status quo? Or should we be about *changing* the community's understanding of religion by teaching students how rich and diverse all of their religions can be? Let's teach about as many different religions as possible, both the well-known *and* the lesser-known ones. In the real world, our students are dealing each and every day with so much religious difference, whether it's in their neighborhoods or in the media, that to overlook these differences in our curriculum is to commit the 'unpardonable sin,' pardon my intentional pun, of educational malpractice."

Rachel: "I'm really disappointed with Eileen's hedging her bets, Jake, just as you are. But deep down, even though she may be supportive of our new course proposal, our principal is a political realist. Justifying a more conventional Comparative Cultures course would be tough enough. But this course on religious pluralism that we've cooked up . . . on top of everything else, might be going a little too far."

Jake: "What we've got going for us is that you and I are both well-respected teachers. We've been working here for a long time. Students like us, our evaluations have been excellent, and Eileen has said that she thoroughly enjoys having us in the building. But I'm very worried, nevertheless, Rachel. Your request for tuition reimbursement to sign up for graduate courses in religious studies was very controversial, and central administration barely approved it. And I'm fully aware that, as committed and respected a teacher as I think I am, I'm still seen by some parents in the community as being over the top and out of step with their conservative values."

Rachel: "All of what you're saying is definitely true, Jake. But my philosophy of education has always been 'nothing ventured, nothing gained.' Let's try something really creative. Let's put together an introductory letter to Eileen about our proposed course that focuses on some of these lesser-known religions. We can write it in a concise and accessible way. Then after she reads it, she can give us some practical advice about how to turn it into a more marketable proposal. I think Eileen's got a good sense of the five world religions we've been teaching in the Comparative Cultures course, so in our letter to her, we can concentrate on some of these lesser-known religions that she admittedly knows little or nothing about. What do you say?"

Jake: It's worth a try, Rachel. Let's do it and see what happens. It'll be a good exercise in how to make our case in a brief, but engaging letter. If nothing else, we'll be able to convey some of our passion to her about the topic of religious pluralism.

A Letter to Eileen

Dear Eileen,

We are writing you this letter in response to your request for more information about our proposed religious pluralism course. We have decided to keep our descriptions of these lesser-known religions short but informative, along with our rationales for teaching them—hence, a more informal letter format. We hope that after reading our letter, you might be able to give us some sound advice concerning how to package the material in a more formal proposal, which, we assume, you will then submit to the appropriate venues. We hope that this letter accurately conveys our enthusiasm and excitement for, as well as the importance of, the material.

The Chinese Religions

We believe that it is important for adolescents to know something about the two leading Chinese religions, *Confucianism* and *Taoism*, for a number of reasons. First, about one-quarter of the current world's population adheres to these teachings (particularly in China, but also among large sectors of the populations in Japan, Korea, Taiwan, and Singapore). Second, adolescents should know that it is possible for a "religion" to be much more philosophical and naturalistic in its content and practice than the more traditional religions, which are more metaphysical and supernatural. In some ways, this humanistic bent is a necessity in China, where public displays of religion have been repressed by leaders of the People's Republic of China.

Third, many adolescents will probably be surprised to know that a non-supernatural religion is able to offer its followers a code of ethics that is both morally edifying and practical, without being codified as "sacred." Fourth, for over 2,000 years, government and business leaders in East Asia have been heavily influenced by their social and spiritual training in Confucianism and Taoism. Even today this is true, at a time when it is not appropriate for government leaders to come out of the private closet as religious believers. Knowing this about China, adolescents might learn to appreciate the freedom of religion clause in the United States Constitution more than they do.

And, fifth, nowhere else in the world have different religions been able to coexist as peacefully and noncompetitively as in China, although, in the past, there have been rivalries. It is in this country that millions of Chinese concurrently practice Taoism, Confucianism, and Buddhism. Taoism is seen to enhance the inner, reflective life; Confucianism the outer, public life; and Buddhism, the end stages of life. Over time, Shinto, the religion of Japan, has become an integral member of this group because it shares so much in common with the other three.

Mahatma Gandhi once said that he considered himself a Muslim, Hindu, Buddhist, Christian, Jew, Shintoist, Confucianist, and Taoist, because he found each of these religions to be far more complementary than contradictory. He refused to set one religion against the other, preferring, instead, to unite people on the basis of their religious beliefs rather than to divide them. We think it important for adolescents to understand that people of differing faiths can live together in such a way that each of their faiths is enriched, without having to compromise the integrity of their own religious beliefs.

Confucianism. Confucius (551 B.C.E.–479 B.C.E.), the founder of Confucianism, was a disillusioned, low-level government bureaucrat until the age of 51. He could not stand the corruption or venality of politics and politicians. He left his secure government position during a time of great social and political upheaval in China, and traveled throughout the country talking about ways to create a better society. His teachings are embodied in the Five Classic texts: *Shu Ching* ("Book of History"), *Shih Ching* ("Book of Poetry"), *I Ching* ("Book of Changes"), *Chun Chiu* ("Spring and Autumn Anals"), and *Li Chi* ("Book of Rites"). All five of these books were in circulation long before Confucius came onto the scene. For example, the *I Ching* is at least 3,000 years old, and exerted a great influence on psychiatrist Carl Jung.

The core of Confucianism (embodied in the *Analects*, a collection of Confucius's sayings and reflections compiled by his followers) lies in these beliefs:

- Everything in life is sacred in the sense that all aspects of the cosmos are interrelated in a kind of natural hierarchy.
- The primary purpose of Confucianism is to promote a harmony among all human beings, wherever and however they might live, as well as between human beings and the natural environment.
- Everything that exists in the cosmos is made up of a "vital substance" called *qi*. This substance contains within it two complementary forces: *yin* (feminine force) and *yang* (masculine force).
- Everything in the cosmos is subject to change, to continual transformations, according to its oscillations between the *yin* and the *yang*, at any given time in the constantly evolving universe.
- A good social order is one where human beings live in mutually fulfilling relationships, in harmony with the oscillating rhythms of nature and the cosmos.

■ Confucianism stipulates an ethic for living in harmony and peace. These are based on what the *Analects* call *li*, the "guiding principle of everything both great and small." The Confucian ethic includes *wen*, "refinement in the arts and humanities"; *shu*, "reciprocity" in relationships with others (according to the *Analects*, "What you do not want done to you, do not do to others"); and *zhong*, sincerity and proper action.

■ The "Five Relationships" spell out the proper roles and associated virtues of everyone in a preestablished hierarchy of relationships: between parent and child, elder brother and younger brother, husband and wife, friend and friend, and ruler and subject. All five relationships, although heavy in obedience and deference on the part of subordinates, also carry with them important reciprocal responsibilities, such as care, guidance, support, loyalty, and protection.

■ The ultimate relationships are those between ruler and ruled, and between parent and child. The ruler's primary responsibility, like the parent's, is to be an active exemplar of all the virtues mentioned above.

In the past, the principle of "filial piety" required strict loyalty and obedience on the part of the child, which later became the rationale for an authoritarian social structure in China. In the 20th century, however, as a result of the Cultural Revolution, Mao Zedong, ruler of the People's Republic, encouraged children to assert their rights and denounce their elders when they were behaving in a "feudal," or autocratic, manner.

Despite many political ups and downs throughout Chinese history, Confucianism, right through the early years of the 21st century, remains the guiding spiritual force for organizing all the affairs of the individual, family, and state into one, integrated way of life. Throughout the twentieth century, however, Confucianism's once-sweeping <u>religious</u> influence waned considerably in China (but not in Taiwan), due to its repression by the government of the People's Republic of China. Since 1928, Confucianism lost its official status of being the state religion. But its social and ethical aspects remain central to Chinese life even today.

In the 20th century, thanks to the teachings of Hsiung Shih-li, a New Confucianism has since emerged, with greater emphasis placed on establishing a harmonious, peaceful, and pluralistic world civilization. This is a trend that meshes nicely with the current Chinese government's official intention to become a strong economic and political member of the new global order.

Taoism. Here is a short story about someone who is part legend and part real—Lao Tzu (604 B.C.E.), the presumed creator of Taoism (the "Way"). Lao Tzu ("Grand Old Master") was an elder contemporary of Confucius and an archivist in the Royal Court. He was a mystic and a dreamer, someone who was deeply reflective and enigmatic. Tiring of his boring work for the Court, Lao Tzu became a kind of apologist for a simpler, more peaceful way of life. Upset by his people's refusal to heed his message of goodness and simplicity, and seeking solitude for the remaining years of his life, Lao Tzu rode westward on a water buffalo toward what is now called Tibet.

Stopped at the Hankao Pass by a gatekeeper, and refusing to heed the warning to turn back, Lao Tzu sat down for three days and composed a slim volume of 5,000 characters. He presented this to the gatekeeper as a kind of bribe to let him pass through. The volume was called *Tao Te Ching* (completed around the middle of the 3rd century B.C.E.). The title means the "The Way and Its Power." To this day, the book tells a story of spontaneity, naturalness, yin and yang, and quietude, and its paradoxical and mysterious quality has satisfied the spiritual hunger of tens of millions throughout the world.

Here are three tidbits from Chapters 16, 19, and 23 in the *Tao Te Ching* (Degen, 1999):

"Quiet your mind and watch living things grow and die; you will then realize that death means rest and that death makes room for life. Knowledge of this cycle permits perception of the way things are." (16)

Here is another one:

"Stop displaying your piety and circumspection; everyone will be relieved. Stop telling people what is good for them through laws; people can then find their own goodness. Stop using your cleverness to take what others want; they will then stop coveting you. . . . Just live simply, put yourself at the service of others, and be aware of how craving for things or for control dulls you to knowledge of the Way." (19)

And one more:

"Say what must be said and then move on. Let nature be your guide: a rainstorm sweeps through and then there is calm; winds blow hard and then there is stillness. Why should you be an exception? Those who seek the Way and patiently practice virtuous acts, such as reticence, will eventually find it. Those who give up in their search for the Way place themselves out of its reach, and become lost. If you do not trust in the Way, you will not find it." (23)

Many adolescents will ask just what the "Tao" is. The question is an excellent one. Various explanations through the centuries include "the Way," "the path," "ground of being," "the way the universe moves," and "power as a unifying principle of all life and being." The *Tao Te Ching* itself says: "Tao is eternal and has no name. . . . It is beyond form . . . it cannot be heard . . . it is beyond sound . . . it cannot be held because it is intangible." So, adolescents might wonder, if the Tao is so intangible and elusive, then why is Taoism important? Just what is its appeal?

Taoism is a nontheological philosophy of life, a practical way of living, and an admirable ethic. As a philosophy, Taoism teaches that life unfolds in a series of cycles, rather than always progressing ahead in a linear direction. Taoism also teaches that personal happiness is a byproduct of getting into a natural flow with life and avoiding the temptation, particularly strong in the West, to control all aspects of existence. The best change, for Taoists, is change that is natural.

There is no such thing in Taoism as seeing the world exclusively in terms of "either–or" or "yes or no." Everything is complementary, and, sooner or later, opposites always contain the potential to be reconciled and integrated into a seamless whole. Life is best lived, therefore, as a refusal to dichotomize choices. For example, Confucianism needs Taoism. The practical needs the speculative. The citizen needs the mystic. The social needs the individual. The public needs the private. And vice versa. Buddhism needs Confucianism and Taoism, just as both need Buddhism. And everything ends up in a perfectly integrated Zen algorithm: "All is one, one is none, none is all."

Ethically, harmony, cooperation, and order are the key virtues in Taoism. The principle of *chiao* (moral relativity) is nonjudgmental. Taoism eschews moral absolutes based on dualistic thinking because ethical absolutism is blind to the insight that morality is always, at some level, dialectical. Morality contains, at any given time, both yin and yang, virtue and vice, love and hate. Every virtue, pushed to an extreme, ultimately becomes a vice. Every vice, pushed to an extreme, harbors the potential for its own reversal.

Even though the key vices in Taoism are self-absorption, selfishness, aggressiveness, exploitation, coercion, and disharmony, there is always the possibility of turning these into their opposites. The secret for living a satisfying moral life is to find a way to live in tune with the natural world and with others. This is actually the most *practical* way to live, according to Taoistic teachings. This is the way to turn negative energy into positive energy.

How, then, adolescents might ask, does one reverse the vices that make us so miserable? How does one transcend the downside of life fostered by residing in a fast-paced, career-driven, materialistic Western society? The answer, for Taoists, is to be patient, yield, be detached, care for others, eliminate hubris (overweening pride) and be humble, live in the present moment, trust, live and let go, and learn to flow rather than fight or flee. Is this realistic, Westerners might ask? Adolescents will surely find it difficult to step outside the American success narrative of grade-grubbing, getting into the right college, and fulfilling the great American dream of living happily ever after with the obligatory professional career, new car, new home, and new partner.

Taoism responds by reminding us that these harsher realities are as much self-chosen as they are chosen for us by others. Finding the natural flow of events in our everyday lives, and yielding to this flow, keeps the frenetic and frantic ego in check. It slows us down. It opens us to the natural wisdom of the Chinese saying: "Never push a river. It moves by itself."

Taoism has been strongly influenced by Mahayana Buddhism, and throughout its history, Taoism has created a mutually beneficial relationship with this religion. So too has Zen Buddhism shared benefits with Taoism. The common ground where the two narratives appear to meet is here: All our pain—our obsessions and compulsions, our displeasures and disappointments—are self-created; and sometimes the best action is to take no action at all.

Moreover, consistent with the teachings of Zen, Lao Tzu says, "The Way is near, but people look for it in the distance. It is in easy things, but people look for it in difficult things." Happiness and contentment are right under our noses, residing in the here and now, no past and no future, all is in the present. Tune in. Sometimes effortless action (wu-wei) is far more effective than calculated, hyperactive, ego-driven activity. Embracing life means letting go of life. Everything exists as paradox. As centuries of experience with Taoism have demonstrated: leadership is at its best when it leads least. So too, religion is at its best when it is least conscious of itself.

Taoism became something of an anomaly in China. Through the millennia, Taoism, originally a nonpriestly and nonceremonial folk religion, grew into an organized religion. It evolved into a complex hierarchy of priests, monks, and even a type of pope. This priestly class purged evil demons, sold amulets, developed a natural medicine of roots and herbs, constructed sacred shrines and temples, and lived in celibacy. Lao Tzu's simple, natural wisdom got transmuted into a complex institutional religion, complete with rites, sacred texts (now over 1,100 volumes), gods and goddesses, and devils and demons.

At the present time, Taoism touches most aspects of Chinese life, including its philosophy, fine arts, healing sciences, and government. The *Tao Te Ching* is sometimes read as a leadership manual for politicians in China, but, as yet, Taoism as a religious system is not officially recognized by the People's Republic. Taoism has even developed practices such as *ch'i-kung* and *t'ai-chi ch'iian* that are a part of the martial arts in China. Most important, however, at least in the eyes of some Western religious feminists, Taoism was one of the first Eastern religions to empower women to become nuns, priests, and even, in some cases, divine intermediaries.

Shinto. Technically, Shinto is the indigenous religion of Japan, not China. Historically, its roots predate Buddhism, Confucianism, and Taoism by many centuries, although its exact origins are tough to pin down. When these three latter religions entered Japan in the 6th century C.E., it was only then that a number of ancient, scattered Japanese religious beliefs and practices were given the name of Shinto ("The way of the Gods and Spirits") to differentiate them.

We include Shinto in our proposed curriculum because this religion has interacted in harmony and peace for centuries with Buddhism, Confucianism, and Taoism. Shinto has also borrowed a great deal from these religious traditions, particularly Buddhism. We think that adolescents would benefit from an exposure to Shinto because, at the very least, they would learn that it is possible for differing religions to interact with one another in such a way that each benefits. There need be no conflict or war between and among religions. In fact, in Japan, many Buddhist temples were built under the supervision of Shinto priests, who also dedicated these temples. Also, Buddhist and Shinto priests collaborated in the celebration of birth, marriage, and religious rituals of all types.

The worship of *kami* (the divine presences, the Gods and spirits, who are sacred, pure, and powerful) has remained stable throughout the centuries in Japan. These *kami* manifest themselves in sacred, mythical figures, in natural forces such as mountains, trees, and rivers, and in powerful human beings such as emperors. Hundreds of shrines in villages throughout Japan honor a variety of *kami* beings and spirits, in part because *kami* worship is one way to consecrate the existence of nature as well as the Japanese nation.

There are no sacred scriptures in Shinto, unless one considers *kojiki* ("documents of ancient matters") to be inspired. Most Japanese do not. Neither is there any exclusivity about Shinto worship ceremonies. Most Shinto practitioners combine elements of Buddhism, Confucianism, and Taoism in their belief systems and daily practices. Shinto, with some exceptions, is one of the most heterogeneous, integrated, and interconnected religions in the world. Finally, except for a few "affirmations," formal religious doctrines and laws are virtually nonexistent in Shinto.

So, adolescents might well wonder exactly what Shinto is. For starters, it is more this-worldly than Buddhism, but less so than Taoism. It affirms family life and village traditions more than Taoism and Buddhism and is more on a par with Confucianism. It reveres nature more than Confucianism and Buddhism, but less so than Taoism. It stresses cleanliness much more than Buddhism, Taoism, and Confucianism—ritually, symbolically, *and* physically. Frequent bathing (*ofuro*), for example, is a common, purifying practice throughout Japan.

What differentiates Shinto from the three religions mentioned above, however, is its avid worship of the *kami*, referred to earlier. These *kami* are more heroic than divine spirit beings, and, according to the *Kojiki*, there are about 8 million of them. Eight is a sacred number in Japanese mythology, and it represents infinity. *Kami* (some are Buddhist and some are Taoist) are omnipresent in the world, and they often visit human beings and human places.

There are also *obake* or "evil spirits" in Shinto, but certain Japanese rituals keep them in check and ward them off. Because of the Taoistic influence in Shinto, however, there is no absolute dichotomy between good and evil. Thus, *kami* and *obake* can manifest opposing qualities whenever these are necessary, in order to set disruptions of the natural world back on course.

Ethically, in Shinto, as in Confucianism, group identity takes precedence over individual identity. The family, clan, and nation are sacred entities. *Wa* is the Shinto principle of "benign harmony," and without it, worshipers believe that society and nature will dissolve into chaos. In fact, nonconformity of any type is a major transgression against the principle of "benign harmony," because it threatens to bring about social disintegration. Individual nonconformity is also a sign of intense disrespect. Any behavior that furthers the quality of *wa* is benign, or that disrupts it is questionable.

Regarding nonconformity, two important ethical principles for everyday living are present in Japanese society: *tatemae* ("saving face") and *ie* ("extended household"). A Shinto worshiper belongs to an extended family, and any act of nonconformity that brings shame to that family is wrong. Thus, "saving face" is necessary for atonement, and this can happen through bowing, gift-giving, heartfelt apologies, and, in some extreme cases such as failing a national exam, even through suicide.

Obedience as a noble behavior is very important to Shinto believers. In fact, during the time of the Meiji Restoration of 1868, and continuing to

1945, the Japanese Emperor was obeyed as if he were a god. After World War II, however, the occupying Allies forced Emperor Hirohito to renounce his claim to divinity, and Shinto no longer remained the official state religion.

Although Shinto has no official religious code of ethics or teachings, some virtues are still cherished. A variety of Japanese rituals and ceremonies testifies to the high sacred place that a love of nature holds. Even life and death are experienced primarily as natural processes. Loyalty to one's family, state, and leaders is a paramount virtue, as are the dispositions of politeness and obedience. So, too, the quality of tranquility, a la Taoism, is highly sought after by Shinto worshipers.

At the beginning of the 21st century, Shinto is changing with the times. Women are being educated in the best universities, right along with men. Women become priests. They also carry *mikoshi* ("portable shrines") during festivals and ceremonies, considered to be a great honor. Today, Shinto, with a few glaring exceptions, tries to remain free of politics and militarism. Also, a number of "New Religions" have sprung up since the early 19th century, most of which are derivatives of Shinto.

For example, *Soka Gakkai* ("Value Creating Society"), a combination of Nichiren Shoshu Buddhism and Shinto, is the largest new religion in Japan, claiming close to 10 million members in 115 countries throughout the world. It was founded by Makiguchi Tsuesaburo (1871–1944) in 1928. *Soka Gakkai* teaches that Nichiren (a 13th century Buddhist priest) is the source of all salvation for the world today. It also teaches that chanting sections of the *Lotus Sutra* ("Lotus of the True Law") improves life, brings happiness, and creates a peaceful society because it aligns members to the cause–effect energy of the universe.

Soka Gakkai now has an international presence, especially among the professional classes in the United States and Great Britain. In the United States, *Soka Gakkai* has been controversial because of its method of recruiting new members. *Shabubuku* ("break and subdue") is a recruitment technique resembling a high-pressure sales pitch. In recent years, however, *Soka Gakkais* are much less intense in their proselytizing.

Lesser-Known Religious Movements in the United States

We are very brief in this section. While we do not intend to spend a disproportionate amount of time covering these movements in the classroom, we do want to introduce them to our students. In certain parts of the United States, some of these religious movements have gained great momentum, especially in urban areas. Many of these endemic religious movements are an excellent example of how certain ethnic, racial, and national groups have modified elements of the major world religions to accommodate their particular faith beliefs and practices. We proceed alphabetically with those lesser-known faith systems (Afro-Caribbean, Baha'i, Hasidism, Nation of Islam, Native American, Neo-Paganism and Wicca, Quakerism, and Sikhism) that tend to show up most often in our own classrooms.

Afro-Caribbean. The Caribbean is well known for its pluralistic, multicultural environment, being the site where Africans, Europeans, Americans, and Asians come together and live in relative harmony. Most religions in the Caribbean are a mixture of African and Christian elements. There are even Islamic and Hindu variants in such countries as Jamaica, Martinique, and Trinidad.

We will not spend much time here on the *Rastafarian* movement because of space limitations, even though its membership is fast approaching a million in the United States. Some Americans know about the Rastafarian movement because of its *reggae* music and dreadlocks. In brief, this is a spiritual and political movement developed in Jamaica and centered on the Ethiopian ruler Haile Selassie (1892–1975). He became the African messiah and took as his common name, *Ras Tafari* ("Prince").

Rastafarians in Jamaica, and elsewhere, are a movement of social protest against Eurocentrism. They combine elements from the Bible (particularly Psalms 68:5) and proclaim themselves true Africans in their search for African redemption. There is conflict among Rastafarians, however, because some believe that Jesus Christ is both divine and human, and that Haile Selassie was God's representative on earth. Some reject this view, however. Also, some Rastafarians use the Christian Bible, but others think the King James Version is a tool of Western oppression.

Voudou ("Divine Spirit") is the Afro-Catholic folk religion of Haiti, forming from 1730 to 1790, and combining religious ideas from the Dahomeans, Senegalese, Congolese, and Yorubans. Haitian *Voudou* is closely related to, but not identical with, Cuban *Santeria* ("The Way of the Saints"), which originated with the Yoruba people in Nigeria and Benin. Since the Cuban Revolution in 1959, and the fall of the Duvalier regime in Haiti in 1986, it is estimated that at least 2 million practitioners of *Voudou* and *Santeria* have come to the United States; and the number is growing.

Voudou and *Santeria*, originating in parts of West Africa, have the following beliefs in common. Both recognize a nontheistic, impersonal Supreme Being similar to a personification of fate or destiny. Individual believers seek guidance from several spirits (*lwa* or *orishas*) in order to fulfill their destinies. Divination and sacrifice are practiced by both groups. *Lwa* and *orishas* are venerated through a variety of media including special colors, numbers, songs, rhythms, and foods.

During the singing and dancing, some individual celebrants actually lose consciousness and become like the spirits. The ultimate purpose of both religions is to put believers in direct contact with their respective spirits through ritual forms of communication. Vegetable and animal sacrifices often take place, although a lot less so with the latter in the United States, due to a legal tightening of animal-sacrifice restrictions. Both men (*hungans*) and women (*mambos*) perform religious ceremonies in these religions. They heal, teach possession trance dances, and counsel individual members and families.

In the United States, there are *voudou* and *santeria* houses in such cities as Miami, New York, and Los Angeles, and both white and black Americans are visitors. These houses provide social services, mutual aid, and spiritual sustenance for immigrants new to this country, as well as to their children later.

As they get older, these children become increasingly Americanized and educated members of the middle class. They find enjoyment in the aesthetic traditions of *voudou* and *santeria.* They also seek the comfort of knowing how they might fulfill their destiny by communicating with the *lwa* and *orishas* spirits. Most important, however, *voudou* and *santeria* have conferred strong feelings of black power and independence upon immigrant American blacks from such countries as Cuba and Jamaica.

Finally, sensationalistic stereotypes of *voudou* and *santeria* in this country, perpetuated by racists and bigots, continue to get headlines. Charges of "voodoo [sic] economics," cannibalism, sorcery, bloody animal sacrifices, and using evil, poisonous potions continue to gain attention in the media. But despite attempts to suppress these religions both here and abroad (particularly by the Catholic Church in Spain), they continue to spread and grow.

Baha'i: ("Splendor"). An Iranian religion whose roots are in Islam, started in 1844. Its founder was Mirza Husayn ali Nuri (1817–1892), also known as Bahaullah ("Splendor of God"). There are no public rituals in Baha'i, although members pray in private each day. They also fast 19 days a year, use no narcotics, make a pledge to maintain monogamous marriages, and accept as a primary family responsibility the education of their children.

For Baha'is, there is a continuing prophetic message that each new age requires, but there will never be a final "seal" in the way it is interpreted and implemented. The message is simply this: embrace the entire world, love and serve humanity, and work for universal peace and brotherhood. The unity of humankind is Baha'i's mission, and the means for achieving this is through educating people to renounce stereotypes and prejudices, practice compassion and promote equality, and eliminate poverty, injustice, and oppression. Baha'i's social ethic emphasizes practicing the art of reconciliation, and working to develop an international language.

Hasidism ("pious"). An ultra-orthodox type of Judaism that stresses both the Torah and mystical teachings. Founded by Rabbi Israel ben Eliezer, who was given the title of Baal Shem Tov ("Master of the Good Name"), Hasidism's appeal has been to Eastern European immigrants settling in the United States, as well as to those Jews who want a revival of the mystical elements in Judaism. This includes deep devotions, intimacy with the divine, and such joyous activities as dancing and singing.

Today in Hasidism there exist two theological strands: scholarship and mysticism, rabbinic learning and piety. Both the Talmud and the Kabbalah ("mystical tradition") manage to coexist equally within some Hasidic groups. At the present time, some Hasidic Jews reject contact with the outside world, while some rejoice in this contact.

Many Hasidic Jews are ambivalent about the democratic state of Israel, and particularly the Zionist movement, because of their "extreme" secularity. Democracy and pluralism often result in a state's reluctance to foster the growth of one, single, unifying religious community—a core value of Hasidic Jews.

On the other hand, some Hasidic leaders are active political participants in Israeli life, even though they might be theoretically opposed to the "heretical" notion of a "Jewish state." They use the civil state to get what they need as a minority group. This demonstrates that, even within a very conservative religious movement such as Hasidism, often believers must make "tactical alliances" with political entities such as the state of Israel if they are to survive.

Nation of Islam. An African American Islamic movement whose major influence was Elijah Muhammad (1897–1975). He advocated fostering a positive racial self-awareness based on the teachings of Islam and also through the promotion of black free enterprise. His imprisonment for participating in antiwar activities during World War II inspired him to convert convicts, one of whom was Malcolm X (1925–1965).

Unlike Elijah, Malcolm X, as a result of spending time in Mecca, the Islamic holy city, believed that interracial harmony should be the main goal of the Nation of Islam in the United States. Malcolm X was later assassinated by a disciple of Elijah Muhammad's. Today, Louis Farrakhan (b.

1933), returning to the teachings of Elijah Muhammad, advocates separatism, black self-help, and economic power as a way to resist what he believes is the "white domination" of Judeo-Christian America.

During the 1980s and 1990s, and continuing to the present day, the Nation of Islam draws the greatest proportion of its members from the inner cities, prisons, and college campuses. The Nation of Islam teaches that black Americans do not have to be reduced to their original status as slaves; they can take pride in their ancient traditions; and they, and they alone, hold the key to their own liberation.

Native American Religions. In actuality, there are a number of Native American religions, including movements originating in Central and South America and in Mesoamerica. Most of these religions developed after contact with Western Christianity. Thus, there may be traces of Christian elements in some Native American religious movements, such as the Yaqui and the Shawnee, and very little, if any, in others, such as the Hopi and the Navaho. For example, the Yaqui were converted by Jesuit missionaries, and, to this day, there are some Catholic elements in their ceremonies, but not many. The Yaqui church is not officially recognized by Rome.

Currently, the Native American Church is the most influential religious movement among 21st century Native Americans. Using peyote (a centuries'-old custom in Mexico and southern Texas) in its worship ceremonies, the Church fuses Christianity with local tribal religious customs. For members of this church, peyote (a psychotropic substance treated as a sacred drug) produces transcendent religious experiences. A large number of Native Americans have rallied around the church, because it has become a source of meaning and unification for Native North Americans.

A revival of interest in Native American spirituality, and neo-shamanism, has become the staple of a number of environmental and New Age movements in the United States. A shaman, in the Native American tradition, is a mystic, a healer, a spiritual guide, a counselor, and a mediator. Shamans believe that living in union with the natural world is preferable to any kind of other-worldly mysticism. Native American shamans teach that attunement to the natural rhythms of the environment and the human body can be as healing as any Western medical intervention.

Despite the growing interest among whites in Native American culture and spirituality, however, some Native Americans feel that white Americans are stealing their traditions. For them, the white race is, once again, engaging in a kind of Western cultural imperialism.

Neo-Paganism (and Wicca). Neo-Paganism is an umbrella term that includes a number of movements, none of which repudiates Christianity, and most of which incorporate many Christian symbols and practices. Some sources estimate that in the Northern Hemisphere alone, there could be over 1 million active Neo-Pagan believers and practitioners. Also, because Neo-Paganism and Wicca (from the Old English meaning "female and male witches") are among the fastest-growing religious movements on college campuses throughout the United States, they are beginning to filter down through the nation's high schools. Eventually, some elements are bound to find their way to the middle schools.

Experts contend that Neo-Pagan practices and Wiccan worship of goddesses actually come the closest to ancient, folk sources of religion. These sources—of Egyptian, Celtic, Norse, and Greek origin—predate even the oldest world religions by hundreds of years. In fact, the word "pagan" (from the Latin *paganus*) means "country dweller," and Neo-Pagans and Wiccans reject Western, Judeo-Christian stereotypes imposed on them such as "idolaters," "atheists," "heretics," and "Satanists." In their minds, they are practicing a religion far closer to its true folk roots than any mainstream religion.

Despite their multiple internal philosophical and ritual differences, Neo-Paganism and Wicca share many common beliefs. Among these are the following: a reverence for nature and all of life; a polytheistic approach to worship, in that there are many pathways to achieving spiritual wisdom and enlightenment, and many manifestations of Godlikeness; a pantheistic awareness of the sacred presence in *all* elements of life, not just in so-called supernatural entities such as monotheistic Gods, and in spirits and angels.

Other common beliefs include these: living the ideals is more important than reciting religious creeds and pledging loyalty to infallible leaders and churches; reincarnation, magic, and Goddesses are as real as an eternal afterlife of heaven or hell, literal interpretations of sacred books, and a monotheistic, Masculine Super Power God; and, perhaps the most well-known, neo-Pagan ethical principle of all—"An ye harm none, then do what ye will."

Today, there is a staggering growth of Neo-Pagan and Wiccan organizations throughout the Western world, but particularly in the United States and Canada. The sheer variety of such groups is overwhelming. Their presence can be felt in an explosion of alternative spirituality books and publishers, countless nature and seasonal festivals throughout North America, websites by the tens of thousands and growing in number and influence every day, and in the increasing development of Neo-Pagan, Wiccan communities that resemble communes and encourage group ownership and mutual cooperation.

Demographically, most Neo-Pagans and Wiccans are college educated, and a significant percentage tends to be gay and lesbian. So too, most are professionals, avid readers, progressive in politics, skilled in the use of computer technology, and environmentally sensitive. They are scientifically articulate, feminist-leaning, and practicing vegans/vegetarians. It would appear that Neo-Pagans and Wiccans are here to stay in the United States and Canada. Some groups even have their own seminaries, perform legal marriages, and establish nature sanctuaries. The Unitarian Universalist Church of America gives official recognition to a group they call the "Covenant of Unitarian Universalist Pagans and Wiccans."

Quakerism (or Society of Friends). George Fox (1624–1691) was the founder of the Quaker movement. Here is an excerpt from Fox's Journal (Smith, 1991):

> And when all my hopes in priests and preachers and in all men were gone, so that I had nothing outwardly to help me, nor could tell me what to do, then, oh then, I heard a voice which said, "There is one, even Christ Jesus, that can speak to thy condition." (p. 368)

This quotation aptly sums up Fox's 18th century disenchantment with the Christian priestly tradition but not with Jesus. In fact, Fox felt totally abandoned by institutional Christianity. And so, he rejected any type of church mediation between himself and "Christ Jesus."

Fox turned his back on institutionalized Christianity. He urged magistrates in the English courts to "tremble" or "quake" (hence, "Quaker") before God rather than the law; and he asked them to stop requiring people to swear oaths. In place of the institutional church, Fox established Quaker meetings that featured silence over words, people speaking directly to God, and vice versa, rather than through the rote recital of creeds, sermons, and prayers.

During the 17th century, personal sincerity and integrity became the primary qualities of Quaker life, along with a simplicity of expression and life style, as well as a moral steadfastness of character. Quakers, despite their withdrawal from corporate religious institutions, remained very active in the affairs of society. Up to the present time, they have been pioneers in their outreach with prisoners and the mentally ill.

Quakers worship in silence in their bare meeting houses, and speak only when they experience the "Inner Light"—the spark of divinity that they believe dwells within each of us. Also, they keep personal, spiritual journals chronicling their efforts to conform to God's will and to "live up to the light." Journals still survive from women's struggles as Quaker preachers and missionaries during the 18th and 19th centuries, and they offer a wonderful glimpse into women's spiritual lives several hundred years ago. Women, to this day, remain extremely active in Quaker spiritual and social life, just as they did 200 years ago while assuming activist roles during various female emancipation movements.

American Rufus Jones (1863–1948) tried to reshape the Quaker tradition into a Christian mystical tradition. He called this "practical mysticism," which manifests in a life of active social service to the community. Even Quakerism, however, is not immune to the presence of pluralism within its ranks. "Practical mysticism" was a principle rejected by some Quakers who were more orthodox in their beliefs. In fact, there have been a series of schisms and factions among the Society of Friends in the United States, and, at times, these splits have been bitter.

Some Quakers are evangelical and fundamentalist; some are liberal and humanistic. Some, who go by the name of "Conservative Friends," still wear the distinctive Quaker dress and pepper their speech with "thee" and "thou." Regardless of these differences within Quakerism, however, the emphasis on personal spirituality and practical action is a common thread. So too is the belief that all human beings, regardless of title, are equal before God and accountable only for their own consciences. Finally, Quakers have adopted Jesus's message of pacifism and turning the other cheek. For centuries, they have assumed peacemaking roles in opposing violence and war.

At the present time, there are approximately 350,000 Quakers in the United States and Great Britain. Presidents Herbert Hoover and Richard Nixon were Quakers. Quakers are represented in all the professions in the United States, including education (many have founded colleges and universities), business, and banking. Today on college campuses, young people in growing numbers who admire the Quaker message of pacifism and social activism are attending the silent Friends meetings. These students, many of whom are former Jews and conservative Christians, value the religious autonomy and privatism of Quakers. They also respect the Friends' signature nonjudgmentalism regarding the issue of same-sex marriage.

Sikhism. Sikhs number about 20 million, most of whom live in the Punjab region of northwestern India. But many others have emigrated to a number of countries, especially to North America and Great Britain. Sikhs do not agree with some scholars that Sikhism is nothing more than a Hindu–Islam reform movement. They trace their beginnings back to the divine inspirations of Guru Nanak (1469–1539), who received a vision from

God at age 30 and, as a result, created an autonomous religious movement whose basic premise is that "there is no Muslim and there is no Hindu." There is only the "True Name" of God. The Nine Gurus that came after Nanak believed in one God and in the centrality of their holy bible, the *Adi Granth* ("First Scripture"), a compilation of Divine Revelations.

Like Buddhists and Hindus, Sikhs believe in *karma*, reincarnation, *maya*, and the *dharma*. Sikhs do have their own unique code of ethical behavior and spiritual practice, however. They reject the use of yoga to reach God, preferring, instead, the experience of meditation, communal worship, and contemplation of the divine name. Also, the Ten Sikh Gurus hold the highest place in this religion, and sometimes their names even become synonyms for God. One of the Sikh prayers is *Wahi Guru* ("Praise to the Guru"). Sikh artwork often features these Gurus, who look more or less the same.

Sikhism is about overcoming five deadly vices: greed, anger, pride, lust, and materialism. Defeating these vices enables each individual soul to unite with the *True God Sat Nam*, an infinite being that is the ever-present source of all things. Depending on whether or not Sikhs have purified their lives, they face an endless cycle of further rebirths or they become united with *Sat Nam*, the "Infinite One."

There are no priests or priestly castes within Sikhism, but there is a diversity of Sikh communities throughout the world. Western Sikhs have a special affection for certain Gurus, and Eastern Sikhs for other Gurus. All in all, Sikhs are very mobile people, and they have emigrated to various parts of the world. Their diaspora has carried them to the United States, Great Britain, Canada, Kenya, and Fiji, among other nations.

In some of these countries, such as England, Sikhs have experienced racism, especially in the cities. In the United States, however, growing numbers of whites have joined a group called the Sikh Dharma Brotherhood. The Brotherhood believes that the Sikh faith is a genuine world religion, more of a global tradition than a particular cultural tradition.

Atheism, Agnosticism, and Secular Humanism. Finally, we mention the nonbelief popularly known as atheism. According to the latest belief.net data, approximately one-quarter to one-third of the world's population self-identifies as atheist, agnostic, or humanistic. It is important to understand that *atheism*, an Ancient Greek word that has been around as long as *theism*, does not mean the *denial* of God's existence. Rather, atheism is a *lack of belief* in the existence of a God or gods. For most atheists, one cannot deny what one does not understand.

Neither is atheism a comprehensive philosophy of life or ideology. It is impossible to infer an all-encompassing worldview from the fact that someone identifies as an atheist. Atheists can be Republicans, Libertarians, Democrats, Socialists, conservatives, or liberals. They can also be idealists, pragmatists, utilitarians, or mystics. Some are yeasayers and naysayers. Some are philanthropists and misanthropes. Some are mentally ill or mentally healthy. And some are lucid or confused.

In fact, to mention just a few self-acknowledged 20th century atheists is to dramatize the point that atheists, like all the rest of us, come in many shapes and sizes, and in many ideologies and philosophies. Here are some familiar names: Thomas Edison, Sigmund Freud, George Bernard Shaw, Clarence Darrow, John Dewey, W.E.B. DuBois, Bertrand Russell, H. L. Mencken, Margaret Sanger, Langston Hughes, Ayn Rand, Jean-Paul Sartre, Steve Allen, Kurt Vonnegut, Jr., Katherine Hepburn, Marlene Dietrich, Gypsy Rose Lee, and John Lennon. To reduce individuals such as these to a single category like atheism is to deny the rich variety and complexity of their entire lives.

Furthermore, atheism is not *agnosticism*, a word coined by Thomas H. Huxley in 1869. For Huxley, agnosticism was nothing more than a method of ascertaining truth: unless one has incontrovertible rational or scientific proof that something is true, then one ought not to assert that something is true. Some atheists are unhappy with Huxley's word because, to them, it seems to multiply terms needlessly. For example, *rationalism* is a respectable term that does the same work as agnosticism.

The term *secular humanism* first came up in the Humanist Manifesto I, published in 1933. It was widely used by the American Humanist Association (AHA), founded in 1941. Interestingly, the Internal Revenue Service granted AHA religious status because it was an educational institution. This has long been a subject of controversy among many of the members of AHA who do not see their organization as being religious in any way, although, obviously, they do appreciate the tax exemption. Tom Flynn, the editor of *Free Inquiry*, the official journal of CSH, has come up with the following summary of secular humanism:

> Secular humanism begins with atheism (absence of belief in a deity) and agnosticism or skepticism (epistemological caution that rejects the transcendent as such due to a lack of evidence). Because no transcendent power will save us, secular humanists maintain that humans must take responsibility for themselves. While atheism is a necessary condition for secular humanism, it is not a sufficient one .... Secular humanism is a comprehen-

sive nonreligious life stance that incorporates a naturalistic philosophy, a cosmic outlook rooted in science, and a consequentialist ethical system.

Well, Eileen, there you have it. These are the lesser-known religions we would like to teach in our proposed course. As you can see, these belief systems have much in common, but they also differ in some remarkable ways. We have tried to point out some of these commonalities and differences in the letter we have written you.

As educators, we think the time has come, in the wake of 9/11, for American adolescents to learn about a variety of faith traditions. No longer can we operate under the assumption that Judeo-Christianity is all that we in the United States need to know about religion. Right now, there are millions of non-Judeo-Christians who live among us (thanks to President Lyndon Johnson's Immigration Act of 1965). They have a right to our understanding and empathy, just as we do to theirs. We need to learn how to dialogue with people whose religious beliefs are different from ours. We need to grasp the true meaning of pluralism, or ecumenicism, if you will.

Religious pluralism is a fact of life in this country that we must not, indeed dare not, deny. We can no longer dismiss those of different faith backgrounds and worship practices as "other," because, to people around the world, we, in the United States, are "other." History sadly has shown what invariably happens when one religious "other" comes into contact with another religious "other." "Otherness," most often based on ignorance, leads to fear. Fear leads to intolerance. Intolerance leads to oppression and aggression. And aggression leads to conflict and war.

We are at a time in our nation's history when the building of bridges between religious groups is necessary if we are to forestall acts of violence. Left unchecked, such acts will tear us apart, both within as a nation and without as a global entity. We believe that promoting religious literacy in the public school is our way, as teachers of adolescents, of trying to remove the stigma of "otherness" from belief systems we, and they, do not understand.

Yours truly,

Rachel and Jake

Lesser-Known Religions Resources for Teachers: A Brief Bibliographic Essay

The best book on what we are calling "lesser-known religions" (or what sociologists call "non-mainstream religions") in the United States is *America's Alternative Religions*, edited by Timothy Miller (Albany: State University of

New York Press, 1995). The Introduction is superb, the writing throughout crisp and concise, and the analysis of over 100 religions by individual scholars is excellent. The book also contains exhaustive bibliographies on each of the religions for those who desire further study.

Primary source material on the Eastern religions that we found to be very helpful:

Richard Degen, *Tao Te Ching for the West* (Prescott, AZ: Hohm Press, 1999); *Confucius: The Analects*, edited by D. C. Lau (New York: Penguin Books, 1979); and *Sources of Japanese Tradition*, edited by Tsunoda Rusaku, Wm. Theodore de Bary, and Donald Keene (New York: Columbia University Press, 1958).

The most thorough resource for information about atheism, agnosticism, and secular humanism is *The New Encyclopdiea of Unbelief*, edited by Tm Flynn (Amherst, NY: Prometheus Books, 2007). A brief examination of atheism is Julian Baggini's *Atheism: A Very Short Introduction* (New York: Oxford University Press, 2003). A religion-friendly presentation of atheism is Andre Comte-Sponville's *The Little Book of Atheist Spirituality* (New York: Viking Penguin, 2007).

Appendix A

We decided to conclude with an article published by Robert J. Nash, the lead author of this book, that first appeared in the *Journal of Religion & Education*. We do so for the following reasons.

- The article speaks directly to teachers and teachers of teachers.
- It represents the genre of personal narrative writing that we urge teachers of adolescents to encourage in their units on religious literacy.
- It provides an in-depth look at why the author chose to create a course on religious literacy in his own teaching of teachers at the university level.
- It spells out in detail the process and content, along with the risks and benefits, of teaching a university-level course on religious literacy and religious pluralism.
- It makes several key distinctions, as well as pointing out the commonalities, between religion and spirituality.
- It shows how the religio-spiritual needs and predispositions of adolescents in the middle-level grades, high school, and college have much in common when it comes to creating religio-spiritual meaning.
- It offers, for the first time in the professional literature, several religio-spiritual types *within the same* religio-spiritual denomina-

Teaching Adolescents Religious Literacy in a Post-9/11 World, pages 179–200
Copyright © 2010 by Information Age Publishing
179

tions, narratives, and traditions. These types exist as well in all the adolescent age groups.

■ It concludes with a final argument as to why religious literacy ought to matter to educators and students at all levels of education from the middle-school on.

Constructing A Spirituality of Teaching

A Personal Perspective

Robert J. Nash

(This essay appeared in the *Journal of Religion & Education*, as the lead article. Spring 2001, pp. 1–20. Copyright, 2001, by the University of Northern Iowa. It is reprinted here with permission.)

Introduction

There is a place where we are always alone with our own mortality, where we must simply have something greater than ourselves to hold onto—God or history or politics or literature or a belief in the healing power of love, or even righteous anger. Sometimes I think they are all the same. A reason to believe, a way to take the world by the throat and insist that there is more to this life than we have ever imagined."

—Dorothy Allison,
Skin: Talking About Sex, Class, and Literature, 1994

The Professor of Education As Spiritual Seeker

In the early 1980s, during a long-awaited sabbatical, I, a tenured full professor at a so-called "public ivy," returned to graduate school to earn a degree in applied ethics and religious studies. In the late 1980s, I took time off to earn still another graduate degree, this one in moral theology. Why, I asked myself, would a person who for so long claimed to be temperamentally indisposed to matters of the spirit spend so much money and energy pursu-

Teaching Adolescents Religious Literacy in a Post-9/11 World, pages 181–200
Copyright © 2010 by Information Age Publishing

181

ing further studies in religiously-oriented disciplines? Was this my way of having something "greater than myself to hold onto," of seizing the "world by the throat" in order to find more to life than I could ever have imagined? At least on the face of it, these degrees had no palpable payoff for my work as a teacher educator. In fact, to this day, I do not even bother to mention them on my Curriculum Vitae for fear of appearing impractical, or worse, intellectually self-indulgent, to colleagues in my professional school.

In retrospect, I now understand that while I may never have been comfortable as a conventional religious practitioner, or even as a believer, I have always been an eager student of religion and spirituality. I have been fascinated throughout my intellectual life with issues of meaning and emptiness, faith and doubt, transcendence and immanence, the secular and the sacred, the ineffable and the expressible. I now accept the fact that in all the professional courses I teach—applied ethics, philosophy of education, moral education, and others—I am actually a spiritual seeker and proud of it. I am a spiritual seeker because, although the world of material phenomena (science and technology) is important to me (after all, I do work in a college of education that is concerned with the prosaic, but no less real, problems of teachers, administrators, and students) the world of the intangible is important to me as well. This world of the intangible evokes questions of being, first principles, intuition, the origin and validity of knowledge and morality, and, most important, the meaning and purpose of the educator's existence.

As a spiritual seeker, I love to ponder the imponderable. And, maddeningly, I invite my students to ponder these imponderables right along with me. I nag them to wonder, to speculate, to ask the truly difficult, often unanswerable questions, the questions that end up exasperating most of us, because they threaten our deep-down, secure and certain places. Examples of these questions are:

- In the larger scheme of things, if there is one, why does what I do really matter?
- Why, as a professional, do I experience those sudden, uninvited moments when I regret the vanishing of a past I have barely lived and can only faintly recall; a present that continues to slip away from me until it, too, becomes a rueful reminder of possibilities forever lost; and a future that looms as being more ominous than hopeful?
- Is there something more to life, to *my* life, that gives it purpose and rationale?

- Why is it so difficult for me to believe in the existence of something greater than the here-and-now?
- Why do I find myself, at the most inopportune times, looking for something more in my life?
- Why am I so restless?
- Why do I cling to the elusive hope that wisdom is ultimately attainable, that it is possible to live a life with genuine dignity and integrity, that somewhere, somehow, I can find a sustaining meaning in it all?
- Why am I alive anyway?

Seekers tend to ask "why" rather than "how" or "what." Staying at the "how" and "what" levels of everyday existence in teaching a professional seminar is a significant piece of my job, I readily admit. But after many years, it has become the least satisfying piece for me, and, I am convinced, for many of my students as well. You see, my heart, and theirs, does not reside in the sphere of "hows" and "whats." I am a fish out of water, and my students know it. I resist their understandable attempts to push me into the role of an expert, a know-it-all problem-solver, in spite of the fact that I have not stepped into a public school classroom in over 30 years. As a teacher, I want to lead with my strength. As a philosopher of education, I would much rather entice students to ask the above types of questions, because these are the inquiries that I believe deliver a much-needed sense of proportion to their professional existence. They add a sense of depth, perspective, and distance. They have the potential of profoundly touching, and changing, teachers' inner and outer lives. When asked authentically and engaged honestly, these questions run the risk of surfacing professional frustrations and doubts, it is true. But, more important, they possess the power to revive buried hopes and activate faded dreams.

A Spiritual Perspective

In a word, this is a spiritual perspective. It is unsettling in the academy, because it refuses to be silenced or contained by the quotidian routines and practical demands of teaching. It enlarges; it does not constrict. It strives to disturb teachers' everyday workworld, rather than simply conform them to it. It encourages them to formulate a vision, to nurture a passion, to forge a commitment. I, for one, refuse to spend my days being dishonest by supplying facile answers to technical professional questions that, in truth, I rarely ask myself. Despite their importance, they too often seem trivial and beside the point. In my experience with students, what often starts out as a simple question about teaching method or curricular content frequently ends up in a vivifying conversation about the questions that truly matter to them, and to me as well. And during those rare and precious moments when we manage, however feebly, to shelve our many ideological differences and to meet each other in genuine "why" dialogue, something inexpressible happens that transforms our lives, if only for the moment. We listen carefully, respectfully, non-defensively to each other. And when we do, we find that we reside in the land of the "holy."

I must confess, though. This asking of "why" questions does not always thrill my students. At least initially, many do not want to live in the land of the "holy," especially *my* "holy." And why should they? Most of them rightfully come to my courses seeking practical answers to clear-cut professional questions about moral and character education, philosophy and history of education, and ethical decision-making. But what they end up getting is spiritual tribulation. Here I am, urging them to consider the influence of their early religious upbringing on their subsequent ethical development; insisting that they reflect for a time on the roles that faith, mystery, and doubt might possibly play in the work they do as professional educators; and occasionally forcing them to delve into complex cosmological and ontological questions like the astonishing one that the philosophers, Leibniz, Schelling, Schopenhauer, and Heidegger continually imposed on their own students: "Why is there something rather than nothing?"

At first, many of my students react with extreme dismay that a professional course of study would emphasize such apparent irrelevancies. A few wonder who they might see with their complaints, someone in charge (a dean or chairperson perhaps?) who might be able to admonish this professorial imposter. Gradually, however, most come around to my spiritual goading, even if somewhat reluctantly. Like Moliere's character who suddenly realized one morning that he had actually been speaking prose his whole life, most students, in their own manner, become aware that, like it or not, they have actually been grappling with philosophical and religious issues without really identifying them in that way. They understand, for example, that the *profession* (the duty to profess a belief in something) of teaching cries out for a way of tying togther the tag-ends of their often chaotic professional practices.

As one student, trying to put the best spin on our activities in a philosophy of education seminar, blurted out in class: "The quest for an educational vision, for something passionate in the work I do, is really a quest for God, isn't it?" To which another student promptly confessed: "But why is it the deeper I go, the further away I get? In the end, doesn't it seem like an exercise in futility attempting to explain the inexplicable?" Perhaps. But what I do know for sure is that, after awhile, most students are unable to resist the invitation to spend some time digging into the deeper things of life, into the larger spiritual reality that some of them believe encompasses us all.

I intentionally combine the two words, "religion" and "spirituality," in my teaching because, in spite of students' widespread popular disdain for the former and their near unanimous approval of the latter, I believe the two terms actually represent two closely related perspectives—the institutional and the personal—on the same phenomenon, *transcendence*. In my usage, religion is what we do with others, spirituality is what we do within our selves; the former is public faith, the latter is private faith. Religion is head; spirituality is heart. Religio-spiritual language is my awkward way of attempting to reunite what too many students have torn apart, what they too glibly discard as an irreconcilable dualism.

For me, a belief in transcendence assumes that there is always something more, something larger and greater, in our lives than what we can directly experience or perceive, something that will forever remain a mystery, an object of awe, something that will always manage to surpass our human understanding. In the face of this mystery, and in the pursuit of transcendent meaning, most students are willing to place their trust only in a private spirituality rather than in a publicly professed religious faith. Few are willing even to consider the truth that the fullest experience of transcendence will sometimes require both self and others, the individual and the community, the private life and the public life, head and heart, religion and spirituality.

Finding Faith in Honest Doubt: A Spirituality of Teaching

Some skeptics in my classes, of course, get no further than to agree with Freud that religion is nothing more than a universal obsessional neurosis; or with Marx that religion is an opiate; or with Feuerbach that religion is simply a projection of human qualities onto an object of worship. Others less cynical come to appreciate the opportunity in a professional course to search for ultimate meaning on the chance that they might discover some irrefutable, all-embracing value underlying everything. Only a few students, I find, are content to ponder the words of Alfred Lord Tennyson, words that have long guided my own interior life and directed much of my teaching in recent years: "There is more faith in honest doubt than in all the religious creeds of the world" (quoted in Haught, 1996, p. 188). Sadly, more students, rather than less, agree with Augustine when he said: "I would not have faith . . . if the authority of the Church did not compel me" (quoted in Mendelsohn, 1995, p. 53).

In this late stage of my career, I have been trying to create a pedagogy I call a "spirituality of teaching." In all the classroom work that I do as a college professor, I am driven by Tennyson's aphorism, by the unwavering conviction that, for me, a genuine faith must somehow find a way to wrestle with the demons of honest doubt. The objective is not to overcome the doubt, because this is neither possible nor desirable, but to fully incorporate it into any final declaration of belief and call to action. For me, honest doubt is a believer's intuitive sense that no ecclesiastical leader, or dogma, or doctrine, or sacred book, or teaching, or ritual can ever capture the fullness of life's ultimate mysteries. It is the humble understanding that, when everything is said and done, one's frail and wavering faith is all that is left to fill the interval between saying too much and saying too little about what is essentially incommunicable.

Here is Peter L. Berger (1992) on the perils of dogmatic certainty:

> It may well be that the quest for certainty is a deeply rooted trait of human nature. If, in the course of a lifetime, we attain this or that certitude, we should gratefully accept it as a gift of grace. But we should not feign to certainties that are, in fact, the result of strenuous and never-ending efforts at faith. By and large, the modern quest for certainty has had both intellectually and morally deleterious consequences. They are all, to use again Erich Fromm's apt phrase, "escapes from freedom." (pp. 136–137)

Spirituality, as I conceive it, has little to do with dogma, certainty, or "escapes from freedom." Neither is it directly related to Christian or Jewish understandings of such terms as ruach, pneuma, and spirit. Nor is my notion of spirituality something that is God-bestowed, incarnational, or even coming to a vivid awareness of some supernatural presence. And it most definitely has nothing in common with New Age occultism. Instead, for me, a spirituality of teaching simply calls for the student, and the teacher, to undertake, in trust, an inward journey together whose ultimate destination is to fashion a deeper, personal response to the mystery of existence. (Parker Palmer, in his *The Courage To Teach*, 1998, shares many of my assumptions about constructing a spirituality of teaching. I have been inspired by his writing, particularly his earlier *To Know As We Are Known: A Spirituality of Teaching*, 1983. But, unlike mine, Palmer's spiritual interests are more on consciousness-raising and personal transformation than on an explicit engagement with the religio-spiritual narratives that I describe later in this essay.)

A spirituality of teaching, regardless of the subject matter, puts the central emphasis on the student's (and the teacher's) continuing quest for a richly textured interior life. It recognizes the pivotal communal nature of this activity whenever it is undertaken in an educational setting. It encourages, at all times, the development of a richer, more complete spirituality on the part of individuals, one that reaches for a meaning far beyond the mere professional mastery of the newest data, the freshest techniques, and the latest technology. Most of all, a spirituality of teaching recognizes, in Fenton Johnson's (1998) words, that

> Faith is first among the cardinal virtues because everything proceeds from it including and especially love. Faith is the leap into the unknown—the entering into an action or a person knowing only that you will emerge changed, with no preconceptions of what that change will be. Its antonym is fear. (p. 54)

A spirituality of teaching, among other things, attempts to elicit candid, first-person accounts of the larger meaning of students' lived experience, whenever these meanings are appropriate to the subject matter at hand. And it attempts always to exemplify such qualities as truthfulness, courage, and integrity. I consider these to be the cardinal spiritual virtues not only of teaching and learning, but of living an excellent life as well. I predicate my spirituality of teaching on the well-tested assumption that, given an ethos of mutual support and caring in the classroom, my students will not hesitate to talk with one another about how their deepest beliefs, ideals, hopes, fears, doubts, and, yes, religious faith (or lack of it), influence the work they do as educators.

They are eager to do this, I believe, because they live during a time when it seems that more and more people are talking about topics which seem less and less important. So much talk in America today is wasted in vapid chitchat (e.g. e-mail and on-line chat rooms), in angry name-calling (radio and television talk shows), in academic one-upsmanship and textual nitpicking (many college seminars), and in an endless cycle of media-generated, self-serving political "spin." Sadly, the kind of religio-spiritual talk I am encouraging in the college classroom rarely occurs anywhere else in America—not in the family, not on the therapist's couch or even in the priest's confessional, and certainly not in the teacher's room, superintendent's office, or college president's suite.

At times in the classroom, this type of talk will take me and my students on a trip through the great monotheistic religions of the world. At other times, it will take an Eastern direction. And often it will settle for nontheistic forms of religio-spiritual commitment as found in nature, loving relationships, philosophy, literature, art, and music. I am growing more and more convinced that the subject matter in a professional course that deals with spiritual meaning can surprisingly make students better teachers, even if they never overtly mention the words "religion" or "God" in their own classrooms and other educational venues. I have a strong belief that absent the opportunity to travel this inward journey—without the challenge of creating a personal spirituality of teaching—the outward life of the educator threatens to become desiccated and burned out.

Coming Out of the Spiritual Closet: Religion As Narrative

And so one day it was bound to happen. Thirty years into my university teaching career, I enthusiastically, but cautiously, accepted the challenge of a very wise, former student who remarked:

> "Robert, when are you going to come out of the spiritual closet? Why don't you offer a special course to educators that deals exclusively with religious content, instead of sneaking this stuff in through the back door of all your other courses?"

And so I did. I created a course—"Religion and Spirituality in Education"—that I now offer twice a year, with long waiting lists. I describe this course in some detail in a book that I wrote called *Faith, Hype, and Clarity: Teaching About Religion in American Schools and Colleges* (1999).

While the book has received much critical acclaim (named a Critic's Choice Final Selection by the American Educational Studies Association, a *Choice Magazine* book of the year, and a nominee for the 1999 Grawemeyer Prize), I am most pleased with the fact that it touched a responsive chord among many audiences *outside* the religious-studies field, including teacher education, public schools, and higher education administration. While I cannot truthfully say that because of the course or the book my own inner life (or anyone else's) has been radically changed, I can say this: I am learning that, as a professional, my work as a teacher educator is, in large part, framing how I think and feel about religious and spiritual issues.

That is, my own spirituality of teaching is a variation of the postmodern assertion that, at some level, all theory is autobiography. I believe that teaching, like religion, is really autobiography, a highly personal narrative that the believer creates in order to elicit, and to answer, the most confounding existential questions, the ones that defy easy scientific, political, or technological answers. Whenever I read Andrew M. Greeley (1990), I realize why my own childhood Catholicism continues to have such a strong hold on me even today, long after I have formally abandoned it. When I was a child, it totally captured my imagination, not with its authoritative dogmas and doctrines, its magisterium and moral teachings, but with its compelling and memorable stories. These include stories about Mary and Jesus, life, death, and resurrection, the saints and the popes, martyrs and heretics, the local church pastor and the ladies sodality, the Jesuits and the Sisters of Mercy, the Catholic elementary school and Notre Dame University, and, of course, the Catholics and the Protestants, the Irish and the English.

These stories inspired and edified me. The official church teachings only served to induce guilt, boredom, and rebellion. For religion to work well, as least in my case, and, I suspect, for the majority of my students, it must first be born in narrative before it grows into creed, rite, and institution. It must be profoundly autobiographical and appeal to the narrative imagination, long before it can convince the discursive intellect.

The most captivating religious narratives—e.g., Buddhism, Hinduism, Judaism, Christianity, Islam—feature unforgettable characters, momentous events, and luminous ideals. And their languages are often sonorous and seductive. At its best, religion as narrative, as a powerful storytelling device, reaches out and captures our imaginations, because the vitality of its message and the vividness of its language are potentially life-transforming. We are moved to fresher understandings of the deeper, previously concealed, meaning of our lives. The lesson here for teachers is surely not an original one, but of the utmost importance, nevertheless. A spirituality of teaching ought to recognize that good teaching, like good religion, is all about storytelling, and that the best pedagogy aims first at the heart and soul before it can ever find its way to the mind.

During a recent sabbatical leave, I developed this notion of teaching as storytelling into a book called *Religious Pluralism in the Academy: Opening the Dialogue* (2001). In this book, I make the case that we are more likely to get college students from a variety of religio-spiritual backgrounds to open up publicly about their guiding beliefs when we de-emphasize the revelational, doctrinal, and corporate elements of religion in the classroom in favor of the aesthetic and the poetic, the philosophical and the literary. I argue that we ought to approach discussions of religion as a series of compelling and useful narratives that people have constructed for thousands of years in order to explain life's tragic anomalies as well as its unexpected gifts of grace. I acknowledge in this book that, as a teacher, I know of no better way to mine the richness of an escalating religio-spiritual pluralism on secular college campuses throughout the United States than to get students to exchange their religious stories with each other in a non-doctrinal, mutually respectful manner.

In fact, I would argue that the brilliance of all the religions and spiritualities the world has ever known lies in their peculiar narrative power. If, as I contend, religion is basically a story devised by people to give meaning to their lives in a particular place and time, then one must continually ask whether the narrative still speaks to people's needs today. In Neil Postman's (1996) words,

> Does it provide [them] with a sense of personal identity, a sense of community life, a basis for moral conduct, explanations of that which cannot be known? (p. 7)

This question, in my opinion, ought to be the engine that fuels to-and-fro, robust, campus-wide discussions about religion and spirituality.

As each week passes during the term in which I offer my new course, I come to realize that, for me, my own teaching narrative is deeply spiritual. It is about helping students to name their doubts about themselves and their work with honesty and integrity. At the same time it encourages them to create and nurture a faith in themselves, their students, and their work that is honest and integral. Whether we are talking about religion or education, my students and I struggle throughout the semester to create individual professional narratives that combine the qualities of faith, doubt, honesty, and integrity in such a way as to deepen our understandings of ourselves and our teaching. We are trying to create a sense of vocation—seeing our professional work as a calling, as a leap of faith without guarantee, as a risky response to the summons deep within us to minister to others wisely and compassionately.

Breaking Stereotypes

Thus far, my new course has attracted a richly diverse group of students. It has included several African-Americans, Native Americans, and Asians; students ranging in age from their late teens to their early 80s; "out" gays, lesbians, and bi-sexuals; Jews, Muslims, Hindus, Buddhists, and Christian Fundamentalists, Evangelicals, and Pentecostals; atheists and agnostics; and professionals representing at least 20 fields, from classroom teachers, to principals, to social service workers, to allied health caregivers, to higher education administrators. Most of the students in these classes appear to fit the profile that Wade Clark Roof (1993, 1999) characterizes as baby-boomer "seekers," although their dramatic departures from this stereotype are instructive and what finally make them and the course such a vital experience.

Roof's deservedly acclaimed studies, *A Generation of Seekers*, and *Spiritual Marketplace*, focus mainly on conventional and post-conventional Christian believers, New Agers, and what he calls "seekers." These are people who have questioned, and even, in some cases, abandoned, their parents' religions, ethnic heritages, politics, and nationalities in order to discover for themselves a more compelling religio-spiritual basis on which to build their lives. My own experiences with those students who represent pre-boomer, boomer, generation-X, and millennialist time periods confirm some of Roof's findings, to be sure, but also go far beyond his depictions. Roof, at times, oversimplifies the complexity and richness of individuals' religio-spiritual journeys by collapsing all of his respondents into one huge, unnuanced designation he calls "seekers."

In my three and one-half-decade experience in teaching college students of all ages, I can assert confidently that there are simply no prototypal "seekers." In fact, there are many different types of seekers, including myself, because nobody ever pursues religio-spiritual meaning outside of a particular perspective or personal narrative. Each of us, I submit, is an intellectually-situated (as well as a culturally-situated) being. Our search for meaning in a fractured American culture will always originate in a set of distinct preconceptions that we hold about religion and spirituality. Unlike Roof (1993), I am wary of generalizing about *all* seekers that they "value experience over beliefs, distrust institutions and leaders, stress personal fulfillment yet yearn for community, and are fluid in their allegiances" (p. 8). To this I can only say—"Well, yes, some do, but some don't."

Another highly respected sociologist, Alan Wolfe (1998), makes similar kinds of generalizations in his well-received study of middle-class Americans, *One Nation After All.* He claims that a "capacious individualism" characterizes the religious faith of the middle-class. According to Wolfe, middle-class Americans are not deeply devout, they have lost a sense of the tragic, they experience no wonder, and they mourn the erosion of "necessary constraints on hedonism" (p. 82). Wolfe believes that middle-class Americans operate from a "rational-choice" theory. They are "free-agent" churchgoers who calculatingly choose and switch their denominational allegiances according to what they believe will make them happiest. Wolfe concludes that, among the middle-class, personal religious belief will always be more important than institutional affiliation.

While it is definitely true that some of my own middle-class students express a strong commitment to Wolfe's brand of religious individualism, many do not. Some, wary of privatizing their faith and hoping to influence public policy, organize social-justice groups in their churches and temples, and even in their schools. Others, tired of their spiritual isolation, join bible-study and mutual-support groups in order to create richer, more intimate forms of community life. Some students are deeply devout believers, others are deeply devout church-going skeptics, some are proud non-believers, and others mostly keep their beliefs to themselves. Unlike Wolfe, I can not honestly identify one student in my courses who is without a sense of wonder, or who fails to recognize the tragic and comic elements in human life. For all his remarkable sociological insight, Wolfe utterly fails to realize that a growing percentage of middle-class Americans is becoming intensely involved with Eastern and New Age religious teachings.

Many of these religions, such as Buddhism and Hinduism, understand all too well the significance of wonder and the omnipresence of tragedy in human affairs, and the need for compassion in the face of suffering. In order to get a sense of the allure of alternative religions for some middle-class Americans, Wolfe might consider reading the popular Vietnamese Buddhist and pacifist, Thich Nhat Hanh, whose *Living Buddha, Living Christ* (1995) has become a runaway bestseller in this country. One student in a recent religion and education course of mine, "Jonathan"—a self-designated "recovering Christian"—continually pointed to this book throughout the semester as having transformed him from being a "dead Christian" to a "live Buddhist-post-denominational Christian." Jonathan, a high-school English teacher, has begun to use Hanh's book in his Advanced Placement class. He claims that, after reading the book, many of his high-school students are able to find new ways to revitalize their Christian and Jewish faiths.

Hanh speaks vividly to people of all religious faiths, particularly disgruntled Christians like Jonathan, about the importance of understanding God, not as an abstract concept, but as a living reality. So too does the Dalai Lama, author of an immensely popular book (1999)—*Ethics for the New Millennium*—that I have used with my students during the last two years. Hundreds of thousands of middle-class readers appear to resonate to both authors' observations that, in the past, Christian triumphalism has frequently prevented authentic inter-faith dialogue and fostered a disrespect for religious pluralism of all kinds.

What Hanh and the Dalai Lama do for American, bourgeois believers like Jonathan and other students like him is to remind them of the significance of the deeply reflective life, and what they call the practice of "mindfulness"—the capacity to attend to everything that happens in the present moment. This is the beginning of enlightenment, and something that contemporary Western faith stories either ignore or dismiss, even though Christianity and Judaism have a rich and lengthy tradition of contemplative spiritual practices (Cupitt, 1998; Gordis, 1995). Many teachers in my small, rural state have become devoted followers of Hanh, mindful meditators who "seek refuge" in the Buddha (the one who shows the way), the Dharma (the way of understanding and love), and the Sangha (the community that lives in harmony and awareness). During a recent public appearance in my state, Hanh drew thousands of his followers to a college lecture and subsequent series of workshops on such spiritual topics as mindfulness, pacifism, meditation, and holiness. Several of my students attended these events.

Eight Types of Religious Stories that College Students Tell

Not all of my students find Buddhism to be an attractive spiritual alternative, however, although many do. In this section, I will sketch eight miniature portraits of the dominant spiritual narratives that I find in classes at my university, and throughout the country, whenever I visit other places to speak. I have constructed eight religious stories that I hope are capacious, diverse, and fluid, in order to avoid the stereotyping that bothers me in the work of such authors as Roof and Wolfe, whom I mention earlier.

I have found these religio-spiritual narratives to be represented among every age-, gender-, racial-, ethnic-, and socio-economic group in my work with students. No single narrative exists as a pure type, of course, and, at least in theory, none need be mutually exclusive. I personally find something appealing in all of them, although a few obviously speak to me, an honest doubter, in a very special way. I also find that most students only need a little encouragement, the right questions, and a supportive dialogue space to tell their stories to each other and to me. Because of space limitations, I can only outline these stories briefly in the sketches that follow (but in far greater depth in my two, aforementioned books 1999, 2001):

- The *Orthodox Believers* come in all religious and philosophical stripes. With only a few disturbing exceptions, they usually remain humble but unyielding in their claims to be in possession of an absolute, revealed truth that most of their classmates and I obviously lack. Their confident, sometimes gentle, sense of certainty attracts, more than repels, many of us throughout the semester. In class, a small coterie of anti-orthodox skeptics, however, always manages to remain unconvinced, and they often have great difficulty concealing their disdain for any expression of uncompromising, orthodox belief. The core leitmotif for the Orthodoxy story is this: *There is a Truth that is unimpeachable, immutable, and final; and it can only be found in a particular book, institution, prophet, or movement. The mission of the Orthodox Believer is to deliver this Truth to others as an act of love and generosity.*

■ The *Mainline Believers* constitute a very large group of college students. These students are neither excessively conservative or avant-garde. They dislike authoritarianism in religion as much as they dislike faddism. They prefer a life of traditional worship that balances traditions, standards, self-discipline, and moral conscience with a degree of personal freedom, biblical latitude, and the *joie de vivre* of close community life. Often they remain in the Catholic and Protestant churches (and temples) of their parents and grandparents. They are the proud holdouts against postmodernity and the religious experimentation and decon-struction that so often accompany it. The controlling theme in the Mainline narrative is this: *People need an organized, sacred space, one that provides clear boundaries between the sacred and the profane, a stable support community, a sense of order, and a moral bulwark against the excesses of secularism.* Although Mainline religion appears to be alive and well in America, some of us, nevertheless, ask Mainliners two complementary questions. When does the need for religious stability and rootedness turn into a denial of those changes that any denomination needs in order to remain vital, responsive, and pastoral? But, also, is it possible for the mainline denominations to make reasoned compromises with the world without the cooptations and dilutions that too often accompany those compromises?

■ The *Wounded Believers* include those students who define their religious experience mainly as a reaction to the physical and mental abuse (often perpetuated in the *name* of religion) that they have suffered at the hands of hypocritical, over-zealous clergy, lovers, parents, relatives, and friends. Their self-disclosing narratives of suffering, denial, reconciliation in some cases, and eventual healing always win our attention, believer and non-believer alike. Sometimes Wounded Believers embarrass us, sometimes they inspire us, but they never fail to captivate us. The thematic thread that winds throughout all Wounded Belief nar-ratives is this question: *If there is a good, all-loving God, why has there been so much unbearable pain in my life?*

■ The *Mystics* remind us continually that more often than not a genuine faith requires a discerning silence on the part of the believer, instead of a learned, theological disquisition. Some turn to the East; some to alternative American religions; some to folk religions; and some to private forms of spirituality. Most express a love for mystery, stillness, and attunement that eludes those of us who too easily fit the stereotype of the fitful, ambitious, hard-driving Westerner. At the heart of the Mysticism narrative is this motif: *The transcendent is best experienced, not through idle chatter or abstract concepts, but by way of meditation, mindfulness, and, above all, a pervasive calmness.* The rest of us listen, learn, and wonder how on earth we can ever find the mystical "stillness" that is said to inhabit the center of all our frenetic activity. Some students, however, reject the Mysticism narrative outright as too quiescent and self-absorbed.

- The *Social Justice Activists* urge us throughout the semester to consider the possibility that believers must be responsible for building the Kingdom of God in the here-and-now, rather than waiting for some distant paradise to come. They advocate an activist faith dedicated to the liberation of oppressed peoples, equal rights and social justice for all, and radical social transformation marked by full democratic participation in decision-making. For them, religious leaders are judged to be effective only according to their commitment to bring about massive social reform in behalf of the least among us. The common theme in the Activism narrative is this: *Religion makes the most sense whenever it tells a story of human rights and social transformation; whenever it invites believers to criticize existing structures of power and privilege such as the wealthy, white, male hierarchies in the churches, universities, businesses, media, and government.* While many students are drawn to the transformative elements of the Activism narrative, others dismiss it as merely partisan liberal politics with a religious gloss.

- The *Existential Humanists* help us to understand that all too often believers turn to the supernatural in order to escape from the difficult responsibilities of individual freedom. For them, a humanistic, "self-centered" ethic can stand on its own as a defensible way of a person's being in the world and living an authentic human life. What is necessary is that all of us confront the inescapable fact of our human finitude, and make a conscious choice to create ourselves through our daily projects, that is through our courageous strivings to make meaning in an absurd universe. The recurring idea in the Existential Humanism story is this: *The stark truth is that God has forever disappeared—if He ever existed in the first place—and now it is up to us to get on with our lives.* After listening to the Existential Humanists, some of us begin to understand, for the first time, the significance of Jean Paul Sartre's assertion that we are all unique selves "condemned to freedom," and Paul Tillich's postulation of a "Ground of Being" as a viable substitute for a personal God, the traditional God of theism. We proceed to look for constructive, alternative ways to cope with the loss of absolutes. Others find the story too bleak and individualistic.

■ The *Postmodern Skeptics* are also deeply suspicious of any and all religious claims to absolute truth. But unlike the Existential Humanists, they reject the existence of an unsituated, context-free self or soul. As committed moral relativists, they openly challenge our religious and moral certitudes, our ethical universals, and our grand spiritual narratives. They frequently encourage the rest of us to accentuate rather than integrate our many differences, to recognize our cultural situatedness as a critical fact of life, and to put our faith, not in metaphysical doctrines or dogmas, but in the awareness that we are all social constructors of our own religio-spiritual realities. The leading theme in the Postmodern Skepticism narrative is this: *An informed sense of contingency, irony, and doubt, and a willingness to repudiate religiously-grounded, patriarchal systems of social domination, are what make us truly human and our lives truly worth living.* In reaction to the Skeptics, some of us confess a gnawing pessimism over life's ultimate prospects. A few, fearing the onset of a corrosive cynicism and nihilism, refuse to take these people seriously.

■ The *Scientific Humanists,*, while genuinely open to the possible existence of a cosmological God who created the universe, nevertheless argue that the evidence of astrophysics, organic evolution, biology, and the brain sciences effectively contravenes this hypothesis. No empirical evidence is able to establish incontrovertible proof of a supernatural power greater than nature or ourselves. But neither can the alleged existence of a transcendental power be controverted scientifically. The core of the Scientific Empiricism story is this: *We are utterly alone in the universe, beyond final Divine revelations and interventions, and left to our own human devices, accompanied by the findings of science, to create a better world for everyone.* In response, some of us express the hope that religion and science can indeed be compatible. Others, however, can never get beyond what they think is the fundamental irreconcilability of faith and reason.

Individual representatives of each of these types always have a powerful religio-spiritual story to tell throughout the term. I try to honor their narratives as respectfully as I can in every class that I teach. I feel privileged that I am able to spend 15 intense weeks each semester with such stimulating people. Each of these seekers demonstrates in every class meeting that the search for a spirituality of teaching and living is never-ending and persistent, even though at times it might exist just below the surface. This search for meaning also shows that it is virtually impossible for any analyst, whether Roof, Wolfe, or myself, to adequately capture the complexities and nuances of the distinct religio-spiritual narratives in any easy, catch-all way. Thus, it is my double intention in offering my course to try to maintain the wonderful distinctiveness of teachers' religio-spiritual views (and to encourage them to recognize the uniqueness of religious views of their own students); while at the same time to provide them (and, by implication, their own students) with accurate and helpful narrative classifications by which to investigate the rich variety of religious experiences among a number of middle-class and working-class Americans today.

Why Should Spirituality Matter to Teachers?

The truth is that religion and spirituality matter a great deal in America today. In fact, I would argue that besides sex, politics, the stock market, and sports, nothing else matters as much. In the field of lower and higher education, a spate of recent publications (e.g. *Educational Leadership*, 1998; Kazanjian and Laurence, 2000; Kessler, 2000; Marsden, 1994, 1997; Noddings, 1991; Nord, 1995; Nord & Haynes, 1998) has recently argued, that, in the name of liberal education, fairness, and multiculturalism, the study (not the practice) of religion must find a permanent place in school and college curricula. This must happen especially in secular institutions, where a timid intellectual neutrality has effectively neutered or totally ignored the topic.

At the college level, there has been nearly a 50% increase in enrollment of undergraduate majors in religious studies during the last ten years. According to one author, Tom Beaudoin (1998), Generation X, the "first generation born without God," represents the most spiritually hungry generation this country has ever known. In his *Virtual Faith*, Beaudoin describes the many ways that Generation X has taken religion into its own hands, by using the tools of popular culture and computer technology to rejuvenate Christianity. From another angle, Howe and Strauss (2000) come to the same conclusion regarding what they call the "next great generation," the "millennials."

According to current opinion polls, three of the most admired people in the world today are the Pope, Mother Teresa, and the Dalai Lama. Not just PBS, but the three major television networks and the cable channels frequently air serious religious specials during prime time. Bill Moyers became a household religious guru because of his widely-watched five-week PBS series, *The Wisdom of Faith*. Through his famous television interviews with Joseph Campbell, he brought the four-volume work, *Hero, The Masks of God* (1959–1968), to the attention of a massive American audience. And faith-friendly popular television series such as "Touched by an Angel," "Highway to Heaven," and "Promised Land" draw increasingly large viewing audiences, even in re-runs.

Many biologists, physicists, and astronomers are getting into the religious act by writing bestselling books with such titles as Davies' *The Mind of God* (1993), Polkinghorne's *Belief in God in an Age of Science* (1998), and Sagan's *The Demon-Haunted World* (1996). And the Religion, Spirituality, and Self-Help sections of the nation's largest bookstores have become the most popular attractions for browsers and buyers alike, thereby guaranteeing record sales. It is no coincidence that Mitch Albom's hugely popular *Tuesdays with Morrie* (1997), a moving account of the author's spiritual reawakening through a weekly encounter with his dying former professor, has remained on top of the *New York Times* bestseller list for over three years.

Finally, the Internet has fast established itself as the site for the most interactive form of religious conversation in this country. The *Christianity Today* site received nearly one-million hits in April, 1996 alone. And the Gospel Communications Network logged 4.7 million visitors to its chat rooms and web sites during the same period. A Gallup study in May 1996 uncovered the staggering fact that 56,000 electronic places use the word "God" in their descriptions, and over 45,000 sites refer to other types of deities. By the year 2000, this list had doubled. *WWW.beliefnet.org* receives upward of 500,000 hits a day at its website. Phyllis Tickle, in her *God-Talk in America* (1997), estimates that, by 2010, over 20 percent of all adult Americans will worship, pray, and receive spiritual instruction exclusively over the Internet. For these Americans, churches synagogues, mosques, and temples will soon become quaint anachronisms.

One of the main reasons I created my religion and spirituality course for educators was to respond to hundreds of my students in recent years who have wondered openly why the schools and colleges have not caught up to the culture at large on religio-spiritual matters. Religion matters deeply to them, even when they are attacking it, and to me as well. Among our concerns is our need to know if the existing churches are really in trouble, particularly if believers become disenchanted with conventional forms of theism, or, perhaps, become less willing to stay with one faith tradition. From another point of view, we are also curious about the millennial possibility that maybe one cosmic belief system will someday fit all, and whether the birth and spread of this new spiritual consciousness are even desirable.

But most of all we want, indeed we insist on, the existence of structured educational opportunities at all levels of schooling, in the company of others, to examine our own spiritual impulses. We want to create a personal and professional spirituality that satisfies our struggling, imperfect longing for meaning and purpose. We want to understand, as best we can, the mystery that lies at the center of the universe's greatest riddles. And we need to put the failures and successes of humanity's perennial religio-spiritual project into some kind of realistic, yet compassionate, perspective. I believe strongly that the opportunity for professional educators (and their students as well) to confront the spiritual dimension of their lives in a formal classroom setting is an idea whose time has finally come in teacher education programs.

Bibliography

Albom, M. (1997). *Tuesdays with Morrie.* New York: Doubleday.

Allison, D. (1994). *Skin: Talking about Sex, Class, and Literature.* Ithaca, NY: Firebrand.

Beaudoin, T. (1998). *Virtual faith: The irreverent spiritual quest of generation x.* San Francisco, Jossey-Bass.

Berger, P. L. (1992). *A far glory: The quest for faith in an age of credulity.* New York: Free Press.

Cupitt, D. (1998). *Mysticism after modernity.* Oxford, UK: Blackwell.

Davies, P. (1993). *The mind of God: The scientific basis for a rational world.* New York: Touchstone.

Educational Leadership. (December 1998/January 1999). The spirit of education.

Gordis, D. (1995). *God was not in the fire.* New York: Scribner.

Greeley, A. M. (1990). *The Catholic myth: The behavior and beliefs of American Catholics.* New York: Charles Scribner's Sons.

Hanh, T. N. (1995). *Living Buddha, living Christ.* New York: Riverhead.

Haught, J. A. (1996). *2000 years of disbelief: Famous people with the courage to doubt.* Buffalo, NY: Prometheus.

Howe, N. & Strauss, W. (2000). *Millennials rising: The next great generation.* New York: Vintage.

Johnson, F. (September, 1998). Beyond belief: A skeptic searches for an American faith. *Harper's,* 39–54.

Kazanjian, V. H. & Laurence, P. L. (Eds.). (2000). *Education as transformation: Religious pluralism, spirituality, & a new vision for higher education in America.* New York: Peter Lang Publishing.

Kessler, R. (2000). *The soul of education: Helping students find connection, compassion, and character at school.* Alexandria, VA: Association for Supervision and Curriculum Development.

Lama, D. (1999). *Ethics for the new millennium.* New York: Riverhead.

Marsden, G. M. (1994). *The soul of the American university: From Protestant establishment to established nonbelief.* New York: Oxford University Press.

Marsden, G. M. (1997). *The outrageous idea of Christian scholarship.* New York: Oxford University Press.

Mendelsohn, J. (1995). *Being liberal in an illiberal age.* Boston: Skinner House Books.

Nash, R. J. (1999). *Faith, hype, and clarity: Teaching about religion in American schools and colleges.* New York: Teachers College Press.

Nash, R. J. (2001). *Religious pluralism in the academy: Opening the dialogue.* New York: Peter Lang Publishing.

Nash, R. J. (2002). *Spirituality, ethics, religion, and teaching: A professor's journey.* New York: Peter Lang Publishing.

Noddings, N. (1993). *Educating for intelligent belief or unbelief.* New York: Teachers College Press.

Nord, W. A. (1995). *Religion and American education.* Chapel Hill, NC: University of North Carolina Press.

Nord, W. A. & Haynes, C. C. (1998). *Taking religion seriously across the curriculum.* Alexandria, VA: Association for Supervision and Curriculum Development.

Palmer, P. (1983). *To know as we are known: A spirituality of education.* New York: HarperCollins.

Palmer, P. (1998). *The courage to teach.* San Francisco, CA: Jossey-Bass.

Polkinghorne, J. (1998). *Belief in God in an age of science.* New Haven: Yale University Press.

Postman, N. (1996). *The end of education: Redefining the value of school.* New York: Vintage.

Roof, W. C. (1993). *A generation of seekers: The spiritual journeys of the baby boom generation.* New York: HarperCollins.

Roof, W. C. (1999). *Spiritual marketplace: Baby boomers and the remaking of American religion.* Princeton, NJ: Princeton University Press.

Rorty, R. (1998). *Achieving our country: Leftist thought in twentieth-century America.* Cambridge: Harvard University Press.

Sagan, C. (1996). *The demon-haunted world: Science as a candle in the dark.* New York: Ballantine.

Tickle, P. A. (1997). *God-talk in America.* New York: Crossroad.

Wolfe, A. (1998). *One nation after all: What middle-class Americans really think about....* New York: Viking.

References

Ahmed, A. S. (1980). *Pukhtun economy and society: Traditional structure and economic development in a tribal society*. London: Routledge.

Ahmed, A. S. (2001). *Islam today: A short introduction to the Muslim world*. New York: I.B. Tauris.

Bloom, M. (2005). *Dying to kill: The allure of suicide terror*. New York: Columbia University Press.

Brooks J. G., & Brooks, M. G. (1993). *The case for constructivist classrooms: In search of understanding*. Alexandria VA: Association for Supervision and Curriculum Development.

Bruner, J. (1990). *Acts of meaning*. Cambridge, MA: Harvard University Press.

Clarke, J. J. (1997). *Oriental enlightenment: The encounter between Asian and Western thought*. New York: Routledge.

Coogan, M. D. (2005). *Eastern religions: Origins, beliefs, practices, holy texts, sacred places*. New York: Oxford University Press.

Dalai Lama. (1999). *Ethics for the new millennium*. New York: Riverhead Books.

Degen, R. (1999). *Tao Te Ching for the West*. Prescott, AZ: Hohm Press.

Eck, D. (1993). *Encountering god: A spiritual journey from Bozeman to Banaras*. Boston: Beacon.

Fowler, J. W. (1981). *Stages of faith: The psychology of human development and the quest for meaning*. San Francisco: Harper & Row.

Gardner, H. (2006). *Changing minds: The art and science of changing our own and other people's minds*. Boston: Harvard Business School Press.

Greene, M. (1995). *Releasing the imagination: Essays on education, the arts, and social change*. San Francisco: Jossey-Bass.

Griffiths, B. (1989). *A new vision of reality*. London: HarperCollins.

Teaching Adolescents Religious Literacy in a Post-9/11 World, pages 201–202
Copyright © 2010 by Information Age Publishing
All rights of reproduction in any form reserved.

Harvey, A. (1996). *The essential mystics: Selections from the world's great wisdom traditions.* San Francisco: HarperSanFrancisco.

Kessler, R. (2000). *The soul of education: Helping students find connection, compassion, and character at school.* Alexandria VA: Association for Supervision and Curriculum Development.

Kimball, C. (2002). *When religion becomes evil.* San Francisco: HarperSanFrancisco.

Levinson, D. (1996). *Religion: A cross-cultural encyclopedia.* New York: Oxford University Press.

Lewis, C. S. (1982). *The Screwtape letters; with, Screwtape proposes a toast* (Rev. ed.). New York: Macmillan.

Lewy, G. (1996). *Why American needs religion: Secular modernity and its discontents.* Grand Rapids, MI: Wm. B. Eerdmans.

Mascaro, J. (Trans.). (1965). *The Upanishads.* New York: Penguin Books.

Moses, M. (2002). *Embracing race: Why we need race-conscious education policy.* New York: Teachers College Press.

Nash, R. J. (1997). Fostering moral conversations in the college classroom. *Journal on Excellence in College Teaching, 7*(1), 83–105.

Nash, R. J. (2002). *Faith, hype, and clarity: Teaching about religion in American schools and colleges.* New York: Teachers College Press.

Nash, R. J., Bradley, D. L., & Chickering, A. W. (2008). *How to talk about hot topics on campus: From polarization to moral conversation.* San Francisco: Jossey-Bass/Wiley.

Nord, W. A. (1995). *Religion and American education.* Chapel Hill: University of North Carolina Press.

Oser, F. K., & Scarlett, W. G. (Eds.). (1991). *Religious development in childhood and adolescence.* San Francisco: Jossey-Bass.

Pape, R. A. (2005). *Dying to win: The strategic logic of suicide terrorism.* New York: Random House.

Parks, S. D. (2000). *Big questions, worthy dreams: Mentoring young adults in their search for meaning, purpose, and faith.* San Francisco: Jossey-Bass.

Policano, J. D. (1998, January 16). Letter from Iran. *Commonweal,* pp. 9–10.

Postman, N. (1996). *The end of education: Redefining the value of school.* New York: Random House.

Schwehn, M. R. (1993). *Exiles from Eden: Religion and the academic vocation in America.* New York: Oxford University Press.

Schoeps, H. (1968). *The religions of mankind: Their origin and development.* New York: Doubleday.

Shelton, C. M. (1989). *Adolescent spirituality.* New York: Crossroads.

Sharma, A. (Ed.). (1993). *Our religions.* New York: HarperCollins.

Smart, N. (2000). *Worldviews: Crosscultural explorations of human beliefs* (3rd ed.). Upper Saddle River, NJ: Prentice Hall.

Smith, H. (1991). *The world's religions* (Rev. ed.). New York: HarperCollins.

LaVergne, TN USA
22 July 2010
190489LV00001B/33/P